ALSO BY JONATHAN SCHWARTZ

Almost Home

Distant Stations

The Man Who Knew Cary Grant

A Day of Light and Shadows

All in Good Time

All in Good Time

A MEMOIR

Jonathan Schwartz

RANDOM HOUSE  NEW YORK

Published in the United States by Random House, an imprint of The Random House Publishing Group, a division of Random House, Inc., New York, and simultaneously in Canada by Random House of Canada Limited, Toronto.

RANDOM HOUSE and colophon are registered trademarks of Random House, Inc.

Library of Congress Cataloging-in-Publication Data

Schwartz, Jonathan
All in good time: a memoir / by Jonathan Schwartz
p. cm.
ISBN 0-375-50480-X
1. Schwartz, Jonathan, 1938—Homes and haunts—California—Los Angeles. 2. Schwartz, Jonathan, 1938—Childhood and youth. 3. Composers—United States—Family relationships. 4. Beverly Hills (Calif.)—Social life and customs. 5. Radio broadcasters—United States—Biography. 6. Authors, American—20th century—Biography. 7. Schwartz, Jonathan, 1938—Family. 8. Fathers and sons—United States. 9. Schwartz, Arthur, 1900–1984. I. Title.
PS3569.C566Z463 2004 813'.54—dc21 2003046606
[B]

Random House website address: www.atrandom.com
Printed in the United States of America on acid-free paper

2 4 6 8 9 7 5 3 1

FIRST EDITION

Book design by Carole Lowenstein

For Casey and Adam,
and for their dazzling mothers,
Marie Brenner and Ellie Renfield

Prologue

In the summer of 1936 on a muggy Sunday afternoon, two years before I was born, my mother fell ill on a tennis court in Great Neck, Long Island. I'm told that she dropped to her knees, then to her back, complaining of dizziness, of "swirling." In the group of five or six who immediately gathered around was a doctor, who asked for an ambulance. In the hospital it became apparent that my mother's disorder was grave. There was nothing to be done for "malignant hypertension." In later years, my father would use the word "catastrophic" to describe my mother's sickness. I didn't know what it meant and never asked, for fear of the answer. In seeking the answer for myself, so I could come upon it in private, I tried to find it in the dictionary under the letter "K." At the age of six, I stood no chance. During an evening sometime later, my parents gave a party. One of the guests, Jimmy Durante, performed. At the piano, he played and sang "Inka Dinka Doo." I sat by my mother on a light blue couch behind him. In the middle of the song, one of its many asides that caused the special splattering laughter that only Durante could produce revealed, for me, the definition I'd sought. "What a ca*tas*trophe!" Durante roared, with comic indignation. I heard the word as the secret in "catastrophic." I whispered to my mother, "What's a catastrophe?" She whispered back, "It's a terrible disaster, like a plane crash."

All in Good Time

1

THERE'S A PHOTOGRAPH OF ME WITH THE FAMILY DOG, MAUD. A WIRE haired terrier who seems to be laughing, Maud sits to my right on the brick stairs leading up to our front door. The house on La Brea Terrace has been rented for a year. It's a snug little place with a front lawn and no backyard, atop La Brea, just a bit into the Hollywood Hills. It is December 7, 1941. In short pants, suspenders, a white short-sleeve shirt, and black high shoes, I look bathed and scrubbed for the Sunday to be. It is morning, perhaps ten. My father, ever the photographer, is taking his time. "No, hold it right there. Hold it. Now. *One* more." My face does not reflect irritation. That would come years later. In fact, I appear to be happy, smiling in the sunshine, with Maud, the "smartest dog who ever lived"—my mother's view of Maud, always—right there next to me. The smartest dog, the smartest boy—me. The best movie, the most delicious piece of pie, the most succulent pear, the most wonderful, the most beautiful, the most thrilling, the greatest. Katherine Carrington Schwartz, a natural hyperbolist, was also inclined to the malaprop. "My, how time passes so fly." And always that strong clear speaking voice, with a song inside. Katherine had been an ingenue on the Broadway stage. Arthur Schwartz had spotted her in Jerome Kern and Oscar Hammerstein's *Music in the Air* singing "I've Told Every Little Star" to a young Walter Slezak. My father had attended the opening on election night 1932, a secondary event to FDR's first plurality but not secondary to the composer of "Dancing in the Dark." He sought out the ingenue almost before the curtain went down. I've occasionally imagined him, oh so eager, leaping upon the stage midway through the second act. "Good evening, I'm Arthur Schwartz," he might have said. Katherine, still in character, might have attempted to incorporate him. "Well, hello," she might have replied. "We've all been waiting for you." She might have extended her arm to the rest of the bewildered cast. The orchestra, trying to cover the disruption, would almost certainly have struck up "The Song Is You," a ballad in the score, while Arthur was hustled away by stagehands, his friends and peers Kern and Hammerstein in the back of the theater, burying their faces in their hands.

In the year to follow, Arthur leapt upon every stage that Katherine traversed. Here was a blond woman with a white round face, a curvaceous form, a delightful laugh, and a clarion voice with a song inside. Arthur played her everything he'd ever written. He began to compose for *her.* She sang his songs, to his great satisfaction. Upon occasion, at George Gershwin's Riverside Drive apartment, George would play the piano and then invite Kay and Arthur up. My father at the keyboard was fluent and unafraid, and always generous to other composers, especially Richard Rodgers, who was frequently present. Kay sang "Lover," her favorite Rodgers. Dick was greatly satisfied. Kay sang "With a Song in My Heart," Rodgers's favorite of his own making—he told me that, many years later. Arthur played Gershwin and then some of his own things, melodies that Kay had inspired.

It turned out that she had been first married as a very young woman. The boy, Clifford Dowdey, whose name is still recognized by scholars, wrote voluminously (and I mean voluminously) on the Civil War, a man possessed, pausing momentarily to marry a girl from Toms River, New Jersey, just about twenty-two years old, a looker, but oh, the noise! Poor Dowdey, who was onto new material, fascinating brand-new stuff about Robert E. Lee's father, Henry; and in the other room in a small New York City apartment, the soprano rang out with pop songs, not the Bach of Dowdey's delight. "Jerome Kern is a trifle," he told his wife. Kern was the reason that Kay had crossed the Hudson River to where the songs were written. Instead she had been diverted by the historian and had accepted his proposal of marriage. Perhaps it was his erudition; Kay had none. Perhaps his reputation; Kay had none. It doesn't seem possible that it was his humor: look him up, Dowdey, Clifford.

Kay and Arthur were married in 1934 amid the theater's elite. A photograph from around that time reveals a slim young man, dark-complexioned, dark-haired, handsome, sitting on the grass in front of a country house with his arm around a beautiful round-faced, light-skinned girl—young woman—exhibiting a thoughtful smile. I can only imagine that Dowdey's arm was never so comforting. As a matter of fact, I know of no photo of the two, though many years later, picking out one of his books at the Strand Bookstore, I found the inscription "For my darling Katherine." Dowdey had written those words in blue ink, possibly, I felt, with a quill pen. And how odd, I thought, to imagine my mother as someone else's darling.

Maud, laughing and leaping that Sunday, must have seen the commotion as some sort of game. The phone rang nonstop. My mother went upstairs to bed, where she was supposed to be most of the time. My father roamed the front lawn, holding my hand. Restlessly, I broke away and ran across the grass to fetch my blue tricycle.

Don Loper came over, a pale man in a white suit, a wisp of a guy, as soft as a pillow, a prominent interior designer; the Beverly Hills Hotel was a Loper marvel. I loved it when he came around. It was as if a white leaf had blown into our house. I called him "Don in the sky," and it stuck. Guess who's coming for dinner. Don in the sky, that's who.

Yipper was there that day, tossing me around a little and then "meeting" with Arthur and Loper in the study. Yipper was Yip Harburg, the lyricist, his *Wizard of Oz* only two years old. I could get him to sing "Ding Dong the Witch Is Dead" anytime I wanted.

But now Yipper was in a meeting behind closed doors, discussing Pearl Harbor. When they all came out, Don in the sky looked ashen. So haunted were his eyes, so radically altered, that he scared me. The white leaf had flown away, and I cried. Arthur gathered me up in his arms. "What's the matter, Jonno boy?" he asked. "Don in the sky's killed," I said.

2

ANN SOTHERN WAS MOVING ON. THE ACTRESS SOLD HER HOUSE ON Crescent Drive in Beverly Hills for $35,000 to Arthur Schwartz. My father moved us in with grand renovative gestures: down came a dining room chandelier, up went another, identical, at least to me. Out went the old carpeting, in came the new, mostly pale green all over the place. With much excitement, there arrived a piano, a Hamilton, which Arthur would own for many years. In the downstairs bathroom a small Grandma Moses, framed in ornate silver-painted wood, was lovingly placed left of the sink, a wintry Grandma Moses that recalled, for me, the New York ice of my first three years, before we had all moved west. My father had gone first, to look for work and find a house. We had followed a month later, my mother, her nurse and companion, and me, in a dark blue overcoat that was never used again. My father had met the train in Pasadena. Filled with a contagious joy, he spoke of his contemporaries who were there: Yip Harburg, Harold Arlen, Dorothy Fields, and Jerome Kern. And Ira Gershwin, now alone after George's death in a Los Angeles hospital in 1937.

"I want you to hear my new songs!"

Forever and ever, those were Arthur's crucial words. They were special words for my mother and me.

I want you to hear my new songs!

The songs spilled out of him as soon as we got near any piano at all. Throughout my life: school cafeteria pianos, Adirondack camp uprights, pianos in rented hotel rooms (many at the Ritz-Carlton in Boston), hotel ballroom pianos when no one was around, Westhampton pianos out of tune, and Arthur's own Hamilton, now the center of attraction in the white living room with green carpeting, fireplace, bookshelves, brown curtains at three wide windows, a light blue couch, a long gray couch, and two, maybe three very comfortable puffy red chairs. He was writing with a lyricist named Frank Loesser. He was writing with Leo Robin. He was writing with Johnny Mercer. All of them new to Arthur. His own well-known collaborator, Howard Dietz, held an executive position as head of publicity in New York with MGM and wasn't available for full-time partnership. That is why Arthur was writing with Ira Gershwin, Dorothy Fields, Oscar Hammerstein, Alan Jay Lerner, Maxwell Anderson, Yip Harburg, Al Stillman, and Sammy Cahn.

I fell asleep in the car on the way to La Brea Terrace, and as soon as we got inside, I was put to bed.

Arthur took sabbaticals on behalf of my mother.

They went to Boston, where a surgeon named Reginald Smithwick performed an operation that involved the cutting of the nerves down my mother's spine to relieve the dangerously high blood pressure that Kay tenuously lived with. A delicate procedure, a creation of Smithwick from which it took a while to recover. My parents remained in Boston, and then New York, for several months.

Another trip was inspired by the Rockefeller Institute in Manhattan, where, it seems to me, the first stirring of beta-blockers (these days the most effective treatment of hypertension) was in the works. My parents' stay that time was about a third of a year.

They kept in touch with me by phone and even by phonograph record. These were no amateur amusement park contrivances; Arthur took Kay into professional recording studios with pianos. There they enacted pleasant disagreements. What was their son's favorite song? My father suggested a title and played it. "No, no, no," protested my mother. "His favorite is . . ." And she sang to my father's playing. "No, no, no," my father protested. "His *real* favorite is . . ." And he played and sang "The Star-Spangled Banner." "No, no, no," my mother interrupted. "That's a wonderful song, but *I* know what his real favorite is," persuading my father near the end of the small 78-rpm disc. Katherine Carrington sang Arthur's well-known "I See Your Face Before Me," with a "Jonathan" thrown in before "face."

"Good-bye, darling," my mother said.

"Good-bye, Jonno boy," my father said.

During my parents' absences, I was left in the indifferent hands of Hazel Sherwood—a cook, housekeeper, and woman of such solemnity and internal Catholic ferocity that there was left no time at all for even a touch of mirth. In the evening, which meant from seven until nine-thirty, Hazel retired to the small maid's room off the kitchen. Behind that locked door, the two of them conspired: Hazel and the Bible, intimate pals, content in a thimble of space with a black throw rug over the light linoleum floor and a photo of Hazel's identical twin sister, Mabel, in Virginia. If I was home for dinner by six-thirty, I'd receive it piping hot. If not, there it would be, cold and slushy when I finally returned.

Often I came in after dark. I'd been around town, patrolling, looking out for other people's safety on my bike. The Lone Ranger permission I granted myself at the age of seven licensed my furtive rambling. The Beverly Hills between Sunset Boulevard and Santa Monica hardly needed surveillance. Doors were unlocked all the time. There was almost no traffic, even at noon. The names of the streets—Elm, Palm, Foothill, Crescent, Roxbury—were chosen, it seems to me, to define a vast garden of contentment, immune to impurities, scavengers, malcontents. The folks within lounged behind the unlocked doors, beside the Capehart record players, in the back of private screening rooms with gin and tonics in crystal glasses. Gin was the choice in the American time of war. Especially poolside. Festivity, Durante, the Brown Derby, gin. I advanced frequently into the dusk. I hid behind hedges, watching the silence. I roamed the alleys between the eternally summer streets.

I climbed the white cement fences, stealing into homes through back screen doors. Hidden behind curtains, under beds, or in closets, I listened undetected to the music of family life. They ate their dinners, they squabbled and relented, they refilled their glasses of wine, they sat around the radio. In one dining room, a plate of food was thrown. It made an awful sound, crashing against the wall behind the intended target, a red-haired woman, a wife. From behind a curtain in an adjoining room I took a peek. The wife, in tears, sat with her back as straight as could be. She made no sound, though her face looked as if it had just emerged from a shower.

Look at her. Maybe she's fourteen. She's in full control of the horse, alone on the bridle path in the middle of Rodeo Drive, between Elevado and Lomitas, riding north toward Sunset Boulevard. She wears a formal riding outfit and an amazing black top hat, out of which flows the longest black hair in the entire world. Alabaster, that's her. If I were closer, the large veins of her temples would be really clear. She is at ease with the trot; I've already learned how uncomfortable it is. Trot, trot; control, control; flowing, flowing. *Clip-clop* on the pavement of the cross streets. Her back is rigid, her great gray animal appreciatively swishes its tail. Its passenger is a light load, riding out of my sight, long black hair the last of her to disappear.

She didn't go to Hawthorne, the school I sort of attended. Beverly Hills High, I guessed. I would wait for her behind the hedges along Rodeo. She would come by irregularly, impossible to anticipate. I lay on my belly, my bike on the grass next to me. On those occasions, and on others, especially at night, I would call upon my mother's voice. "I see your Jonathan face before me."

The rider might not come tonight.

Most people didn't show up.

What I mean by "sort of attended" can be best understood by hearing from Virginia Pogson, the principal of Hawthorne, a school of white stucco, red-orange brick breezeways, and overlit classrooms, a block and a half from home.

"Jonno, the answer isn't out the window."

"Jonno, you're not applying yourself. Look at this report card: C, D, D, B+ (in English), F. And only *two* silver stars, the lowest number in the class. And six absences! What in the world are you telling your mother and father?"

Virginia Pogson was squat, matronly, gray-haired, and not unpleasant. I was but a deflection to her, soon, she must have felt, to be gone from Hawthorne and on to some other "location of learning." Miss Pogson had a fondness for "location of learning." In a conference with Hazel Sherwood that I attended, she said that Jonno just wasn't using this "location of learning" in the least. Later on, Hazel claimed it as her own: "Are you going to your location of learning today or just hanging around listening to records?" That's why I remember it so clearly. Hazel's theft. I began to use it satirically in class. "May I excuse myself from this location of learning to go to the boys' room?" Or: "Do I *have* to stay after class at this location of learning?"

Everybody perceived me as a wise guy. I was not recognized as a satirist. No, you may not go to the boys' room. Yes, you'll stay after class.

More little records from New York. More of Jonno boy's favorite songs. "Are you being good to Hazel and Maud?" asked my mother on one little record. "I hope so, because Santa Claus will know. Daddy and I will be home for Christmas, which isn't so long from now, and we'll have so much fun. Hazel, Maud, and Hazel's sister." Hazel's sister, whose train trip from Virginia was being financed by Arthur. Fun fun fun. That particular little record was made on the first of October, 1944. The label was dated in my father's hand. It arrived perhaps a week later.

My bedroom, at the top of the stairs and down the hall, overlooked our backyard. My mother had seen to the flowers, the marigolds, petunias, geraniums, and poppies—quite a show of color. Two fruit-bearing and climbable trees, a persimmon and an avocado, bracketed the far end of the lawn, just inside the white cement wall, itself climbable, just about. On the other side of the wall was an immaculate Beverly Hills alley, wide enough for cars, terrific for bikes or roller skates, or just running as fast as I could. The wind would whistle in my ears. I'd stop, out of breath, at Elevado or Carmelita, the cross streets, east-west. I might take an interest in someone's backyard, someone's kitchen screen door or patio sliding door. Inside the house, a hiding place. I might wait for hours, maybe even falling asleep behind some especially grand couch. The family would flow together sooner or later, coming out from the private pockets of their home, bickering or howling with laughter. They might listen to Tom Mix on the radio (I listened, too, hidden away). They might put on records (I knew every note). But I was not *of* them. My good-bye was lightning fast and always into the dark. I used the alleys to return home. I was stealthy and agile and, not understanding why, often teary.

The bell played a little four- or five-note tune. As soft as a whisper, as energizing as an open trumpet, the little tune announced the Helm's man, a mobile bakery packed with jelly doughnuts, chocolate chip cookies the size of the moon, strawberry tarts, apple cakes, cinnamon rolls. Children I didn't know materialized at the Helm's truck, racing breathlessly up Crescent Drive, arriving by bike, or just running out of houses both north and south of Lomitas. Now and again, a Hawthorne boy's face gave a grinless nod—I was now seven, eight, nine, with a wise-guy reputation.

The Helm's jelly doughnut stands to this day as the finest American work of art in its field. After the truck had pulled away, after the others had departed, I would sit at the curb, my two strawberry jelly doughnuts beside me on the cement. I often thought: What's good in my life? Who do I hate? Who are all the teams in the Pacific Coast League? The taste of a jelly doughnut brought out the lists in me and, in a quirky, Proustian way, still does. At the curb at Crescent and Lomitas in the summer of 1946, I hated Hazel's sister (fun fun fun); Billy Rothburg (in my class); the woman in the white uniform at the Cañon Theater, the movie house that became the Hitching Post on Saturdays, where you tied your bike outside to a rack placed on the street, and sidled in to see two westerns, a Laurel and Hardy short, and an episode of the Cisco Kid. If you spoke too loud or rested your foot on the back of the seat in front of you, the matron in the white uniform would shine a flashlight in your eyes from her menacing position in the aisle.

What's good in my life?

My parents are home.

Bubble gum is back (a rubber shortage during the war had almost shut down the Fleer's Dubble Bubble people, though my own discovery allowed for a poor substitute: six pieces of Dentyne gum would at least produce anemic bubbles).

Records. Music. Avocados. The girl on the horse.

The way my father looked at the piano. It was so exciting. I loved him so much, particularly when he was on the piano bench.

I really felt organized, making those lists. I felt functional.

What am I afraid of?

I'm afraid of going to sleep. I'm afraid my mother will die in a catastrophe. I'm afraid of practically everyone in my class, especially Billy Rothburg. I'm afraid of holes in bedsheets, that mice will bite off my toes.

I'm afraid of the girl on the horse.

Something wonderful in my life was our avocado tree. I could climb to the highest spot; the limbs offered easy steps. High up in the tree, they made seats. To be hidden away, sitting high on those seats, was to be comforted by invisibility. The garden was serviced by Japanese gardeners, solemn, ageless. My mother's marigolds, petunias, geraniums, and poppies; her snapdragons, pansies, and sweet peas; all were watered and pampered. I observed our gardener as if he were appearing in a silent movie, a man in green dungarees and lumberjack shirt, despite the heat. I sat in the tree with a ripe avocado in hand. I had brought up a pocketknife and a Dixie cup's flat wooden spoon. I would pull the knife in and around the avocado, slicing lengthwise. Then I would disengage the pit from its half with the spoon and let it drop and bounce its way down through the branches to the earth at the trunk of the tree, where many other pits were settled. The avocado, so much subtler than candy, so delicate and reassuring, was the only spiritual symbol in my life.

My father told the story for years. Jonno kept that Victrola from the age of three until we left California for good in 1947. Six years without breaking it or breaking one single record. When he was little, he'd applaud after every song, like the audience.

The audience in the tree, the audience in other people's houses, the audience rather than a student at Hawthorne, and what an audience for the music!

Bing Crosby, André Kostelanetz, Dinah Shore, Artie Shaw. They all sang or played my father's melodies.

"That was a song by Arthur Schwartz," I would say out loud, changing the record. "Here is Judy Garland."

Applause applause in my bedroom. On weekends, all day long.

My mother, in her own bed in a darkened room at noon, would listen to me telling her about the records. She would read their labels as I handed them to her.

She was dressed in a silk nightgown and a lace bed jacket. There was always a book in her lap, and when I came in she would push her glasses above her hairline to greet me, cheerfully. I was called "Pumpkin," and was always asked about the records I was playing and which song of Arthur's I liked best. "Listen, hear him?" she'd say.

Downstairs, Arthur was composing with the door closed. I often sat outside that door, as the audience, and heard him repeat a melody over and over again, adding to it, subtracting, changing keys, experimenting with tempo. It seemed to me that he could stay in there forever. I could never stay anywhere forever, except at my record player. Other than that, everything felt fragmentary; shards of time, the picture disassembled, danger at the gate. Keep moving. Beware of trust.

"His highs were high, and his lows were low," a friend of Arthur's recalled, long after his death in 1984.

But from out of the living room there emerged, finally, only an ebullient guy. Hearing him finish, I had scampered away. On most occasions, he would call me in to hear what he had written, and I would listen to what I had already heard. Although I never told him, I could identify his edits, his inclusions, or a new line or two that he'd make up right then. I was able to hear the architecture of a melody, to feel it whole, a complete thing, with no words yet. Just my dad. Just his handiwork.

No need to ask him to play it again. He would always play it three or four times. When the lyric was written, he'd sing it into your face, *selling* the song, playing softly for the first vocal chorus. Then he would play the entire melody, just the melody, and he would beam at you and draw out the best you had, smiles galore, appreciation, clapping, play-it-again, I-want-to-hear-it-again. Arthur would ask, "Isn't it terrific?"

It *was* terrific. It *was,* it *was.*

"Listen, hear him?" said my mother, in bed upstairs, on borrowed time.

Backstage at the Alvin Theatre, on the night of November 8, 1932, after the first performance of *Music in the Air,* Arthur must have really put it to Kay. He must have gotten to some piano backstage or the next day in his apartment, or possibly in Kern's, or to somebody else's piano. Arthur wooed the beautiful blond soprano, adored, it seemed, by everyone around *Music in the Air.* She told Arthur that he was "a very pleasant nuisance."

Kay must surely have heard all his songs. "Something to Remember You By," "I Guess I'll Have to Change My Plan," "Dancing in the Dark." And Chopin in the concert halls. And Rossini, Mozart, Brahms. And Gershwin, Rodgers, Kern. He immersed Katherine Carrington in all that she'd been hoping for.

Two years after they were married, almost to the day, she dropped to her knees in sickness on a tennis court in Great Neck, Long Island.

There was one screwup during one of my parents' many absences.

In someone else's house, after a silent break-in, I had found a large broom closet as a hiding place. In a pantry off the dining room I sat down in the dark amid mops and dusters, and with the door slightly ajar, I was able to observe the family dinner that got itself together a long time after I'd settled in.

The family, a man and a woman who appeared much older than my mother and father, sat at each end of a large rectangular table and dined silently, their courses served by a maid in a white uniform who resembled Hazel Sherwood. They seemed far away from each other, so disconnected from whatever it was they had started out with, whatever fine silk thread of affection they had shared. There was nothing to suggest that there were children anywhere in the house. Just these two austere people, eating.

Suddenly the man rose, his eyes on the closet. Perhaps I had stirred. It took only a second or two for him to get to the door and fling it open. I was sitting on the floor, legs crossed in front of me. He looked down with anger and addressed me in a foreign language that I've come to believe was Italian.

I stood, preparing to flee. I knew my parents would be called, that Miss Pogson would be told. I was almost nine and able to think it through quickly.

I zipped by the man, through the pantry, and out the patio door, across the twilight garden, over the cement fence, down the alley, onto my bike hidden behind four or five enormous garbage cans.

I was so angry. A furious little boy, discovered as an intruder. A thief. Of what? Of family laughter and the sight of asparagus and ginger cookies and milk and butter and candles and babies—infants in high chairs—and bananas and radios and pajamas and comic books and bottles of wine, and love.

I picked up speed, approaching Elevado. I flew across the street, daring drivers, of whom there were none. I was profoundly embarrassed. The man's voice comes back to me at every Italian film.

I tried to reach my parents at the Volney Hotel in New York, but they weren't in, at eleven o'clock in the East. Way back in the East. I was going to say good night, that's all. No big deal. But they were out, way back in the East.

3

MY FATHER AND MANY OTHERS BELIEVED THAT JAPANESE PLANES MIGHT drop bombs on Los Angeles if we didn't protect our skies, and that we had to obey any order issued, especially at night. When sirens rang out ominously all over Los Angeles, we were to turn out our lights and plunge the house into darkness. Blackouts, infrequent as they were, allowed for great excitement, even between Hazel and me. "Lights off!" she would shout, coming out of her room, climbing the stairs, hurrying down the hall to make sure I knew what to do. "Lights off!" She was right outside my door. "I *hear* you!" I said, waiting until the last minute to turn off my lights.

But my records kept going, by flashlight.

They were very well organized, in their sleeves stored like books on a shelf. Perhaps there were fifty 78 rpms, and three or four twelve-inch 78-rpm discs with only one side occupied. The blank side was a smooth black ghost, on which, I imagined, there had once been strange and quiet works of music that no one had ever bothered to listen to, music from faraway lands, emphasizing an unidentifiable instrument, possibly the harp. My father had taken me to the Hollywood Bowl, where, at a common harp, a woman in white had had moments to herself. She had made ethereal sounds, her hands combing the strings, caressing them, her long blond hair reminding me of the rider on Rodeo. I imagined that hers was the music on all the blank sides, the music of the girl on the horse. It was what went on in her home, in her family. Safe in her room, she would remove her hat, her riding outfit, everything but her pajamas, which I guessed were under all of it. Then she would comb her hair before the mirror. She was the only person able to hear the music on the blank sides. On side A of the twelve-inch discs, there were patriotic "masterworks" calling for all of us to support "the war effort." My father, with Frank Loesser, wrote such a masterwork. It was entitled "Buy a Bond." My father played it and sang it, with gusto: "Buy a bond, give a dollar, and we'll hear the people holler" is the one line left in my mind. My father's melody ascended, much like Rodgers's "Blue Room." It became urgent, joyous. My father, singing it, had such a wonderful time, way up there on the high notes: "And we'll hear the people holler!" when he performed "Buy a Bond" on a demonstration record and at parties downstairs. He sang as if trying to differentiate the song from his other material by lending it a patriotic glow, his fervor unbounded. The audiences in the living room were the Beverly Hills elite; the songwriters, choreographers, directors, and producers, the nimble dancers and adored clowns, the beautiful women who had become active in "the war effort," and the screenwriters, all of them married couples. The Spewacks, the Hacketts, the Ephrons, two sets of Kanins, and Ruth and Gus Goetz. I believed that movies *had* to be written by married couples, with the possible exception of the brothers Julius and Philip Epstein, but that, in any event, it was the *law* that only relatives wrote stories.

"We all together live," my mother said, about the Hollywood people in Beverly Hills.

All under an invisible bubble that insulated us from the troubles of war and from general misbehavior. There were few vehicular disturbances, no street-corner confrontations—in fact, no pedestrian traffic whatsoever. In that luxurious ghost town, the ping of a pink rubber ball thrown against brick stairs could actually break the enormous silence, the silence of the passing of time; the silence of the growth of flowers; of gardeners in lumberjack shirts; of the silence of thought; of muted grief, of amorphous longing. The silence of Hazel's room with the door closed.

The silence was broken by the sound of my father's piano in the early morning, of his composing, some phrases repeated over and over again. In the evening, the frequent gatherings were pleasant to hear from above. I lay in bed, listening, slowly falling to sleep. One night there arrived at my bedside, before my eyes were closed, Judy Garland. She said, "I came to sing you a lullaby." She sat beside me. Her lullaby was "Over the Rainbow." Afterward, she giggled. Then she left. "Sleep well," she said from the doorway.

Later she sang it again, downstairs. I was wide awake. Everyone applauded. But when she had come upstairs, it had been only for me. Just one person. I was special, that's for sure.

The end of the war, the very end of it, on August 14, 1945, caused a stir in Beverly Hills. American flags appeared in windows, firecrackers went off in the distance, and far more traffic than usual accounted for honks and rumbling up and down Crescent Drive.

I carried out my idea of a celebration.

Stringing five or six extension cords together—the house was full of them—I brought my Victrola out to the front lawn and all the way over to the sidewalk, at the corner of Crescent and Lomita. I also brought out perhaps six or seven records of my father's music. They were all instrumental versions of his songs by the orchestras of Leo Reisman or André Kostelanetz. His songs poured into the neighborhood at top volume: "Shine on Your Shoes," "Dancing in the Dark," "Alone Together," "You and the Night and the Music," "New Sun in the Sky."

My mother, up in her room, waved at me through her window.

My father came home from the studio. Hazel appeared on the front steps. I ran upstairs to get another record, to discover that, although all the radios in the house were on and tuned to the network news, they didn't drown out the music I'd set up outside. The record I'd come in for was somebody's version of "I See Your Face Before Me." It joined the rotation on the sidewalk. Neighbors showed up appreciatively. Kids came around on their bikes. The Helm's man appeared, his little song warmly joining my father's music. When Arthur arrived, he beamed with delight. By then the Good Humor truck had replaced the Helm's man. My father bought ice cream for everyone.

He put his arm around me. We had always been affectionately tactile, and what better time than now, with balloons rising above us and "New Sun in the Sky" on the turntable once more? My mother, dressed in short pants, came out of the house barefoot. Someone gave her a Good Humor bar.

"This is the most *delicious* ice cream I've ever had," she said.

I recall that I felt a great relief.

4

HARRY COHN, WHO RAN COLUMBIA PICTURES, SAW IN ARTHUR A PRO-ducer and had hired him in that capacity for the Rita Hayworth–Gene Kelly film *Cover Girl*. Arthur would write the music to Ira Gershwin's lyrics and produce, for the first time.

But no. No, of all things, to the collaboration with Ira. "There's a better man than I available," he told my mother he'd told Harry Cohn. Through the years, repeating the story, he stuck with those words. "There's a better man than I available."

Arthur became the employer of the composer he most admired, Jerome Kern. To Cohn, Arthur Schwartz was, as my father said himself, a songwriter "for the theater." He had written a highly regarded score, with Frank Loesser, for the movie *Thank Your Lucky Stars*, which had included a grand event: Bette Davis singing. Sort of. The song, which bemoaned the fact that the best American boys were overseas, characterized what was left as "They're Either Too Young or Too Old." Harry Cohn loved that song. Harry Cohn sought out Arthur.

My father in his forties cut a suave path. He was cultivated, as suggested by his unaccountable, ever-so-slight British accent. He was always wonderfully dressed. He moved gracefully with cigarette in hand, a man in honorable thought. His dark hair was turning gray, his light blue eyes held no venom. He was alive and ready for conversation, by all accounts a marvelous listener. He was able to intimately argue both sides of any issue, confident that his own heartfelt view would prevail. He would make it happen with tenacious charm and a cascade of absolutes. Same thing with tennis. He was ambidextrous, simply shifting the racket from one hand to the other so that every stroke became a forehand. For years and years, I told him that "it was the same goddamn thing as arguing both sides of an issue" as his own heartfelt view won again and again on the court. "Don't talk to your father in that language," he would say with a humorous little smirk.

Who, then, could argue with "There's a better man than I available. I would like to hire Jerome Kern."

Kern and Ira quickly wrote a song called "Midnight Music." After Kern played it for the producer, and before Arthur could even speak, Kern jotted something down on the sheet music. "What did you write?" Arthur asked, seeing the letters "ADL." Kern explained: "Those letters mean 'Arthur doesn't like.'"

"How did you know?"

"I could feel it as you listened."

"I love your melody. But Ira can do better."

Ira's lyric:

Just a whisper, soft and low,
And midnight was aglow,
For oh, your words made midnight music—
Words that brought me such a thrill
The echoes haunt me still—
and always will.
In that midnight rendezvous
You said, "There's only you."

And oh, there never was such music!
Darkened streets began to shine
The moment midnight music made you mine.

But time was essential. The song had to be recorded.

Ira's next lyric after Arthur's urging:

Long ago and far away
I dreamed a dream one day—
And now that dream is here beside me.
Long the skies were overcast,
But now the clouds have passed:
You're here at last!
Chills run up and down my spine,
Aladdin's lamp is mine:
The dream I dreamed was not denied me.
Just one look and then I knew
That all I longed for long ago was you.

What would Arthur have written in its place?

I think he would have composed a terrific tune, every bit as dignified as Kern's, something along the lines of his own "If There Is Someone Lovelier than You." Would it have been as revered as "Long Ago and Far Away"? God knows. The meaning of such an award, then much more powerful for songs than now, would have altered our family's life. Arthur's options as a composer would surely have been many. Had he wanted to, he could have sailed on as a Hollywood composer and producer of musical films for at least ten years.

As it was, the Cole Porter story, *Night and Day,* followed *Cover Girl* for producer Arthur Schwartz. Starring Cary Grant, *Night and*

Day was as hollow a film as you could imagine, held afloat only by Porter's songs. It allowed me the first inkling, however it came to me, that up on that screen the truth wasn't being told. The whole thing was in cartoon language and not to be taken seriously. Ducks, chickens, mice, cats, elephants, and zebras all blabbing away and occasionally singing songs, as if nothing out of the ordinary were going on. The film was about a man my father revered, a man I'd met, a man who'd been downstairs. I didn't think the movie was telling the truth. I felt that it was giving me the runaround, all over the place. These feelings were embryonic, but I remember them.

A day or so later, I was told that my parents were going to New York but they'd be back soon. They told this to their son, who knew the meaning of the word "catastrophic," who knew they wouldn't be back soon. I was being given the runaround.

Occasionally my father would lie down and stay there for a day or two. What was wrong? "The man with the pitchfork is here," he told me, meaning that a man with a pitchfork had come to the house to poke him in the stomach. I looked up pitchfork: a large, long-handled fork for lifting hay. I had seen such forks in westerns. Now I was told that some invisible guy was using one on my father. For sure, in the middle of the night when I was asleep. No one ever spoke the word "colitis."

My father took me to a special screening of *Night and Day* before its release. Cary Grant sat next to my mother. The room was full.

My father drove us home afterward. He asked what I had thought of *Night and Day.* My reply remained in the family as "a great story about Jonno": We took him to see *Night and Day,* and when we asked him what he thought of it, he said that he thought it had been written by the man with the pitchfork.

The telling of the tale involved a series of evasions:

1. The story, told jovially, had it that Arthur had experienced a stomachache for one hour a month or so earlier.
2. The pitchfork line was just a throwaway by Arthur, when, in fact, he'd said it many times.
3. Jonno loved *Night and Day* and said that it had been written by the man with the pitchfork as a way of complimenting the movie, the pitchfork being a happy joke that Daddy had made up when his stomach hurt during that one hour. Jonno, by saying "pitchfork," invoked his loving dad.

In fact, the hour was really many many many days, through which my father lay on his back on a couch in a dark room downstairs, like my mother upstairs in bed. He would lie there with his eyes open, and when I came in, he would mournfully say, "Oh, Jonno boy. Oh, Jonno boy." My real feelings about the movie, which I would not have been able to tell them, were confused and sour. The pitchfork was all I could think of. It touched on the truth, if Kay and Arthur had wanted to consider it at all, while at the same time operating as a little-boy prank. I was just being a wise guy driving home in the car, kidding around and all.

Evasions like these were the currency of the family.

My father's Jewishness went unacknowledged. I had no idea I was considered a Jew until high school. I was never given a bar mitzvah and never attended one. I had no connection to the spiritual life, but I loved Christmas, of course for its gifts, but specially, I think, for its ornamental corroboration of the passing of time. My mother, so clearly Christian, had no idea in the world what she was. Yip Harburg called her "Arthur's shiksa." I thought that meant Arthur's wife, and, in fact, many years later I referred to the wife of a teacher (a man named Rosen) as Dr. Rosen's shiksa.

The length of my parents' absences, before they occurred, were played down, as in "We'll be home soon."

The severity of my mother's illness was never talked about unless I raised my voice really loud in the hallway outside her room. Then my father would say, with startling ferocity, "If you don't lower your voice, you'll kill your mother!"

My school grades, dropping lower and lower, were characterized as "flukey and temporary."

Hazel was described as "kind" and "caring."

And *Night and Day* was embraced as "fabulous."

Every now and then, my father would say to me, "Let's go over to Ira's house." Ira Gershwin's house on Roxbury Drive, next to the house in which George had lived, was the central gathering spot for the songwriting community. Yip was always present, as were Harold Arlen, Kern, Harry Warren, Burton Lane, and Arthur. If there were other children around, I don't remember them. What I do recall was the surprising sight of Ira Gershwin on a tennis court. He always appeared to me as the man in an easy chair, inside the house, always reading, a book or manuscript in his lap, one of George's pianos only a few feet away. His eyes were welcoming. I could make him smile—I don't remember how. But his nice chuckle was another man's uproar. In his quietness, Ira was revered for his authentic modesty, for the brilliance and bulk of his work. The evasion at Ira's house was the only occasionally acknowledged shadow of his brother by his side, close to the easy chair, near his racquet on the tennis court, at poolside next to his glass of orange juice, in the constant sway of the wind. I felt it as a child. Everyone else did, too: The blood rushes to the neck and cheeks. Hands and feet grow warm, though clouds have obscured the sun. Ira survives in the mist, sedentary. The chuckle. The lack of grandiloquence, the soft uncertainty of self, the conviction that the magic lay elsewhere, deceased, silenced well before the war, and, in dying, cutting down everyone's chances, chopping years off the far end of their futures. Only the magic could have pushed things forward further than, in the end, they would go. The magic would have enlarged the possibilities and extended the refinement. Without that magic, they were all running out of time.

Harold Arlen, dressed in tennis shorts, played George's songs on George's piano. We all sat around with gin and tonics, me with a Coke. A cantor's son from Buffalo, Arlen had a lovely singing voice, melancholy through and through, similar to Johnny Mercer's, even though Mercer, from Georgia, was touched by whimsy. Arlen's wife, Anya, seated on the carpet at Harold's feet and right next to me, put her arm around my shoulder, where it remained. Let it go on, let it go on, were my unspoken thoughts.

Then Kern played. He had long hairs growing from each nostril. Was he dying?

Gin and tonics sat on cork coasters.

Refills, more ice from the kitchen.

Arthur may have had one drink at the start, but water was his preference, except at the Beachcomber's, on Vine Street, where rum, sugar, and orange juice made him lively and anecdotal. Far from the man lying on the couch.

Kay was at the Beachcomber's. She sipped from my father's drink. Salt was forbidden her. She ate a bowl of rice. Being on the town with her family made her teary. I didn't know why that should have been the case at a restaurant with little umbrellas in the drinks. Here she was, away from her bed, away from Laura Z. Hobson, Betty Smith, and back issues of *The New Yorker.* She liked the magazine's "light handshake."

My mother leaned over and kissed me on the cheek.

I wanted a sip of my father's drink.

Not too much, I was told.

My mother laughed and kissed me again.

We ate giddily in candlelight, Kay and Arthur and their son.

5

"AND YOU'RE COMING WITH US!" MY FATHER ANNOUNCED.

He and I were driving to the Hollywood Bowl in the early evening. My father told me that he was going to write a show for Broadway and the family was coming with him. I'd miss a semester at Hawthorne, but I'd go to school in New York and I'd visit him while the show was trying out in Boston. He felt confident that given the people he'd be working with, the show would be a "smash."

During the concert that night, during Gershwin's Concerto in F, he issued a mischievous smile and took my hand. He was telling me that he would write great music for a smash show and he was feeling great about it. He had mentioned in the car that Ira Gershwin would do the lyrics and two other guys would work on the smash show. The smash would put him back in business in New York. At the Hollywood Bowl, with George's music filling the night, out of doors, Arthur was exhilarated. The concerto, especially the second movement, still reminds me of my father's smile that night.

A smile that led to a whirl of hastily made plans.

I would go to a camp in the East for July and August.

My parents would take a suite of rooms at the Essex House in the City, where specialists would be able to monitor my mother's precarious health.

After camp I would attend a New York City private school and be escorted to and from that school by a grad student my father would hire.

In almost no time at all, I was gone, placed on a plane in the charge of the airline. On the other end I was handled by friends of my parents, in whose apartment I stayed the night, and in whose company I taxied next day to Grand Central Terminal where I was alphabetically committed to a group of kids who seemed to number in the hundreds.

On an endless train ride to the Adirondack Mountains, I was offered sandwiches and cookies by a boy named Schweitzer, who had been oversupplied. My one Hershey bar, bought with great fanfare at Grand Central by the friends of my parents, stayed in my bag until the middle of the night, in a cabin in the woods, in a rainstorm, with Schweitzer comfortably asleep in the bed next to mine.

Twenty-four summers earlier, in 1922, Arthur had been a counselor at this very camp and had written all of its songs, which were still being sung in 1946. Brant Lake was the only camp with a Score, music by Arthur Schwartz and lyrics by Lorenz Hart. My father had befriended his diminutive fellow counselor Hart at once, finding a young man already promised to a theatrical career and to the young composer Richard Rodgers.

One of the melodies my father wrote on the dining hall's out-of-tune upright was what became, a few years later, "I Guess I'll Have to Change My Plan." Larry Hart's camp lyric, which has always struck me as misinformed, describes an idyllic summer life:

I love to lie awake in bed,
Right after taps I pull the flaps above my head,
And let the stars shine on my pillow—
Oh what a light the moonbeams shed.
I feel so happy I could cry,

And tears are born within the corner of my eye,
To be at home with Ma was never like this,
I could live forever like this—
I love to lie awake awhile,
And go to sleep with a smile.

Howard Dietz differed:

I guess I'll have to change my plan,
I should have realized there'd be another man,
I overlooked that point completely
Until the big affair began.
My boiling point is much too low
For me to try and be a fly lothario;
I think I'll crawl right back and into my shell,
Dwelling in my personal hell,
I'll have to change my plan around,
I've lost the one girl I've found.

As a result of the camp score—seven songs in all—the framed photos of the songwriters hung conspicuously in the clubhouse, gleaming down on every camp function, during every rally, during all camp shows, during all celebrations or mass scoldings, during color war huddles, secret ballot caucuses, occasional meetings of prayer.

Arthur Schwartz and Larry Hart, in framed black-and-white photos above the stage, appeared presidential, omniscient.

For me, Arthur's picture granted entitlement without my understanding its obviously alienating power: it bespoke trouble for whoever showed up as the child. That I was uncomfortable in any group larger than three was a part of my nature that I disregarded in pursuit of that entitlement, that special treatment that irritated far more than any simple little group of three. The contradiction of entitled discomfort, witty in retrospect, disastrous then, revealed a clear vulnerability that any kid my age would recognize and exploit.

And exploit they did, running in packs: stolen candy, French sheets, water balloons dropped from the rafter onto my bed, towels taken away during my shower, Ex-Lax in candy wrappers, my cherished baseball thrown from one to the other to another to another, me in the middle, crying, "Give it back, give it back."

The smashing of the radio, which broke my heart.

A mass scolding was held under my father's photo.

A new radio was purchased in Glen Falls with the offending kid's money.

The radio was the source of baseball, actual Major League baseball rather than the Pacific Coast League games between the Hollywood Stars and Portland Beavers, which I had listened to with the kind of attention that knows no equal, except, perhaps, that given to the study of sexual rumor.

For me, the radio *was* the team most audible, the Boston Red Sox and their imperious slugger Ted Williams.

My mother and father came to visit.

Entitlement abounded. I was taken to the owner's house. I swam in the owner's private section of the lake. I ate in a restaurant. I slept in a room with my mother and father.

They were now living in New York, my father preparing his smash show. Arthur told the camp owners that he was working with Ira Gershwin, George S. Kaufman, and Nunnally Johnson.

He played a couple of his new songs on a piano every bit as out of tune as the one in the dining hall. He sang, he played, he sang.

Then my parents left in spite of my tears, promising that the summer would quickly go by and that they'd be waiting at the

Essex House. I remember that my mother stumbled on the gravel getting into the car; that her straw hat fell off; that my father retrieved it with a glance in my direction.

The smash show, *Park Avenue,* ran for but seventy-two performances at the Shubert Theatre. Arthur Schwartz and his family were back in Beverly Hills for Thanksgiving. The man with the pitchfork had remained on Crescent Drive, awaiting Arthur's failure.

My mother and father's two dark rooms now assumed a somber formality. Night into day, there they were, the man with the pitchfork downstairs with my father. I rambled between them, my mother far the more interesting of the two, her magazines piled high; the recipes for dishes she could not possibly eat clipped and gathered together on the bed table; her sneaky one cigarette a day taken only in my presence, her good spirits the cause of mirthful conspiracy.

Funereally chained to his brown couch, my father said little. "Jonno boy, oh, Jonno boy," is what he had to offer. And occasionally: "Your mother is so sick. I can't do any more for her than I am."

Meaning that there was nowhere else to search for a cure, no other medicine to discover, no other sources of joy to call upon on her behalf. And so, in the dark, his belly under siege, my father lay beneath a gray blanket, dressed in brown-and-white shoes, slacks, and a white shirt with a dark tie. He would sleep and not sleep. He would rue the day he'd taken on *Park Avenue.* He told me that he would never return to Broadway. He told me he *would* return to Broadway if only he had "a project."

Then he would sleep again and not sleep again.

. . .

The idea was this: We'd sell the house. We'd drive across the country as a family, stopping at Zion National Park, Bryce Canyon, and Yellowstone National Park. We'd arrive in New York just in time for my ninth birthday, June 28, and for the train to camp, June 29. Arthur would find a show to do, a project—Howard Dietz had signaled his availability. Arthur "hated" California. He wanted to write "for the theater."

But I *hate* camp.

You'll grow to love it, Arthur said.

He sold 723 North Crescent Drive for $75,000.

We were on the road in early June.

From the backseat, I described the surroundings:

> You'll find to your left a field of grazing horses.
> You'll see to your right a gas station with nobody in it.

"A little quiet back there," my father said, at the wheel, sensitive to the superfluous spoken word.

"I'm broadcasting the scenery," I said.

There it was, another family story. "We were driving across the country, and Jonno, in the backseat, said . . ."

Maud sat beside me, breathing rapidly in and out, drooling a little. My father drove cautiously and therefore slowly, and a broadcaster could closely regard scenery of any kind.

Early in the morning, in a motel near Hoover Dam, my father came to the room I had by myself. He woke me with excitement. "Come with me," he said. "Put your clothes on."

It was just getting light. The heat, though ferocious even at so early an hour, was comforting. I must have said, "I like it hot." My father must have replied, "This is the desert."

He took me to Hoover Dam and explained its purpose.

He told me that I should always look after my mother, in the event anything happened to him. He expressed his love for me with a genuineness that I experienced as something far greater than ordinary. It was in his quiet voice, in the touch of his hand, in its brevity.

My mother, always inclined to dizzy spells, suffered a whopper in Cody, Wyoming. For two days, she lay in a motel room, her strength eaten away by the trip we were on, her son's constant energy, and Arthur's euphoric melancholy. Possibly, too, by food she shouldn't have eaten, walks she shouldn't have taken, and the happy notion of the musical theater again. Mr. and Mrs. Arthur Schwartz.

A doctor staying at the motel examined Kay and advised Arthur not to continue the drive with his wife. "Put her on a train," my father told me the doctor had said.

From a local hospital, Arthur secured a private nurse, at what must have been great cost, to accompany my mother and me to New York by train.

We left, my father waving to us on the platform. The heat that I had loved in the desert was ruthless in Wyoming. My clothes stuck to my body. My mother, wet through and through, looked wiped out. My father on the platform, faded from view as we slowly pulled away from the station. He appeared disheveled and fatigued. He held a lit cigarette in one hand and Maud's leash in the other. Maud panted and twirled beside him.

My mother lay down on a lower bed in a sleeper.

Sitting by the window, I broadcast the scenery in silence.

. . .

When he showed up on my ninth birthday, the day before camp began, Arthur had tales to tell. For one thing, he had lost and then, at the last minute, found Maud, who had wandered away and taken refuge from the heat in the back of an auto repair shop while Arthur was buying a sandwich a few stores down. He had come, he said, within ten minutes of having to leave the vanished dog behind. What would Kay and Jonno have thought? How could he come back without Maud? There he'd been for five hours in a tiny Michigan town in the middle of nowhere, calling Maud's name, until finally there she was, asleep at the nozzle of a dribbling hose under a workbench. My God, had he been relieved!

But the really good news was that he'd had an idea for a show. He'd seen a book in a window along the way, gaudily displayed as a number one best-seller. It was called *Inside U.S.A.* He had never met the author, John Gunther, but assumed that through his friends the publishers Bennett Cerf and Richard Simon he could get to Gunther and ask permission to use the title for a musical about America. He would do it in revue form; he and Howard Dietz would write songs that glorified unusual spots on the map, such as Rhode Island, Pittsburgh, Atlanta. He'd already written a title song with a complete melody and a partial lyric. Would we like to hear it?

A Steinway upright in the living room of the suite he'd rented had, he was told, just come in two days earlier. Arthur was at that piano twenty minutes after coming through the door. He sang, he played, he sang:

The USA was born in liberty
On a wonderful day,

And you know the sequel,
We are free and equal,
And may we say we're doing OK!

That was as far as he'd gotten with the lyric, though he'd finished the melody and presented it to us with all the fervor of "Buy a Bond."

My mother, in nightgown and bed jacket, applauded rhapsodically. "It could replace 'The Star-Spangled Banner,'" she said.

Dinner came to us from a place outside the hotel that specialized in salt-free cooking. My mother, who had weakly left the train, had been feeling better at the hotel, and on this night of Arthur's return, she had a small glass of Scotch.

Arthur's trip, after Maud's recovery, had apparently been a straightforward marathon of driving, sleeping a few hours here and there in a motel, and then continuing on. He spoke of "lousy hamburgers," "pouring rain," "nothing on the radio, just static." And he told us that he had thought about us and how he loved us and couldn't wait to see us.

Eventually I went to sleep in my own bedroom. Early in the morning, Arthur took me to Grand Central, loaded with sandwiches and Pepsi. Schweitzer, my fellow camper, was there with a brand-new goofiness. "Hellooooo," he said. "Isn't this graaaand!"

Not so grand, if the truth be told. A bungled, lonely two months in wretched humidity, with poison ivy and a plague of giant mosquitoes. Broken raw eggs were put between my sheets. My father's photo in the clubhouse was turned with its face to the wall, while Larry Hart remained at peace.

I fled the camp, walking in the mud by the two-lane highway that cut through the Adirondacks. I was picked up near a place called the Point O' Pines and threatened by the head counselor with expulsion. During my father's one-day visit a week later, not a word was said to him about my indiscretion.

Arthur was excited about what he had found for me.

He had found a boarding school for the fall, just twenty minutes from New York. One of the best schools in the country. I'd be home every weekend, or at least every other weekend. My mother and father would be living in the Volney Hotel, where the pianist Vladimir Horowitz resided, as well as the famous writer Dorothy Parker.

This time at camp there would be no swim in the owner's part of the lake. My father, who had come up without my mother, could spend only the Saturday of the weekend. He was writing a new "smash show."

He had driven up in a car I'd never seen, a fire engine red convertible. "Flashy, right?" he said to me with a signal he'd never issued before: a wink.

As he backed out of the parking area, his flashy convertible struck a tree Arthur hadn't seen through the rearview mirror. It must have been his idea to leave with a flourish, in front of the head counselor, the owner, and the owner's wife, who were there to pay their respects. Instead they all gathered around the broken taillight and the shards of glass in the pebbles of the parking lot.

"It's nothing," Arthur said, and then, far more cautiously than before, he drove away, his theatrical good-bye bungled like the summer he'd given his son.

One shiny red piece of metal had nestled at the trunk of the tree. I found it after dinner that night, when no one was around. I took it back to the bunk and hid it away in a Brant Lake Camp sweatshirt, which I would never wear again.

6

A WHOPPER OF A STORM! A SNOWFALL THAT WOULDN'T STOP, JUST after Christmas 1947. Footprints were gone in seconds. Himalayas rose, only to be blown into something less or more. A blizzard with a hurricane inside. Is it possible, I remember thinking, that these two calamities could actually join together? But here it was, so how could I even wonder about it?

On Madison Avenue, where my father stood, wobbling and holding my gloved hand, having ordered a limousine to take us downtown to a movie, there were but three or four other human figures struggling with the events, each of them alone directly in the middle of the avenue, bulky and battered and inching along, and eventually joined by the black car my father had hired. Slowly it rolled up in front of us at the irrelevant traffic light on Seventy-fourth Street.

My father got in and stopped. Even I, behind him, recognized the one bewildered passenger as Arturo Toscanini, his feet just reaching the floor, his eyes timid, fearful. "I'm sorry," my father managed in shocked awe, quickly backing out, "I thought you were the wrong car."

His retreat caught me by surprise, and I fell out of the limo and into a mountain of snow, disappearing from sight. My father, hovering above the hole I'd made, peered down, perplexed rather than petrified. In his eyes was the soft light of amusement.

Spread-eagled way below him, I said, "Don't let me go."

A week later, Arthur drove me the half hour to boarding school, alternating false enthusiasm with weary regret.

Why couldn't I live at home, like everybody else?

Because we have no room at the Volney.

But I had a room over Christmas.

It's rented to somebody else after the first of the year.

Did it occur to me to press further? To ask for a different room than I'd had? Probably not. The crush of exile had by then become a confirming mortification: I simply wasn't worthy of living with my parents, and that was that. It was so simple to understand.

I would reside, instead, with exchange students from all over the world. The dorm was for them, their own families in China, Brazil, India, Spain, Korea. *My* family was at Seventy-fourth and Madison. My father said he would come up every other weekend and take me home.

The dorm, a two-story building on a hill above the Henry Hudson Parkway, was designed for a population of about a hundred. A cubicle, perhaps ten by fifteen feet, was assigned to each young man. Mine, on the north side of the building, did in fact overlook the parkway. The limb of a tree grazed my window and often called to me to climb out to it and slide my way down until I was on the ground, escaped. There was no reason for all that, when all I had to do was to walk through the front door of the dorm and away. I was so experienced an escapist, so familiar with the difficult ways of vanishing, that the grazing limb of the tree appealed to that inclination.

Rather than flee, I enlarged my own space by finding, at the other end of the main hallway on the first floor, a door without a room number or any identifying sign. It was tightly shut but not locked. With a screwdriver, I was able to inch it open at its base. I did this during a break in the middle of a school day, when the dorm was almost always empty.

Talk about dust and cobwebs!

A staircase that might never have been used.

From a sitting position in the dark, I took the stairs one at a time, seventeen in all. With arms outstretched before me, I descended carefully until my hands were pressed against either a wall or a door.

I felt for a knob, found one, slowly turned it, and pushed.

Light. And a small enough space to squeeze through.

Covered in soot and filth, I realized that I stood in the dorm's boiler room. Everything was painted gray (one of the school's colors), and efficiently so, perhaps recently, for the new school year. The boiler, noisily at work on a cold January day in 1948, had overheated its surroundings with its pumping and heaving. The door to the parking lot outside the one window was unlocked. I opened it for a second and then ducked back in as a couple of kids and a teacher came into view at the top of the driveway.

In a short time, within a week, I'd say, I had swept and sponged the little staircase by the light of a seventy-five-watt bulb taken from the second-floor lounge after I discovered by flashlight an empty socket on the ceiling halfway down to the boiler room. I had oiled the hinges of the bottom door and sealed the top door with glue, so that the only entrance to the staircase became the door to the parking lot.

I supplied the secret space with comic books and, as I recall, two or three loftier works. I filched three pillows from the linen closet on the first floor to make comfortable chairs out of the stairs, or a backrest, or even a bed. And a pair of white dice, which would eventually lead to the invention of the Password League of America.

Photos went up on the walls, Scotch-taped to the decaying white paint I'd washed: Ted Williams; a 1946 Boston Red Sox team photograph; and a black-and-white snapshot of me and my dad sprawled together on a lawn.

An empty Del Monte box became a candy counter. There were Hershey bars, Dots, Delicia bars, Life Savers, and bottles (though warm) of Coca-Cola, with a bottle opener thrown in.

There were flowers from the cafeteria windowsill, which I slipped into my briefcase once a week. The glass vase was removed from the porch of the headmaster's house on campus.

I had created what I thought of as a secret garden.

In the secret garden, Sunday-night tears were shed.

Letters to my father were written but never sent.

This Side of Paradise was begun but never finished.

A letter from my mother, perhaps the first ever, was read and reread many times, and stored in the candy counter. It told me that she loved me and that she felt so bad about being sick. And I'd be living at home as soon as they found an apartment. And Daddy was writing great songs for a smash new musical.

And that she missed me every single day.

A smash it was!

Inside U.S.A. opened on November 20, 1948, to terrific reviews. At the opening night party, Beatrice Lillie, the star of the show, put her arm around my shoulder, much as Anya Arlen had done at Ira Gershwin's house. She wore an extravagant multilayered necklace that seemed to drape around her entire body. I told her as a joke that her beads were all the colors of the alphabet, which amused her, and she told every well-wisher what I'd said. When it reached Arthur across the room, he came to me and gave me a hug. During that hug, I saw my mother watching us from a Sardi's banquette. Her face was tearstained. In her right hand, she held a cloth napkin that she used as a towel for her face.

A hit song came from the show. Recorded by Jo Stafford, "Haunted Heart" made the hit parade. On the night of its debut, my father gave a party in his brand-new apartment at Ninety-fourth and Lexington, a penthouse that he and my mother had briefly occupied shortly after my birth and that had become sensationally available again.

It took up the entire top floor of the building, the twelfth floor, and was surrounded by a brick terrace that widened and narrowed at several spots. It was a luxurious pad just off the Park Avenue loop. The fact of its being a penthouse allowed it a grand stature, despite Lexington Avenue's slight tilt to the east.

Everything in storage came roaring back, joining the new green carpets and the new oval dining room table, easily enlarged by up to three leaves. Arthur's spacious office, with carpets of dark brown and walls a soothing shade of beige, included his Hamilton piano, a sturdy wooden desk, the brown couch for the man with the pitchfork to approach, and a small bathroom in light blue. A mirrored door opened out at the widest spot of the terrace, where chaise longues and canvas chairs surrounded a round glass table. A green-and-white-striped awning covered the setting. In warm weather, dinners were served on the round glass table, while tall white candles lit the evenings.

After the summer of 1949, I was home, with my own room. I saw to it that it was immaculate at all times, for fear that it would be taken from me. I often thought: They wouldn't do that, would they?

My records were filed and organized. My books, now gathering space, shared four metal shelves with special objects of meaning, including a Major League baseball, a framed photo of 723 North Crescent Drive, a neat pile of Classic comics, and a small piece of red metal brought back from camp in a sweatshirt. If Arthur ever noticed, and he had seven years to do it, he never said so.

The room became a laboratory for imagination. The Password League of America, begun in the secret garden, spinning out from a pair of dice, was completed.

A radio station was born from the newly invented Electronic Baby-Sitter, a device that, when placed by a crib, would transmit any disturbance to a radio in another room at 600 on the dial, where there was no New York station. I used the Electronic Baby-Sitter as a microphone, placing it in front of my record player. The result in the living room and in my mother's room and in my father's study was nothing short of what my mother called "a miracle." The music that I was playing in my room was as clear as a chime on every radio in the house. My father's battery portable, which rested on a bed table by the brown couch, gave me the big idea.

I took it, one morning, down the back stairs of the building, all twelve floors, to the street.

The reception remained clear as my father changed the recordings in my room. Absolutely clear, even on the street, even across Ninety-fourth and down Lexington toward Ninety-third.

I lost the signal a block from home, but it returned as I returned and became its powerful self in the lobby of our building.

A real opportunity here. A real station, WKCS, in honor of my mother.

"Isn't that a little too close to CBS?" my father asked when presented with the first program schedule I typed up.

I told him it had the W for the eastern stations, the K for western stations, and the KCS for my mother's initials, Katherine Carrington Schwartz.

The program schedule:

> Monday–Friday, 7:00–7:30 A.M., *The Sunrise Salute.*
> Saturday and Sunday, 7:00–8:00 A.M., *The Weekend Salute.*

Laboriously, I carbon-copied this exciting new information under the heading "WKCS, The Voice of 94th Street" and slid a schedule under each door in the building.

I picked up in my father a sense of embarrassment, as if I were delicately compromising him in some way, perhaps bruising his celebrity.

"Are you really going to do this every day?" he asked.

Of course I was, reading from *The New York Times,* first the sports, then the front page, then the weather from the top right corner of the front page.

The music followed: *The Best of the Best.* Meaning Jo Stafford's "I'll Be Seeing You" instead of her "Shrimp Boats." Meaning Frankie Laine's "That's My Desire" instead of his "Mule Train." Meaning Nat "King" Cole's trio recording of "I Never Had a Chance" rather than his "Nature Boy."

As I changed records, I talked about what a wonderful fellow Rudy (the doorman) was or how the snow from a week before was still piled high, "like gray skyscrapers."

For about a month I was told by other tenants that I was doing "a great job" or that I was "providing a great service to the building."

My mother listened for a while, sweetly waiting for me to put the *Times* on her bed table. Three or four months after the first broadcast, I became aware of her slacking off. Her door was closed, her radio silent. She had begun to sleep later and later. I would leave the *Times* on the carpet outside her door when I left for school: the crosstown bus at Ninety-sixth, the subway to 242nd, and a not short walk "to the school set high upon a hill." The school's alma mater had it dead right.

On many a morning I left with the thought that in the night, without my father's knowledge (he had taken to sleeping on the brown couch in his study), my mother had died. Once, on a rainy morning, I was convinced it was so. I opened the door and crept into her room, holding my school bag to my chest for protection. In the dim light that thrust itself through the almost completely closed curtains, I could see my mother's face.

She lay on her back, the covers to her chin. Her eyes were open and focused on me. She appeared to be examining me, as if I were a stranger. Then she melted into a smile that amplified into a beam. She said nothing. I said nothing. I turned away at what I must have felt to be a necessary time for both of us.

The Password League of America (don't ask me why, I don't remember) had started out in the secret garden. There were six teams in each league, the National and the American. The schedule was balanced, reasonable, and, as I said to myself, "authentic." The American League: the Red Sox, Yankees, Cleveland, Detroit, the Philadelphia A's, and the Washington Senators.

The National League: the Giants and Dodgers, the Boston Braves and the Phillies, the Chicago Cubs and the Cardinals.

The rules:

1 + 1: a triple.
1 + 2: a double.
Anything adding up to 4: an out.

Anything adding up to 5: an out.
Anything adding up to 6: an out.
Anything adding up to 7: a single.

Now get this: Only a 4 + 3 advances a runner two bases (in the case of runners on second and third, two runs score, or, in the case of runners on first and third, a run scores and the man on first moves to third).

Anything adding up to 8: an out.

As far as 9 is concerned: a 6 + 3 is an out. A 5 + 4 is a walk.

As far as 10 is concerned: 6 + 4 is an out. 5 + 5 is a double play, unless there are no runners on base. Then it's just an out (it is always the lead runner who is doubled off; if there's only one runner on, he's doubled off, pure and simple).

A 6 + 5 is a two-base advancing single, like 4 + 3.

A 6 + 6 is a home run.

To this day, in a new century, if there's a pair of dice around, I'll play a World Series between the Red Sox and somebody. Each game takes about three minutes. I have played World Series games on planes, on someone's card table, sitting on the john with *Vanity Fair* on my lap, and a few times on the flat naked belly of a girl named Cindy.

The Password League of America games were carried not on WKCS but by WBCY, an imagined station. (I have no idea where those letters came from.) With commercials, pregame shows, pitching changes, station IDs, all in somewhat real time, each game took about an hour to play, broadcast, summarize. The weekend doubleheaders began at 1:25, and usually went on until 4:00 or so. My father, who had bought an official ON AIR sign and had

had it installed outside and above my door, its wiring pushed through a tiny hole drilled through the wall at the left of the door, was under the impression that the games were being broadcast on WKCS. I was fearful that he'd try to listen one day, only to discover that his one child was locked in his room talking to himself. Which for two and a half years was the truth, from 1950 until mid-1952, from ages twelve to fourteen.

Kay really got herself up for Arthur's fiftieth birthday. She arranged a surprise party on Saturday night, November 25, 1950. Theater people en masse and the two or three regular buddies my father had accumulated: an economist, Larry Fertig; a PR guy, Sy Seadler; and the publishers Bennett Cerf and Richard Simon.

He was never psychologically intimate with any of these men. Even Howard Dietz, his collaborator, fell short of being a real confidant. Arthur, a gregarious, informed entertainer out in the world, had little access to naked honesty. An imagined victim at home, he was easy prey for the man with the pitchfork, my mother's illness haunting him every day. He loved her, cherished her. He lay alone, waiting for her destiny, the medical bills piling high, his son a loving foreigner.

By Saturday afternoon, the official hurricane that my mother had only the day before become aware of menacingly approached New York. The forecasts were dire: hundred-mile-an-hour winds, torrential rains, in fact the toughest hurricane ever to hit New York.

With invitations already accepted by Judy Garland, George S. Kaufman, Danny Kaye, and all the songwriters in the East, the secret had to break.

Arthur was told about the party and asked what he thought

should be done. His answer I remember still: "Bring 'em on!" he said. "I'll bet you no one shows up anyway."

Through the howling storm they came, in their finery, soaked through and through, more than seventy-five, a crowd that took up the whole apartment.

I piped in music on WKCS. Rodgers music. He was present and came to my door to thank me. Judy Garland was there, oddly the first to arrive. The man she would soon marry, Sid Luft, was skeptical when I told him that WKCS could be heard across the street. There was something spooky in his challenge that suggested that if I wasn't telling the truth, if I was "exaggerating," he'd make much of it.

"I'll prove it to you," I said.

Luft, as I recall him, appeared as an oily bystander with shady intent. His eyes squinted, his nose perspired. And here he was, in pursuit of a cheap victory.

Together we walked down the stairs of the building. I led the way, holding my father's heavy battery radio. I had asked a butler to keep the music going, to change the records, "just for a few minutes."

They were Judy Garland's, by design.

In the lobby of 139 East Ninety-fourth, after descending the twelve floors while his wife sang with marvelous audibility, Luft took it an amazing step further. Borrowing the large umbrella from the doorman, he said to me, "You're full of crap about the outside."

He was actually going to force us out into the hurricane to try and win his point.

In fear that the storm might have altered the WKCS signal, I left the building and stood trembling beneath both Luft's borrowed umbrella and the by now torn awning of 139.

Out in the dreadful night, Judy Garland was clearer than ever.

He didn't speak another word to me.

We took the elevator up, Judy still singing.

Luft reentered the party as if he were a valued presence, sliding through the celebration (made all the more merry by the storm) and passing through the living room in which WKCS warmed the evening. He had, I saw, moved on.

7

I HADN'T PREPARED FOR THE ALGEBRA TEST THAT FRIDAY IN MAY 1953, and even with an A on the test the best I could hope for overall was a D. I was an F5 student in the subject. Interest, effort, and class behavior were graded numerically, one to five, the latter representing an "utter disregard" for algebra, classmates, homework, "and the school." Those last words were scribbled on a late-winter report card that I intercepted, slipping it out of the family mail in the foyer.

"And the school." An utter disregard. The opinion of Rufus B. Cowing, a flaccid, urgent man devoted to the blackboard, often erasing equations so quickly that parts of the vanished numbers still remained within the new equation. I remember thinking that my F5 must have been an insult to Cowing, who had devoted his life to the arrangement of numbers and the ideas within them. Clearly I had insulted his passion by a lack of interest. On this count, I felt unremorseful.

I told my father that my stomach hurt, that my homework was done, that nothing much happened in school on Fridays, and that I thought it best to stay home.

Arthur Schwartz surely understood the stomach part, and the rest floated acceptably past his half an ear.

My mother, accustomed to an afternoon stroll around the neighborhood, set off, in my company, at about two o'clock.

There was a soothing warmth in the early-May sun and talk between us about the weather.

A Lexington Avenue bus discharged a large group of children. They spilled in front of us, shouting and laughing, and throwing us a bit off balance.

I told my mother that a few days earlier I had come racing up to catch a downtown bus at Ninety-fourth Street, just as it pulled away. A passenger, a woman by the window, had given a sympathetic smile. Running, late for no appointment, just running, I had hustled to the Ninety-sixth Street subway and had caught a train as the doors closed. I had gotten off at Sixty-eighth with a plan.

Waiting at the corner, under an awning and out of sight, I had seen a bus approaching the stop. The woman with the sympathetic smile was still a passenger.

I had waited until the doors closed before racing up to it again, intentionally in vain. The passenger's expression was a pleasant mixture of incredulity and fear. We had stared at each other for as long as possible, until the bus had moved a block away.

My mother laughed. "Did you think of continuing on?" she asked.

"I thought the woman was going to Bloomingdale's at Fifty-ninth," I said.

"Wouldn't it have been swell if you could have done it all the way downtown."

"I would have *loved* that," I said, a young man willing to take anything too far.

On this particular stroll my mother had a destination. Only five blocks to Eighty-ninth, to the Service Hardware store. All she wanted to buy was three yellow legal pads.

Afterward, we walked over to Park Avenue, up to Ninety-fourth, and down the hill to Lexington. I recall that we moseyed along in an intimate silence and that we gave a warm greeting to Rudy the doorman, who hadn't been in place when we'd left.

"I'm pooped," my mother said, back in bed in her nightgown and lace bed jacket.

Our trip had taken about an hour.

At 3:30 I went on the imaginary airwaves of WBCY for a special Password League doubleheader.

At about six o'clock, I went into my mother's room and sat at the bottom of her bed, as I often did. She was reading a book by Irwin Shaw, which she rested on her chest. She slid her glasses up onto her hair as she often did, a signal that she was ready to talk.

"How did your game go today?" she asked.

"It was a doubleheader. Two games."

"Maybe you'll be a baseball announcer."

"I'm going to be a dancer."

"A *dancer?* Oh, come on."

"I'm kidding."

"You'll be in the arts," she said. She had said it frequently.

I asked something like: Is baseball in the arts?

"Of course," she replied.

At about this time my father came into the room.

My parents talked about Irwin Shaw, about my father's show *A Tree Grows in Brooklyn,* which had closed a year earlier.

At seven o'clock, we gathered for dinner.

The maid, a black woman easily in her sixties, could be summoned by my mother's foot finding the buzzer under the carpet under her chair.

During the meal, my father spoke glowingly of Dwight Eisenhower. My mother, an admirer of Adlai Stevenson, said something like "You can talk all you want, Arthur."

About an hour after dinner, the Yankee game with the White Sox went on the air. In my room, I lay on the bed, listening.

Although I didn't realize it then, my attraction to the Boston Red

Sox had a lot to do with the fact that Ted Williams was the only player in the league without a roommate on the road. *I* had no roommate; no brothers or sisters on the road or at home. Also, the Red Sox, having lost four decisive games since I had come of baseball age (game seven of the 1946 World Series with the Cardinals; the playoff game in 1948 with Cleveland; and the two closing Yankee games in 1949), had taken on a loser's hue. I saw them in deep purple, black, and turquoise. Their stadium, where I had been taken in June 1950, had turned out to be the most beautiful place I'd ever seen. Watching my first game at Fenway Park in seats behind the Red Sox dugout, my father beside me despite an attack from the man with the pitchfork, I was witness to a Red Sox 29–4 massacre of the St. Louis Browns. "They knew you were there," my father said in the cab back to the hotel, and I sort of believed him.

The Yankees had won four world championships in a row. Icy, autocratic, their place of business a contemptible coliseum, their undefeatedness a melancholy fact of daily life, I set out to defeat them myself. Was it just possible that the sheer force of my hatred would eventually disrupt the Yankees, close them down?

The game on the radio that night was going my way. The Chicago White Sox were getting to the Yankee starter, Eddie Lopat, and had taken a lead behind Billy Pierce, their star pitcher. "Show me what you're made of," I said out loud to the White Sox franchise.

At about 10:30, my father came in to tell me that he was "going to try and get some sleep." The implication, of course, was that the chances were slim.

At about eleven, I went into the kitchen.

A cabinet above a black-and-white-tiled counter housed a few bottles of liquor, wine, and a rare port, a gift to me from Dorothy and Dick Rodgers to be opened on my twenty-first birthday.

I had become accustomed, since *Inside U.S.A.*, to an occasional mix of a drop or two of VAT 69 Scotch in a Pepsi.

Somewhere in the show, perhaps in a George Kaufman skit, the brand name VAT 69 was uttered onstage. Grateful for the plug, the distributors had sent a case of their product to both Schwartz and Dietz and, for all I know, to Kaufman, Bea Lillie, Jack Haley, Herb Shriner, and everyone connected with the smash hit.

I experienced nice little tingles, beginning in early 1949, from my Pepsi with ice in it. I was ten and a half.

The drop or two of VAT 69 increased to four or five drops, enough to alter the taste of the Pepsi. I missed that new taste in any plain old Pepsi at school or at the movies. I liked *my* Pepsi.

The White Sox were on their way to a win over the Yankees. I actually toasted them. "Way to go," I said to the radio.

I must have fallen asleep to the drone of the game, with the light on above my head, the Pepsi on the bed table next to a schoolbook called *The Seasons and How We Use Them.*

I awakened at 1:30 to what I thought was unusual coughing in my mother's room. I went to her.

She had turned on her light. She was crawling on the floor toward the bathroom. She was vomiting a bubbly white stream, then blood. Blood in profusion.

"Mommy," I said.

I ran down the hall to my father's study, yelling "Daddy!" I woke him up from a deep sleep. "Mommy's sick," I said.

Dressed in pajamas, he ran to my mother. I lingered at the door.

Over his shoulder he said to me, "Go to your room and stay there, *now.*"

I did as I was told.

The baseball game had become popular music, on WINS. I turned off the radio, lay on the bed, switched off the light, and listened to the night.

My father shouting something.

Voices in the hall, just outside my door. Unrecognizable voices.

The sound of my mother. She seemed to be weeping in another language.

It couldn't have been more than fifteen minutes.

Suddenly my father shoved my door open.

He was dressed in slacks, a shirt, and a jacket.

"I want you to stay in your room until I get back," he said.

"Is Mommy dying?" I asked.

He turned his back on the question, left the room, and closed the door.

Soon the apartment was still.

I woke up suddenly, believing I was in the dormitory. When I got out of bed to go to the bathroom, I noticed that it was five o'clock. I was due on the air at seven for *The Weekend Salute*.

I opened my door and shouted, "Daddy."

No reply.

My mother's light was on.

Her room was unimaginably upset. The sheets were torn away from the bed, the pillows, mattress, carpet, and bathroom floor were bloodied and slimy. A window curtain had fallen to the floor.

On the bed table by a glass of water lay her wedding ring.

I heard a noise in the foyer by the elevator and rushed back to my room and into bed.

My father, weeping in the hallway, came to me.

Standing in the middle of my room, he howled, put his palms to his face, his howl a wail, a shout, a gurgle, a howl, so much more than grief.

Standing there, his palms still on his face, he spoke, incoherently at first, about his love for his wife. Eventually, with a bit more clarity, he told me that he had dreaded this moment for years; that every ringing phone within his earshot made his stomach jump. He told me that my mother had pleaded with him "to be with other women." But he hadn't. He told me that she loved me and he hoped that I knew that.

He dropped his arms to his sides. His eyes were black. His clothes were caked in blood. He was fifty-three and a half years old, but he looked to me as ancient as human life, his gray hair knotted and tangled.

His tentative cohesion left him, his howl returned.

He sat down at the foot of my bed.

"Jonno boy, Jonno boy," he said, his right hand on my ankle that was concealed under the covers. I recall that his moist fingers picked up lint from the blanket.

I consoled him in some way.

In time I sat and took his head in my lap and stroked his soaking brow.

"She was so so so so sick," he said into the covers around my waist.

There was no *Weekend Salute* on WKCS.

The phone rang a lot, Howard Dietz showed up, Larry Fertig, Andrea Simon, and others.

Andrea, the wife of Richard L. Simon, had been a close friend of Kay's. My mother, I learned later, had asked that Andrea "look after Jonno" just in case. I'm fairly sure that on the morning after my mother's death, Andrea assured Arthur that her pledge to Kay would be kept. She would step in as a surrogate. Their Stamford, Connecticut, house would become my summertime lodging.

In fact, it was decided that I would temporarily live in the Simons' commodious Riverdale home and would accompany Andrea at the end of the day. No, no, I insisted. I wanted to spend that night in my room "with my belongings."

The truth was, I wished to conduct a final *Weekend Salute* from seven until eight the next morning. The usual news, sports, weather, and music. A Brooks Atkinson theater review might have been featured, though I preferred Walter Kerr in the *Herald Tribune,* who wasn't as formal a writer.

My "belongings" did the trick. I would go to the Simons' Sunday afternoon. The cook would prepare a Saturday dinner for me to eat on a tray in my room. My father, with "so many things to attend to," would be out until late.

In the evening I planned the music for the next morning's program. A teacher, Herb Murphy, called with sorrow at the news he'd heard.

By ten or so I was asleep with all the lights on in my room, which was unusual. On that night, darkness would have held a chilling power.

"Good morning," I began at 7:00 A.M. "*The Weekend Salute* is on the air."

The baseball scores came first, with teams "whipping" or "mauling" or "nipping" the losers.

The music: Nat Cole, Jo Stafford, Les Paul, and Mary Ford.

I remember giving movie listings around the neighborhood: for the Grande on Eighty-sixth Street and the Brandt's next door to it and the Orpheum and the RKO 86th and the Trans Lux at Eighty-fifth and Madison.

At 8:00 A.M., I identified myself, for the first time, in full.

"This is Jonathan Schwartz from the penthouse on the twelfth floor," I announced to probably no one.

I then said this: "In local news, my mother, who was known as Kay or Katherine, died Friday in the middle of the night. Actually, early in the morning on Saturday, May 2, 1953. She started to die at 139 East Ninety-fourth Street, and then she was taken to Doctors Hospital at Eighty-eighth and East End Avenue. She died from a cerebral hemorrhage. She had had a long illness. She was forty-seven. Until further notice, *The Weekend Salute* will not be heard at its usual time. You are tuned to WKCS at 600 on the dial in New York."

8

ANDREA HEINEMANN, THE SWITCHBOARD OPERATOR AT THE YOUNG publishing house of Simon and Schuster, had married Simon and had borne his three daughters, Joanna, Lucy, Carly, and his one son, Peter. Now, as a vibrant mother-director-chef and the fulcrum of a dozen teeter-totters in constant use, she put into play a cunning ambiguity that left me, and the others, at one time or another, unsettled and fearful. Was it yes or no? Was it love or hate? And in my case, was I welcome or unwelcome? "Be sure and come to the picnic next Friday," she said to me. Next Friday, at the front door: "What are you doing here?" And the possibility existed, at least in my mind, that she would send me away.

There was also her joy, her energy as she moved across the lawn, through the house, up the stairs. In the kitchen she was a hummingbird, tasting, sipping, laughing with delight. At table: scooping a lobster's roe with her hand while the other hand held high a buttered ear of corn. In her hair a hibiscus, occasionally a rose. Her skirts were quilts of colors, her blouse often a white ruffled peasant garment. I'm sure there were many others, beautifully folded in a bureau drawer directly above the dining room on the second floor or in the room above that, on the third. She marveled at what the children said, her deep voice rising in appreciation. She was easy to thrill. Children in wet bathing suits did it. A thunderstorm did it. Strawberries, tomatoes, apples, soft-boiled eggs, sourdough bread, zucchini, gazpacho, watermelon, they did it.

Andrea and my mother had been buddies, their hands and arms talking and telling. They had giggled, chattered, and roared together. Between them there were five children, me the guest at the Simons', the girls from ten to sixteen years old, benevolent and loving. Their father acquiesced with a disquieting toleration. I was never to be a favorite of Richard L. Simon. I was too loud, selfish, and present, and, what's more, I monopolized his daughters.

The daughters and their baby brother, Peter, spent their summers on a sixty-four-acre estate in Stamford, Connecticut. An apple orchard, vegetable garden, swimming pool, bathhouse, and tennis court were all but a short trot from the main house that appeared magisterial as viewed from an approaching vehicle on Newfield Avenue or from its wide U-shaped pebbled driveway. It issued a formal hello, belying the rhythm and energy within. Framed by white pillars, five wooden steps led to a shady porch almost the width of the three-story house.

The grand front door opened into a nineteen-room labyrinth of a large family in the full swing of music and dogs, tomatoes and guitars, peonies and peanuts, tchotchkes and vodka, footsteps and surprise appearances, laughter and tantrums, poison ivy and chocolate cake, mosquito bites and bubble gum, orange juice and wet towels, crayons and tennis balls, comic books and Hershey bars and all the colors of Andrea's skirts distributed on the walls and rugs and coffee tables and in bathrooms and down hallways and up the stairs: orange, purple, dark red, and touches of blue and gold. The colors of music.

Through my early life, piano teachers had come and gone. "The boy is talented," they would always say, "but he won't learn to read music." I was, however, able to watch and listen as the teachers played and then play back to them precisely what they'd performed. I could repeat melodies with left-hand harmonies disagreeable to the teachers but absolutely right for what I had in mind. "This is *not* a Stravinsky piece!" I was told by an unamused instructor named Tim Tippin. "Why *can't* it be?" I asked.

Richard L. Simon was a serious classical pianist. A mighty painting of Brahms hung above his piano in the living room of the Stamford house. Often we were all asked to hear him play.

If I felt any love for him, and I wanted to, it was almost always when he sat at the piano. In his study; at the dining room table; during a bridge game in a crucial little space by the front door where friends would remain until late at night, the fingers of Richard's right hand were in constant pianistic action, drumming out a melody on the arm of his chair.

Benny Goodman, a Stamford resident, sat at the bridge table with such delight, amiability, and spoken affection for any child who wandered into view that it became impossible for me to later understand the internationally accepted joke: One musician says to another, "I have good news and bad news. The good news is, Benny Goodman died. The bad news is, he died in his sleep."

Richard L. Simon's authors were familiar faces around Goodman. Herman Wouk, Sloan Wilson, and the bridge expert himself, Charles Goren. Bennett Cerf, unctuous and affable, would occasionally appear. He had been Richard's protégé from Columbia University on, and now his Random House was a rival of Simon and Schuster.

The Simons had helped Jackie Robinson's family gain a home and a social standing in the white community of Stamford and encouraged the Robinsons to become a part of their household, around the pool, on the tennis court, or at the bridge table. The three Robinson children, Jackie Jr., David, and Sharon, and their mother, Rachel, were present at every happy occasion: every lobster feast, birthday party, children's performance, barbecue, croquet match, songfest (there were many songfests), every thunderstorm, many sunsets, a few breakfasts, and often for drinks by the pool, and for potato salad and tall glasses of beer and thin slices of roast beef and turkey and Swiss cheese and ham, and corn on the cob and heels of rye bread and dark chocolate brownies and peaches and cherries.

John Crosby, the first radio and television critic in the country and a Simon and Schuster author, rented a guesthouse on the estate for three summers. From that house, off the front driveway near Newfield Avenue, there regularly spilled a dreadful rage, a lava of madness from the black hole of alcohol that possessed John and his wife, Mary. Crosby, at poker or by the pool, appeared to me as a man behind a sheet of gauze, encapsulated, languid, dazed. At water's edge, he spoke from a distance, benignly cynical, chain-smoking, often reading, a drink on the grass beside his chaise longue. When he shook your hand, he received only your fingers. When he laughed, he started late, a beat or two late, as he considered his options. The laugh itself was more of a chuckle, always disappointing to an explosive laughter like me. His laugh was the equivalent of his handshake: noncommittal, tentative, and just a bit insulting. I always thought there was a chance that he would change his mind in midlaugh or midfingershake, and turn on me, spewing the venom that he saved for midnight, for his wife who fought him, cursed him, came after him with broken whiskey bottles as their two infant children slept upstairs. Joanna told me, "It's a drinking thing." *My* drinking thing, embryonic and secret, would never, I pledged to myself, come to where the Crosbys were. Never.

Clear of mind and warm of heart, Don Budge, the great tennis champion, then just past the finish line of a remarkable career, rented the faraway guesthouse for his redheaded family. I said to

Lucy that in order to go over to the Budges' house you'd have to accept the word "excursion." Certainly it was the longest journey on the sixty-four acres, but the Budges made it easy by showing up at the pool. They came to us. They brought food and soft drinks. They were merry and pretty, light-skinned, with blond or red hair. The kids seemed to encircle their tall prince of a father, until he said, "Go on, now," and they skipped away, joining the garden of children.

Andrea's two brothers, Fred Heinemann (known as Dutch) and Peter Dean Heinemann (known as Uncle Peter), were the source of great joy when they were in Stamford, which was most of the time. They were angelic adults, though a parasitic melancholy, probably enervating to the host, subdued Fred and gave us an uncle once removed. It was Peter who hit fungos hour after hour to Jackie Jr., the Budge kids, me. The girls who joined in, loping across the lawn, their arms outstretched, gawkily graceful in their pursuit of the sailing sphere—a softball, tennis ball, rubber ball—retained just enough interest in following the flight and capturing the prize before it fell to earth. The sense of the imminent passing of their interest held no solemnity for anyone. I think that losing the women never occurred to us, especially Uncle Peter. For him, the ball in the summer sky was as light as a flower, as bright as the sun, and that's all there was to it. Its flight prolonged every childhood on the lawn. Uncle Peter, in his forties, had sensed the dangers of adulthood when he was around eighteen and had held back, relinquishing much of himself to a permanent adolescence.

He played the ukulele with his brother, old songs like "Four or Five Times," or "When the Red, Red Robin Comes Bob Bob Bobbin' Along," or "Am I Blue?," or "Oh, You Beautiful Doll" (you great big beautiful doll). They sang in fabulous harmony, and then one or the other would imitate the sound of a muffled trumpet or trombone in the second chorus. We all sat at their feet. "More! More!" we cried. And there was always more from Dutch and Uncle Peter, inevitably in the form of invitations. "Joanna, *you* sing."

Joanna, a studying mezzo-soprano, stood regally before us. She did so either accompanied by Richard or just out there on her a cappella own. Singing in Italian or French, she threw me into a tizzy of excitement and hero worship. Although I have never responded to the sound of the cultured human voice, Joanna Simon stands alone as the one formal figure (with the exception of Maria Callas on recordings) who has touched me with the mysterious beauty of whatever in the world it was she was singing.

"Lucy, your turn," said Dutch, in later years called the Dutchman.

Lucy's voice, untutored, brushed the ceiling, a twinkling sparrow way up there. "If I Had a Ribbon Bow." Such a thing as folk music made its debut on my stage. Lucy and Carly had worked up any number of songs. Alone or apart, they jived in the innocence of flowers and sunsets, raindrops and ribbon bows. Carly's deep, vibratoless voice was suited to Lucy's mile-high soprano. "You girls could be an act," Dutch said during one of our sessions.

I played a song at the piano, maybe two. "Blue Moon," "Mountain Greenery," "Shine on Your Shoes," the melodies straight down the middle, my left hand Stravinskyed. Why not?

Have you ever heard of the game called Sardines?

It's a nighttime out-of-doors *opposite* of hide-and-seek. One person hides, let's say, under a tall copper beech tree whose limbs and leaves are distributed almost to the ground. Sitting under the tree on the grass or moist earth by the trunk, a fellow feels pretty safe, able to scramble around to the other side of the fat trunk if a searcher approaches, who looks and yells, "He's not under the copper beech!" Ah, but possibly the hidden fellow was actually spotted by the searcher. The searcher becomes a hidden fellow, too. The two whisper conspiratorially. They are now a team, the rest of the group thrown off guard, having been told by that voice in the night—maybe Joanna's voice or Carly's or Uncle Peter's—that Jonno or Dutch or Jackie Jr. is *not* under the copper beech. But let's say that one of the Budge kids is old enough to be skeptical about that tree. Just in case, he checks. He finds! "Ssh," he is warned. In an exciting silence, he joins the other two. Time goes by. The night is cool but sticky. There is no moon. Fireflies in profusion flicker and flit. "How do they do that? Do they rub their legs together or their hands or do—" "Ssh!" There is no sound from the remaining searchers. They must be on the other side of the house or way down on the far side of the apple orchard or on the front lawn. "Why is it so quiet?" Okay, okay, a hint. One voice from beneath the tree yells, "D-U-Z, D-U-Z." A common detergent, with the slogan "D-U-Z does everything." Lucy hears it from the apple orchard. She's *got* it! She now really suspects the copper beech. If I am one of the three beneath the tree, I will welcome Lucy more than anyone in the whole world. I am truly, truly in love with her, and will never love anyone else as long as I live. Lucy is barefoot and wears a one-piece bathing suit, and she is fourteen or fifteen or sixteen, but always two years younger than I. She has long hair, some of which drapes over my bare shoulder under the tree as we sit huddled and hidden together. She knows I love her. She loves me as a family member. To please me, she holds my hand. Lucy pleases everyone. She is her father's favorite; I am his rival. Gradually, as the night grows long, we are all beneath the copper beech, except for one. If it is Uncle Peter, there is joy all around in his dilemma. We feel it. He loves it. We hear him out there, "Give me a D-U-Z!" Fat chance. If it is Carly, she's talking a lot to herself. Carly has a stutter, so that things like "Let me see, they can't be under the copper beach, so they must be, they must be *over there*" have little hiccups in them, bubbles of resistance that block fluency. She is tall, like her sisters. She is three years younger than Lucy; there are still some teeth to arrive. Her limbs are long and appear especially elongated when she sings "Always True to You in My Fashion." Out there alone, Carly has my empathy. I almost want to forfeit the game by yelling, "Carlotta, we're under the copper beech!" If it is me still searching, I am near tears. Everyone else is together. I'm alone among the fireflies. Not even in a whisper but in a hush, I design the vibration of the word "Mommy." Being the last, I hide first in the next game. Or Carly does. Or Uncle Peter. A hidden Uncle Peter is as wonderful as a singing or searching or laughing or fungo-hitting Uncle Peter Dean Heinemann. We imagine his eyes are as large as moons. We know that he is *findable.* Unless he pulls one of his tricks, like lying right down in the middle of the lawn, camouflaged by his cunning accessibility. There's no sound, there's no sight of him. Until he can't control himself. Then he breaks out into all the laughter of childhood. "There he is!" we shout, and pounce upon him as if he were an inflated rubber god. Which of course he is.

Jackie Robinson had a high-pitched voice with muscle. In the summers of 1953 through 1955, throwing a baseball around with him or just walking around with him talking baseball, the hero slowly changed into a friend. Two athletes alone, as I mirthfully pointed out, shooting the breeze. As a baseball talker-walker I was excellent company. I spoke of Walt Dropo, Ellis Kinder, Billy Goodman, Ted Lepcio. American League stuff, Red Sox stuff. I spoke of Jackie's smaller, unmythologized moments: a dive to his right for a whistling liner headed toward center field; a bunt with the infield pulled in that slipped by three defenders while Jackie took second.

He told me that he thought Andrea was "a little phony." He told me that I was going to marry Lucy.

On a humid Monday afternoon in August 1955, I was the only witness to a severe tennis match between Grand Slam Champion Don Budge and Jackie. They just fell into it, after they'd hit the ball around.

Jackie, in tennis shorts only, took on a Don Budge at forty, wearing tennis white, top to bottom: Bill Tilden long pants, a short-sleeve tennis shirt with a yellow dot on the right shoulder, and a white scarf, or some kind of fancy white towel, around his neck. His kind eyes turned dark in concentration as he commenced a battle with easily the most competitive athlete alive and probably the best known.

I sat by the court in a gray wooden bucket chair usually reserved for an adult with a gin and tonic in one hand and a cigarette in the other.

Now it was mine, with a glass of Pepsi and ice and perhaps a full ounce of Gilbey's gin. I wore a bathing suit, a Red Sox hat, and Jackie's loafers, which were too big for me but which I dangled proudly on my feet.

Budge had DiMaggio grace. In his element, he was a dancer. The music of his form was enhanced by the testimony of his skill: a backhand rich in authority and strength, the ball catching the white line as it sped past a Robinson racing to the net.

Budge's serve, a mighty slash, was distinguished by the great height he managed as he threw the ball over his head. It lingered above the champion and seemed to gain an inch or so after it reached its apogee. Then it descended invitingly, in no rush, ready for Donald Budge.

It is said that players "charge the net." Not Budge. He quickly *approached* the net. At net, his face came close to assuming a smile. He seemed not to perspire, despite the tropical August afternoon. He appeared, as I think of it now, as a witness to the event, a partner in my chair, or a referee in an elevated seat without a say in any matter.

The opposition was ferocious and unamused. He was clumsy compared to the champion, charging, lurching, running backward while facing forward, serving artlessly in a tight tense battle with accuracy. He would talk to himself in that high but, for the moment, demoralized voice. "Gotta straighten it out," I remember him saying.

After a couple of double faults, my Gilbey's gin encouraged me to yell out, "Bunt, JR!" Jackie gave no sign that he'd heard me.

That Budge would win easily was a foregone conclusion. But with Jackie Robinson as an opponent, there was always a chance—at poker, swimming laps, climbing apple trees, making beds, hiding in Sardines—that this guy would win. Even against a whole team. Even against the Cleveland Indians. All by himself at second base. Certainly, with just one man, Don Budge, in his way, there was that chance.

It was Jackie's approach to the ball that gave him a chance. He came at it like a nimble mountain lion. He smothered the ball with the weight of his talent. He chased it to the farthest corners of the court and got it back to Budge—maybe a lob, but maybe not. Maybe an inelegant slam over his shoulder that would catch the white line, finding Budge unprepared. Once, a 180-degree spin for a deadly forehand right at Budge's genitals, a bullet that confused the champion.

Oh, did Jackie sweat. Puddles of his perspiration covered the court, so that when changing sides Budge would grab a towel and wipe up the mess, "because I don't want to slip and break my neck," he laughed, after winning a service game at love that had Jackie all angered up, his teeth clenched, his face a sheet of distaste for Budge, for me.

Moments after the match ended, Jackie Jr. came down to the court with his mother, Rachel.

"We've been looking for you," Rachel said, with no *where have you been* that is often buried in "we've been looking for you." The Rachel I knew, a beautiful, encouraging woman, gave out a beatific radiance that I found soothing.

Jackie Jr., who was about nine or ten, was solemn and silent. He arrived at courtside without holding his mother's hand. He shot a decent smile to his father but nothing to Budge or to me.

Suddenly Jackie Sr. picked up a tennis ball, perhaps in frustration, and slammed it high and long with a racket. He said to his son, "Catch it."

Jackie Jr. was the fastest child who ever ran across a lawn. He ran far away from us, following the ball. Although it rolled off his fingertips, I've never forgotten the attempt. He returned silently and stood next to his mother, as if nothing had happened.

Another thing about Jackie Jr. He was entirely lefty. He hit lefty, threw lefty, caught lefty. He was almost an imposition to his father's famous right-handedness. He was also among the best athletes, of any age, that I've ever seen.

An example: the front lawn on another summer day. The croquet wickets had been pulled from the grass and stored on the front porch with the balls and mallets. A softball field took their place, with shirts and towels serving as bases, home plate, and the pitcher's mound. There were about twenty kids in action, many from the neighborhood. Jackie Sr. assumed the role of pitcher for both sides and umpire as well. The day was autumnal, the air dry and crisp, the summer in temporary repose. The yard had about it the aura of a real stadium. Grown-ups sat on the stairs of the front porch, shouting encouragement with impassioned neutrality.

From their group, a mink coat thrown over her one-piece bathing suit, Lucy Monroe stood, crossed the driveway, and took her place on the pitcher's mound next to Jackie Robinson.

There are many who remember that the Yankees won five World Series in a row, from 1949 through 1953, and that at every home World Series game during those years, Lucy Monroe, in a mink coat, would take her place near the Yankee dugout to sing the national anthem. She had a light opera voice and a sweet, asexual gaze that neutralized her most attractive countenance. She had become, somehow, a friend of Andrea's. She came to visit at least once every summer, always with her mink coat in tow.

On this occasion, she assumed a formal posture similar to Joanna's by the piano, her back straight, her chin held high, her left arm rigid at her side. She held a martini glass in her right hand, but other than that bold discrepancy, she was the authentic Lucy Monroe. Everyone on the scene wearing a baseball cap, including Jackie, held it to his heart.

Lucy Monroe's voice rang out, powerful without amplification. When she finished, she took a long sip from her martini and carefully left the field, walking slowly, to applause, back to the steps of the front porch.

I knew that my mommy could have done that just as well, which I had told her on many an occasion during the Lucy Monroe World Series games at Yankee Stadium.

"You've got to have the energy to stand erectile," she had replied on one occasion.

The first batter was Jackie Jr.

His father gave him no advantage, no gentle lob up to the plate. A swift strike one, called by the pitcher.

Robinson Jr. dug in from the left side of the plate. His father wound up more elaborately for the second pitch.

His son smashed a dangerous line drive in fair territory, just by the red shirt that was first base.

The ball was fielded cleanly in right by a neighborhood kid about my age. As he picked up the ball, Jackie Jr. was rounding second. The strong throw toward home plate arrived two or three seconds after the runner had scored and had come to a stop to watch the action.

The place was in an uproar. The fans stood and cheered. The pitcher, bareheaded, his cap having flown off at some unobserved moment, his hair turning white, a slight belly noticeable on such a scrutinized figure, tipped his imaginary cap to his thoroughly rested son, who now sat in the grass behind home plate with his legs crossed.

As his father might have beaten the Cleveland Indians on his own, so could his son have whipped the Stamford aggregate—throw in the fans—without breaking a sweat. He lined a homer, his second, this one down the left-field line. He reached base a couple of other times in ways I can't recall. As the left fielder, he caught one line drive hit to his left, barehanded, then whirled and threw a strike to his father, who was covering first, doubling up a tall neighborhood boy.

Late in the game, a high foul fly ball drifted toward the stairs. Drinks were spilled as the fans scattered. Jackie Jr. crashed into everyone and caught the ball on the third stair. Then he turned back to the field, to us, without expression.

In other games later on, I tried to be expressionless, but I was so delighted with anything I did that my glee oozed out from behind my disengagement. Uncle Peter was exultant at any sign of my skill. He was far too exuberant for expressionlessness.

Peter Dean Heinemann was a personal manager of fringe musicians. By the 1950s, Paul Whiteman could certainly have been considered beyond his prime. Buddy Weed was a capable but hardly an innovative jazz pianist. Johnny Nash was an up-and-coming black pop singer who made two or three albums on which some of the material was unusually good ("And the Angels Sing" resonates).

Uncle Peter's own music, its easy wit and joyful tempo, its old-time pleasure in red red robins and toot-toot-tootsies and great big beautiful dolls, sung just above a whisper with the youth of Sardines and the playfulness of a rubber god, was, I'd have to say, the essence of summer. He performed, with or without his brother, as an innocent. He was also a mediator, sympathizer, and guide. After my mother died, he included me in as if I were a prize package. He asked me to play the piano, he praised my Stravinskyed left hand. He became a living organism assembled from the notes of a favorite tune he often played.

Uncle Peter was the sunny side of the street.

9

MY MOTHER DIED TWO MONTHS BEFORE THE OPENING OF *THE BAND Wagon,* the Fred Astaire–Cyd Charisse MGM film that made use of the Dietz-Schwartz catalog. My father and Howard had been asked to write but one new song, something that would express the joy of creating and presenting plain old excitement. In twenty minutes, in a rehearsal room on the MGM lot, Arthur wrote the melody for "That's Entertainment." Howard Dietz's sophisticated, out-and-out hilarious lyric took a great deal longer than twenty minutes.

The Band Wagon opened at Radio City Music Hall in July 1953 and received a unanimous welcome. Its score put Arthur out there in front of everyone by revealing his body of work with Dietz as a rich, fluent, melodic achievement, the equal of those of greater renown. "Dancing in the Dark" was all over the place. "That's Entertainment" joined Irving Berlin's "There's No Business like Show Business" as an anthem for the theater, for the movies, for television and radio. It was a shout of affirmation: Here comes the show! "Where a ghost and a prince meet / And everyone ends in mincemeat."

One of the songs, "By Myself," had lain dormant for years. It had been written for a flop show in the late thirties and had never been discovered, never examined or embraced. Astaire himself remembered it, brought it forward, and began *The Band Wagon* by singing it in a melancholy understatement as if thinking aloud. It is one of the loveliest moments in any musical film, and it made "By Myself" a standard. Its melody, as I hear it, comes closer than any other to identifying the internal Arthur.

I don't know if my mother saw a screening of the movie. She surely heard the demonstration acetates of the sound track that came to our door every week or so. Six weeks after her death, Arthur and Howard began a publicity tour on behalf of *The Band Wagon* that was somewhat organized around the Red Sox schedule, so that I could come as the "and" in Dietz and Schwartz to see a few ball games. Dietz, as head of publicity for MGM, simply made it happen. I tagged along to all the events—radio interviews, receptions, magazine photo sessions, and eventually back to the hotel room, where Howard would challenge me to anything I could think of. "I'll beat you no matter what it is," he would say, with an impish bravado that was oddly charming from a guy as distanced from me as Dietz. I noticed in Arthur's smile that he was as surprised as I.

The two of us stood fifteen feet from a Ritz-Carlton Hotel wastebasket in Boston, taking turns throwing playing cards toward it. A few made it in, and in a little over an hour Howard was way ahead.

"What's next?" he said.

"Gin rummy." I knew my strength.

But Dietz was a professional, the cards natural extensions of his hands. His shuffling was close to noiseless, the cards floating together in their new arrangements as if they were feathers artfully deployed. I hung tough, but in vain. Howard, in triumph after triumph, whispered the word "gin" as he won his hands. He hardly said it, but it rang raucously across the table.

Then: "Give me a melody, *any* melody, and I'll give you a new lyric in ten seconds."

Arthur, who had come into the room, suggested the melody of "Jalousie."

Almost at once, Dietz sang out:

Cyd Charisse
Get off the mantelpiece,
You're quite a shock there,
We need a clock there.

Victory all around for the head of publicity at MGM.

The next day he retreated and never returned to the fifteen-year-old he'd swayed his way. Never an imp again but a grown-up: sardonic, droll, famous.

Though it must have been Howard who set Arthur up with the owner of the Cleveland Indians, the most congenial Hank Greenberg, whose fabulous history as a player I knew back and forth.

On a hot Sunday, July 19, 1953, "the Schwartz boys," as Greenberg called us, joined him in the owner's box for a doubleheader against the Red Sox. What a giant of a fellow, and how receptive he was to my expertise. "I've never seen a kid who knew as much about this as you do," he said, right there in front of Arthur Schwartz.

Maurice "Mickey" McDermott threw a two-hit shutout at the Indians in the first game, which agitated the owner (the pitcher himself had homered for one of the Red Sox two runs). Greenberg wordlessly disappeared between the games.

Arthur warned me that if the Red Sox did well in the second game, I should not show my feelings. (I had noisily rooted McDermott on.)

The Red Sox scored four times in the first inning of the second game. Greenberg, his congeniality gone, fell into a fearsome silence. I spoke not a word as the Red Sox went on to win, 7–5. We gravely thanked him at the end of his long, long day.

I truly felt that I had given my father this doubleheader sweep. *Do you see what I can do?* I am them, they are me, Mr. Arthur Schwartz. At least your son has a knack.

In 1954, just after the first of the year, my father brought a woman home for dinner. He took my mother's chair, with access to the kitchen buzzer, and I sat across the table from Mary O'Hagan. She spoke with a bit of a stutter that wasn't as pronounced as Carly's. She had allowed her amazing brown hair to grow down her back to a length I'd never seen. "Doesn't she look like Rita Hayworth?" my father asked, over his favorite soup, cold borscht. I said that yes, she did.

Mary's eyes seldom met mine. They were evasive, perhaps shy eyes that for the most part stayed with her borscht, the leg of lamb, the apple pie. With her eyes cast down, she asked two or three questions about me. Did I enjoy school? Was I as good at basketball as my father said I was? What did I want to do as a career?

These questions, if answered honestly and in detail, might very well have confused her and would surely have appropriated the rest of the evening.

Did I enjoy school?

Sort of, I said.

In truth, I prepared every day, adhering to the school's dress code: a suit or slacks, a white shirt with tie and jacket. Because I'd discovered that I was allergic to wool (my skin broke out in a dark red rash), all my suit pants and slacks were flimsily lined with sheets of paper-thin cotton. If I dressed in a hurry, I would often as not drop my leg between the wool and its lining, tearing the stitches and dropping much of the lining halfway down the leg. My hair, informed by an unmanageable cowlick, would be set in a green gelatinous product from which, in the breezes of the subway, the cowlick would break away and triumphantly wave above the back of my head like an Indian feather. When this happened, I would burst out in perspiration, even in winter. In September and October, with ragweed at its most devastating, I would suffer from what was diagnosed as an acute allergy that would let up only with the first frost, which could mean November 1. Now, in the middle of winter as in all winters, I experienced something larger than loneliness in which I saw myself at the very bottom of a black hole, into which fell a drizzle of sleet from a night sky. For miles and miles there was no one around.

Was I as good at basketball as my father said I was?

Yes, but only on my home court at the widest spot on the terrace, where a regulation-high basketball rim (with a net added) had been drilled into the bricks that could be attacked by eight-foot jumpers or set shots, and where a wire fence above the railing prevented errant basketballs from bouncing down off the twelfth-floor terrace into the servants' alley directly below. On this court, even in heavy snow, I was as good as my father said. On the school court I hung back, waiting for the time to pass by. I was afraid of failing at a game I not only understood (I *felt* it in my hands) but played with intensity and talent, a talent that if called upon in front of others might, in fact, vanish. Once or twice, friendly classmates came up to Ninety-fourth and played ball. "I never knew you could do this," one of them said. "I can't," I told him. "Then what would you call *that*?" he asked, watching me hit twenty jumpers in a row.

In cold weather, constantly shooting a basketball, my skin would split painfully. A basketball is hard to direct by gloved hands. But, and here's a piece of advice, try using three bandages on each finger of your shooting hand, one lengthwise over your nails and down your fingers and two around them, creating long white thimbles. Keep them in place as long as possible to avoid having to reapply.

As it happens, all five of the fingers on my right hand were so encased when Mary O'Hagen came to dinner, though she made no mention of them as we sat in the living room around a bowl of salted nuts, or at dinner, or later.

I could think of nothing to ask her. There was really only one question in the air: Who are you? Or, possibly: Who might you be?

I answered what she asked. School was okay and my grades were picking up. My father exaggerated about my basketball playing, but I was okay at it.

As for a career?

I don't know yet, I told her without mentioning radio. If I had, my father might have felt obligated to speak of WKCS, my mother's initials, the Electronic Baby-Sitter, far too much for Mary O'Hagan at dinner.

To talk on the radio. A career. If I understood anything about myself, it was the certainty that I would pursue a place on the air where I would speak, introduce music, and talk about baseball and professional basketball, which had absorbed me to the point of scholarship so unusual that Leonard Koppett of the *New York Post* wrote a column about the kid with the good ideas about the National Basketball Association, then in its infancy. (The scheduling stank; I knew how to fix it. Defense was shoddy; I promoted its value. The game was eastern; I urged a move west. The play-offs were a chaos of round-robins; I knew how to reorganize them.) All of this, in my desired career, around Rodgers and Hart, Harold

Arlen, Dietz and Schwartz. A whole new idea for radio, you see? With Walter Kerr reviews that *he* would read and interviews with literary figures such as Irwin Shaw, John Crosby, John O'Hara. Maybe even a visit with Jackie Robinson. "It's all the same thing," I had explained to Arthur when I had spoken to him about radio. "Everything is related. It's what's going on."

I had told him that every station did one thing and never strayed from that plan.

He had said, with what I'd come to understand as a dismissal, "It's an interesting idea."

But this time, lying on his brown couch, he had added, "It really is, you know."

Mary O'Hagan was often there when I got home from school. She dined with us most nights of the week. On other nights, my father would tell me, "Mary and I are going out for the evening."

One afternoon, Mary came into my room for her first visit.

"Cluttered," she said. "It's a sweet little room."

Then she asked, "What's that thing on the shelf?" noticing the piece of red metal from Arthur's 1947 visit to Brant Lake Camp.

"I found it in the woods at camp. I like the color."

"Clutter," she said again, disdainfully.

I discounted the fleeting notion that she was afraid of me.

My father had brought home a slim, long-haired woman with a square face and high cheekbones that, in concert, created the advantage of beauty that would feel no fear in my tepid presence. For Arthur, another winning shiksa, a former dancer, an aspiring actress, a student of Lee's (as Lee Strasberg was called by everyone), a glamorous woman in her early thirties, twenty-one years younger than Arthur.

Mary was a friend of Allyn Ann McLerie, the actress who'd first played the role of Amy in *Where's Charley?* A pleasant red-haired woman about Mary's age, she had been the wife of Adolph Green and had remained his friend after their divorce. Adolph took Allyn Ann and her girlfriend (he placed the occasion in late 1950, recalling that the opening of *Guys and Dolls* was the talk of the evening) to a party at Betty Comden's town house on East Ninety-fifth Street (Betty thought it might have been New Year's Day 1951).

Arthur was there alone. He played the piano. Betty and Adolph performed "New York, New York (It's a Hell of a Town)," which they'd written with Leonard Bernstein, who was also present.

Mary O'Hagan, whose stage name was Mary Grey, stood around the piano with all the others before taking a seat on the floor. She'd given birth to a girl during a turbulent marriage to a pianist and arranger named Ed Scott, who had worked closely with Frank Loesser on both *Where's Charley?* and *Guys and Dolls.* If Betty Comden is right, Mary Grey's daughter turned two that day.

There, in Betty's living room, sitting at the piano, playing and singing and making people laugh, was the immediate new love of her life.

Arthur had a full repertoire of songs from *Inside U.S.A.*, as well as some new things he was writing with Dorothy Fields for a show based on the novel *A Tree Grows in Brooklyn* by Betty Smith. One of those songs, "Make the Man Love Me," really caught Mary Grey's ear.

I knew nothing of her until the salted nuts and the leg of lamb.

Did I enjoy school? Was I as good at basketball as my father said? What did I want to do as a career?

As a career.

I had a secret.

It had happened twice. In a Brant Lake Camp summer, probably

1952, I'd been running up a hill to the dining hall and running late, having fallen asleep and not having heard the bell for lunch. At the top of the hill, with much of the camp in view, I'd stopped to catch my breath. Then I'd said out loud, for I was alone, "He stopped at the top of the hill where the watermelons were sold."

There had been no watermelons in sight or on sale, but I had envisioned them there and had cloaked myself in the third person.

Then, in less of a hurry, I had gone to lunch.

One day in the autumn of 1953, demoralized by allergy, wool pants, and an October heat wave, I excused myself from a history class to go to the bathroom. At the urinal, urineless, I rested my head on the cool white tile and cried. My nose, already bedeviled by ragweed, overflowed; mucus dripped past my lips and chin and into the urinal in a steady stream. I helplessly let it happen, without solution or will. I cried as my father had on the night of my mother's death. I howled my grief, a noise that was magnified by the lavatory's acoustics. When, finally, the howling subsided, I slid into a sitting position on the floor next to the urinal. I wiped my face with my sleeve—quite a mess—and rested my chin on my knees.

A boy named Danny came in. "What are you doing?" he asked.

"I'm preparing," I said.

"For what?"

"To tell the story of every passing second."

I've forgotten Danny's response, but I know that, word for word, that's what we said to each other.

Of course Mary Grey and Arthur married. Howard Dietz had a house in Sands Point, Long Island, and turned it into a dance floor; a caviar table; a champagne cellar; a theater of salmon, roast beef, clams, and shrimp; and a great outdoor arena for a tall white wedding cake.

The Red Sox and White Sox were playing a Sunday doubleheader on the radio in the bedroom I clung to for most of the afternoon. On Long Island, the Red Sox games could be picked up from Bridgeport, Connecticut, or Hartford or Waterbury or New London. All of them, except for WTIC in Hartford, have dropped away from the Red Sox Radio Network, though Hartford still does a powerful job.

On their honeymoon a week or two later, my father wrote, on Bermuda Inn stationery, that he and Mary were "wildly happy" and that he had accepted a job to write a score for a Dean Martin and Jerry Lewis movie called *You're Never Too Young,* with the lyricist Sammy Cahn. "Sammy's very commercially successful, and maybe he'll help get me a hit song. He did 'Time After Time,' and I can't remember the others." I wrote back facetiously that *You're Never Too Young* was based on a J. D. Salinger story called "For Esme, with Love and Squalor." He responded to his sixteen-year-old son by saying that he didn't think that was the case but he'd ask. I still enjoy the thought of his asking.

Their honeymoon, just after the school year, left me alone with the maid and as the recipient of an occasional obligatory phone call from Larry Fertig, a dry, decent man who had befriended Arthur at college. Perhaps the most unmusical fellow in America and the least ironic, he had been placed, one evening at our apartment, in a front-row chair during a party to hear Ethel Merman sing with Arthur's accompaniment. Fertig, no more than three feet from Merman, had taken about two or three minutes to fall asleep, snoring and all. My mother had had to poke him once, and again.

"How are you?" Larry Fertig asked on the phone.

"Fine."

"Any problems?"

"No."

None that I was going to tell this guy, that's for sure.

Mary took my mother's room, and Arthur returned from his study couch to join her. I don't recall that there were any big changes made in the apartment. They left things pretty much alone, which should have told me that a move was imminent, inevitable.

During their honeymoon, I went into my mother's bedroom for my first good look around since her death. Her absence was eerie and woeful. There she had read Irwin Shaw, Wolcott Gibbs, Jean Stafford, Robert Benchley, Charles Jackson, Thomas Wolfe, Edmund Wilson, John Gunther, Truman Capote, Dorothy Parker, Laura Z. Hobson.

There she had clipped articles from *Gourmet, The New Yorker, The Saturday Review, The New York Times.* She had courteously leafed through *Argosy* and *McCall's,* both of which arrived as gifts from their editors, Harry Steeger and Herb Mayes, friends of my parents. Ted Patrick, the editor of *Holiday,* would always send his magazine by special delivery.

My mother had come to town no older than twenty-one, with a lively mind and a generous spirit. Her father, Ray Carrington, had been a successful insurance man, but alcohol had sucked him down like quicksand. Divorced, out of work, and clearly befuddled, he had died in a rented room, alone. Kay's mother, Miriam, a goofy, frightened woman who would flinch at a cloud, drifted through the households of her three daughters, including Kay's. When she was with us, which was occasionally and always briefly, she wandered from room to room, jabbering away, in constant putter and worry. Without knowing it, she invited the man with the pitchfork into the house. "He's in the study," she might very well have told him.

My mother's first husband, Clifford Dowdey, had never before, I imagined, lain intimately with so gorgeous a gal as Katherine Carrington, let alone an actress on the stage with good reviews from *The New York Times*. Dowdey, his very soul awash in the Civil War, couldn't have resisted the blond singer, even with her Kern songbook a constant disruption.

Alone in her room, I lay on my side next to the spot on the carpet where I had found her crawling, retching, dying. I wondered if I'd ever met my mom, known her. What had I said to her, after all, but babble babble babble?

I now think that my mother's heart patrolled the streets of her intellect, presiding over everything, applying a romantic haze to even the grimmest of fleeting thoughts. She was alive with unexamined feelings that sweetly waved hello to my father's unexplored regrets.

Mary Grey set up shop. My mother's apparatus was disassembled and disappeared. Now the skirts in the closet were in darker colors, and leotards filled the drawers where once my mother's laces and stockings had been neatly arranged. The bathroom cabinet bore exotic tablets, perfumes, soaps, implements of beautification—tweezers, scissors, files, clippers—and small glass bottles of a European shampoo.

On the window sill sat a large white tin box, perhaps of chocolates. I took it over to the bed and sat down.

The tin was filled with letters on Beverly Hills Hotel stationery addressed to Mary Grey's apartment. They were passionate, obscene, adoring, graphic, urgent. They were all dated 1951 or 1952, well before my mother's death, and were held together by two thick rubber bands.

They were letters from the composer of the score of *Excuse My*

Dust, a Red Skelton film, and *Dangerous When Wet,* an Esther Williams film. Arthur had rented a bungalow at the hotel for both jobs, so that he could have a piano brought in, so he could work first with Dorothy Fields, then with Johnny Mercer.

The letters were all addressed to the apartment in which Mary Grey had lived as a woman separated from Ed Scott.

I read three or four of them. Then I stopped, rewrapped them in the rubber bands, and returned them to the white tin box.

I slid the box back under the very part of the bed my mother had courageously inhabited.

I looked through my things for the letters to me that Arthur had written during the same trips. I found them in a plaid plastic catchall my mother had given me as a Thanksgiving gift. "For all your old turkey bones," she had said, planting the catchall in the back right-hand corner of my closet.

My father's letters all began with upbeat razzmatazz. He told me that I'd "eventually do marvelously in school" and that I'd "learn to join the others with greater regularity." And he wrote that he wasn't worried about my future "*in any way.*"

Then he turned his attention to his work, his collaborators, and, in two or three letters, to the budding possibility of becoming a team with Alan Jay Lerner, "who is not only a great lyricist but a great book-writer as well. Look at *Brigadoon,* it's masterful. *You* loved it, remember?"

On the phone I asked Arthur about Lerner's partner, Frederick Loewe.

"Alan called *me,* so I guess he wants to work with someone else. It looks as if we're going to open an office in New York." In another letter, somewhat later, he told me that he was going to write a Cinerama version, with Alan Jay Lerner, of *Paint Your Wagon,* the Lerner-Loewe show, with a brand-new Lerner-Schwartz score. He told me that they'd already finished one song, called "Over the Purple Hills," when Alan had been in Los Angeles a week earlier. "It's a cowboy sort of song. It could be a smash hit."

As I stood in the closet reading Arthur's letters, I wondered if Mary's had been written first, or letters to my mother or to some other woman. Or what.

She told me to be with other women, but I haven't.

When they came home, Mary's white skin seemed lighter. Arthur, tanned and feisty, gave me an enormous hug. "Jonno boy," he whispered in my ear.

I told him I was so happy he was back and that things were okay. I withheld what I knew, and I told myself I forever would. The thing was way above my understanding, except my father's lie, for which I forgave him as soon as I saw his face. His was the one remaining lifeline with which I dared not tinker. What would he do if I confronted him? Would I be sent to a reform school? Or to the old dormitory?

He wouldn't do that, would he?

Of course Mary Grey would have a vote, not Katherine.

Alan Jay Lerner came around. He and Arthur took me to see their impeccable office at Sixty-second and Madison. A piano, a secretary, carpets and paintings, white telephones, and a shelf of cartons of Parliament cigarettes, Alan's crucial prop.

Lerner was a man in constant motion. A lit Parliament would go round and round in his fingers, the flaming ash closer and closer to skin as Alan talked, bit his nails, stood, sat, walked across the room, flicking the butt into an ashtray at the last possible second, while simultaneously lighting up again, another sleek recessed-filter Parliament round and round in Alan's right hand. I remember thinking that he must have been doing this since Harvard or even since high school; the whole thing had been rehearsed, round and round for years and years, in lobbies and nightclubs and bedrooms and limos, and at home, married so often—in the end, eight times. "Getting married is Alan's way of saying good-bye," Rex Harrison once observed.

I don't think so, really. Lerner, a pill-popping, drug-taking, chain-smoking nomad, was on the run from what I would imagine was intimacy. Arthur, punctilious at work hour, would wait and wait before calling Alan's home. Mr. Lerner is in France, the butler would say. But that's not *possible,* Arthur would insist. He's due here *now,* an hour ago, *two* hours ago. Over and over, Alan was gone. Once he called from London with no mention of the date he'd broken with Arthur that morning. He called to say that he'd acquired the rights to Shaw's *Pygmalion* and that they could do a great job with it, "even though Hammerstein couldn't lick it."

They got together in the office at Sixty-second and began to write a score for the new *Paint Your Wagon.* I came by on a Saturday morning to find the ceiling littered with hanging cigarettes. Alan had done it with his recessed filters, bending the tips, licking the tips, extending his right arm straight out before him, then shooting the Parliament straight up. The suction created by the saliva applied the cigarette to the ceiling, and it held. They all held. "He does it all the time," my father told me, later. "It's not a joke or a trick. It's a nervous habit."

Alan again grew elusive, slowing everything down, sometimes for weeks. During this period, Dorothy Fields told Arthur that she had a ready-made show with a star they knew from *A Tree Grows in Brooklyn*—Shirley Booth—but no composer. Harold Arlen had dropped out of the project at way past the last moment. Would Arthur be interested?

My mother's medical bills were eating away at Arthur's savings and his ASCAP royalties. He looked upon a Lerner collaboration, especially with *Pygmalion,* as a possible financial blessing. He had toyed with *Pygmalion* even in Alan's absence and had talked with Hammerstein. "If anyone can do it, it's Alan," Hammerstein had said, which had encouraged my father and had made Alan's disappearances infuriating. He shot Lerner angry letters that might or might not have reached him. Telegrams, icy and brief, carried the same imploring message. The phone resulted only in Alan's assurances that he'd be there, that all would be well.

Arthur accepted the job of *By the Beautiful Sea* with Dorothy Fields.

When he told Alan, they were standing together in the barely used Sixty-second Street office under a ceiling of dangling Parliaments. Alan's face turned red with anger. He said that by taking the Fields show, Arthur had ruptured their collaboration.

"*What* collaboration?" Arthur told me he'd said.

He left the office at once and never returned, though their companionship survived.

By the Beautiful Sea, with a score by Dorothy Fields and Arthur Schwartz, gave 270 performances.

My Fair Lady, with a score by Alan Jay Lerner and Frederick Loewe, is still running in at least a dozen countries. The Broadway cast played it 2,717 times.

Mary Grey's daughter was five when I met her. Madeleine was a blond and lovely child, gentle of manner and generally unhysterical. When she was with us at Ninety-fourth Street, which was most of the time, she used Arthur's study as a bedroom. I took it upon myself to teach her things, such as never pick up a razor until you are ten years old and how to wind a clock. I taught her everything I knew about the artichoke, such as how to draw the leaves gently out; how to scrape away "the fuzzy stuff," not with a fork or knife but with a spoon, to uncover "the heart of the matter." I told her that they grew in California, that they sat on top of their plants like bonnets, and that there were thousands and thousands of artichoke fields that stretched east into America, across the Rocky Mountains, to Kansas, where Dorothy, from *The Wizard of Oz,* ate them. What do you think Dorothy was doing outside at the beginning of the movie? She was picking artichokes, Madeleine. But even more important, the artichoke fields continued east to New Jersey and to the Atlantic Ocean and to the sand on the shore, where sunbathers would pick them and take them home to cook and eat for dinner, *and* they could have them cold for lunch the next day.

Madeleine, dazed but willing to believe, dipped her first artichoke leaf in warm melted butter, just as I instructed her, alone with me at the kitchen table.

For Arthur, after the Martin and Lewis film came a multilayered project for CBS. He would produce three specials, two of them musicals for which he'd write the scores, all of which would be done on the West Coast. *On the Twentieth Century,* a play starring Orson Welles; *A Bell for Adano,* a four-song adaptation of John Hersey's story with lyrics by Howard Dietz; and a seven-song *High Tor,* with lyrics by the playwright Maxwell Anderson. The very young Julie Andrews would appear opposite Bing Crosby in the final presentation of the CBS series, sponsored by Ford.

All of this solved a number of problems for Arthur and Mary Grey. Perhaps the most important was her separation from me. After their honeymoon, Mary came home with the political strength of a wife, and often, after a few glasses of wine, she would speak directly to my deepest fears. Gratuitously, she would say, among other things, "No matter what you do, you'll never surpass your father, so don't get any of that shit into your head."

Or: "We're moving to Beverly Hills, but we haven't decided yet where to put you."

Or: "You're going to have to learn to become a fucking adult on your own."

"Fucking" and "cocksucker" were her favorite demoralizers. "Don't play your music so loud, you cocksucker!"

Or: "Get out of the fucking room!"

"I haven't done anything to you," I said.

"Bullshit. You're standing there, aren't you?"

That's what did it for me.

"You're a fucking cunt!" I shouted. "You were with my father *way before* my mommy died!"

In the light of truth, Mary Grey pushed my shoulder, harmlessly enough.

"You cunt, you cunt!" I said, backing away.

Arthur came running.

"I read your letters from the Beverly Hills Hotel," I told him. "The ones to this cunt."

"You cocksucker!" Mary yelled.

"Where are they?" Arthur asked.

"Under Mommy's bed. I thought they were a box of chocolates."

"You fucking *liar*! You *cocksucker*!"

Arthur began to cry.

"Daddy, it's okay. Mommy said it was okay."

He was inconsolable.

"See what you've done, you *cocksucker*?"

"You are a sick cunt," I said in a vulgar staccato.

Mary Grey led Arthur away from me, leaving the narrow hallway that we'd somehow moved into strewn with the shards of our obscenities.

"Go fuck your mother, Mary Grey!" I yelled at her back, their backs. "You may have married Arthur Schwartz, but you're still a scumbag!"

The word "scumbag" stood for years, whenever there was a flare-up.

It would drive her, well, fucking crazy.

Mary Grey and Arthur took a house in Beverly Hills. Madeleine was placed in the Westlake School for Girls nearby.

Joanna Visher, a friend of Mary Grey's from Lee's class, was hired to live at Ninety-fourth Street, to keep an eye on me and generally promote peace.

Joanna, in the line of stutterers I'd encountered, had trouble finding the beginnings of what she wanted to say. Her mouth would get ready to form words, but nothing would emerge for five or ten seconds. Then she would speak thoughtfully, stopping occasionally for another preparatory silence, her pretty hands folded in her lap, lacking the gesticulative impulse that might have helped her speed things up.

She, like Mary Grey, was in her thirties, an actress studying with Lee Strasberg, admiring the iconic director, as did they all. Joanna's friends Marty Fried, Mary Troy, Geoffrey Horne, Jimmy Holland (known as Anthony Holland), and a dozen others rehearsed scenes for Lee in our living room at all times of day. Joanna had a long, melancholy face and large puzzled eyes that suffered, I think, from ambivalence: what to show whom, and where to show what, and when to speak, and even when to laugh. The conflicting emotions within her presented Joanna with so many choices of feeling that her eyes fell numb, glazed, in a dislocation that might very well have been the villain in the stutter. That she was as good as gold, as gentle as an infant couldn't be contested. That she was easily deceived, remarkably gullible, and oddly stagnant prevented her, I think, from deserved success in the theater. I watched her rehearse, with her permission, and found, almost always, that I would lose her to the character. She elevated her partner and taught me what a truly gifted actor could do. We lived together for two years in the penthouse of 139 East Ninety-fourth Street, and I sat and watched more scenes rehearsed than I can possibly remember. Joanna, not a remarkable beauty, was beatific, serene, stoic, not particularly funny, but always the girl in the play, someone else entirely.

The maid was let go, except for cleaning chores twice a week. Joanna made my dinners, or Mary Troy did. A skinny, lively girl, younger than Joanna, she was considered by the other actors (including George Furth, who would, many years later, stake a claim as a Sondheim collaborator, writing the librettos for *Company* and *Merrily We Roll Along*) the one to watch. In her scene rehearsals she was hilarious. In romantic moments she was steamy just by holding her hand to her heart. If need be, and sometimes if not, she was nude in a flash and delighted, waving her thin arms around, banging the top of her head with her palm. Bucktoothed, flat-bellied, her breasts larger than I'd imagined, Mary Troy wanted us to really see her, to connect with her. Once when I was talking with her forty years later, she told me that Mike Nichols had wanted to take her with him to Chicago as a partner on the stage. "I said no," Mary told me, "and I'm glad I did, for he found someone far more articulate than me."

One night a little after my seventeenth birthday, Mary Troy bathed me, dried me, and on the floor of my bedroom, under the twenty-five photographs of the 1955 Boston Red Sox (including Ted Lepcio, Dick Gernert, and Ivan Delock), she directed me so sweetly to a clearing in the woods for what amounted to but a moment. I still adore her for waiting around, watching Steve Allen on television with me until I was ready for a longer encounter.

In the morning, she revealed to Joanna what we'd done while Joanna had been out at a party. Her mouth opened, her silence emerged. Mary Troy and I waited expectantly for the verdict.

"We should celebrate with pancakes, don't you think?" Joanna finally said.

The girls prepared a celebratory meal; pancakes *and* eggs. Sausages *and* ham. Orange *and* tomato juice. As they bustled about, I added a splash of Gilbey's gin to my tall glass of orange juice.

We listened to Mozart and Rodgers and gabbed until noon.

Arthur, Madeleine, and Mary Grey returned for the Christmas of 1954, rousting Joanna out of the house and over to Mary Troy's top-floor walk-up in a building on Forty-seventh Street close to the United Nations.

Mary Grey sprang into attack. I mentioned a joke I'd told at Joanna's expense that had made Joanna laugh out loud. I had invented a friend who had the same kind of stutter; that is, at the beginning of sentences. I had given him a name, Tom Bronson. He wanted to give me his new phone number, but, of course, he had some trouble trying to get rolling. After a great effort, he said: "It's ATwater 9-4482. If there's no answer—" and he struggled again, before blurting out: "It's me."

"That's so in*sen*sitive," Mary Grey said.

"But Joanna loved it. Ask her."

"She wouldn't say anything. She's got free rent in a penthouse."

"What does that have to do with it?"

"She's not going to talk against you."

"I don't get it."

"She tolerates you. I'll put it that way."

This hit me hard. The idea that everything was an act, that I was only "tolerated" by Joanna (and Mary Troy) was devastating. They were in it for the apartment, where they could rehearse, smoke cigarettes on the terrace, and tolerate Arthur Schwartz's son, who needed a chaperone because his father couldn't stand him and neither could his stepmother, so they had moved to Hollywood until he was out of the house.

"Ask Joanna if she thought the joke was funny," I said, which led to a terrible response: "I already have," Mary Grey said, leaving the room with the last word, always leaving the room with the last word, always leaving the room, shutting the case down.

"But you just *heard* the joke," I yelled after her, to no response.

When Arthur, Mary Grey, and Madeleine were gone at the first of the year, I asked Joanna to tell me the truth.

Surprised, she spoke at once with indignation.

"She never asked me about any such thing. I never told her about it, and I thought it was a *terrific* joke."

"Then Mary Grey is a liar?"

"She sure didn't tell the truth about this."

Then Joanna said something about letting it go, it wasn't worth it. I told Joanna that the letting-it-go pile was growing high.

She's your stepmother, Joanna said, back to her stutter-start, her hands folded in her lap.

Mary Troy came back. I remember thinking it all out before I wrote it down, a little stand-alone view of Mary Troy as a character in a story:

> She was plain but gorgeous. She was as thin as a piece of string. She had buckteeth, bad teeth that needed work on them, but she didn't have the money. When they kissed, their teeth mashed together. Everyone said that she was an actress who'd be a star, because she wasn't afraid to show her inside or outside. She saw funny things in sadness.

We rolled around again from time to time, but kissing eventually became our only sport. She was a great kisser, clunking those teeth, always, as Joanna put it, while "naked as a jaybird."

Other actors showed up: Diana Hyland, Clifford David, Inger Stevens, Charlie Robinson. I discovered that Joanna was Lee Strasberg's secretary, collecting payments, booking scenes, so that she lived an all-round scholarship life, bunking in a penthouse and working for her seat in Lee's class.

"You've got quite a racket going on," I said to her.

"Not really," she said, which was, on the whole, true. Especially if you take into account her obsessive love for Marty Fried, an actor with a taxi who earned his scholarship by driving Susan Strasberg to and from the Cort Theatre during her run as Anne Frank. Fried, a pockmarked, tough-talking philanderer with a remarkable history of invention—as a foster child, an adopted child, an only child, a Moroccan, a Brazilian, a "former" poet, a father of three, a father of a retarded boy, a married man, a divorced man, a wealthy business-on-the-side guy, an I've-got-$100,000-comin'-next-week guy, an Oxford graduate, a Latin student, a lover of Marilyn Monroe (which was probably true), a man "deeply in love" with Joanna Visher—all of it fed Joanna's canyon of ambivalence. And so, catatonically, she existed on hold as Fried made his rounds, occasionally gracing the penthouse behind my mother's closed door.

"Jonno boy," wrote Arthur, in October 1955, "Mary and I would love to have you come out for the Christmas holidays. We've got a house on Cañon Drive, as you know, and plenty of room. And guess what? We've had a house guest who is two years older than you. Did you ever hear of Julie Andrews? She was in *The Boy Friend,* and she plays the love object of Bing Crosby in *High Tor.* She sings like a dream. After *High Tor* she's going to do the Lerner-Loewe show in New York. I hope she's still out here when you come.

"Max Anderson and I have written smashing songs for Crosby. You'll hear them in your usual understanding way. HAPPY CALIFORNIA."

My father communicated by letter most of the time, staying off the phone, I've come to believe, in fear of nuanced fury, Mary Grey the unmentioned issue. His letters championed and anticipated "great times," "smash hits," "straight A's" for me at the school set high upon a hill.

Jonno boy, in fact, was a wobbly student, a not especially ingratiating presence, except around Mary Troy, and, most odiously, he had met, in a bar, a man named Luke, who had looked familiar. It turned out that Luke worked as a salesman at the Liberty Music Shop on Madison and Seventy-sixth Street. What a coincidence! Luke had noticed Jonno boy in the shop and around the neighborhood. He lived in a brownstone on Ninety-fourth. My God, wasn't that amazing! The bar, a Mulligan's on Lexington between Ninety-third and Ninety-fourth, would sell liquor to an infant and, of course, to an acned and perspiring adolescent who bought Cutty

Sark whiskeys straight up with Rheingold beers as chasers. Luke, a heavyset Oklahoman with two martinis before him at all times, had a shine for Jonno boy. Invitations to his apartment were extended. No, thank you. A carriage ride around the park—"My treat," Luke said. No, thank you. All right, then, how about this: If Jonno boy would simply allow Luke to fondle him to conclusion, he, Luke, would open the Liberty Music Shop—he put the key on the bar—one midnight "real soon," and Jonno boy could pick out as many albums as he could carry. And he wouldn't have to do anything to Luke. A promise is a promise.

A summer night in 1955. First, to the Liberty Music Shop's listening room. Luke required only lowered pants from Jonno boy, who lay on the green carpet, imagining it was Mary Troy at work.

Fifty albums, boom boom boom. And a taxi ride home, the albums on the seat between Luke and Jonno boy.

Alone at the corner of Ninety-fourth and Lexington, Jonno boy, in shame, dropped one of his albums, the original cast recording of *The Boy Friend,* into the garbage can under the streetlamp.

To this day, Jonno boy shies away from the original cast recording of *The Boy Friend.*

Embarrassed at the thought of ever running into Luke, I dropped Mulligan's for Callahan's at Ninety-fourth and Third Avenue. Again, no problem with age, and Callahan's had a jukebox with some of Bing Crosby's Irish things, hit records by Eddie Fisher, Jo Stafford, Perry Como.

With straight Cutty Sarks and Rheingold chasers, I began to toss around the word "phony"—a gift from Salinger—as I heard the familiar recordings with a new ear. I found Como especially offensive, though he made a pretty enough sound. It didn't seem to be music emanating from anywhere, from any heart, from any thought, from any design. I said to someone at the bar that Como was chewing gum when he recorded, which was one of the reasons that he sounded "phony." I was asked how I knew. I replied that my father had been a trombone player "on the date" and had told me so. I believe the song was "Wanted." Listen for the Doublemint.

Since WKCS had gone off the air, I had fallen away from pop hits. Debussy and Chopin played all the time through the new long-playing technology that allowed classical music its proper space. The Beethoven string quartets were grave and intimate. There were times when I couldn't handle them and shut them off. When I could endure them, I sat still and listened, staring at the record player as if it were a television set. Now and then, Mary Troy or Joanna Visher joined me in respectful silence. I read about the quartets and their composer and blabbered my knowledge to the girls. I had a fleeting thought of going back on the air with a classical music station, but I found that the Electronic Baby-Sitter was gone, remembering only after a search that about a month after my mother died, I'd rested it gently in the bottom of the kitchen garbage can.

It wasn't any more complicated than walking down the hill to Third Avenue for a Cutty Sark and Rheingold at Callahan's.

Midafternoon, only three or four others in the bar. One of them had dropped a handful of dimes into the jukebox for the usual titles. A hot day. Two large fans noisily cooled the room. Callahan's offered free bowls of roasted salted peanuts. I recall wondering, that afternoon, about the mysterious process of salting nuts *in their shells.* They were wonderful with the beer and the whiskey and the shallow pop hits on the jukebox. But how was it done? Was each peanut injected with sodium by hand? By machine? There were millions of these peanuts. It would take forever.

After the first few seconds of Frank Sinatra's "Birth of the Blues," I slid off my stool and stood. I went to the jukebox and sat down in front of it on the old wooden floor. The recording had literally floored me. It was brassy, tough, confident. The singing was unlike any Sinatra I'd heard. It sounded operatic, effortless, fiercely virile, with no cover of violins to hide under. Ten of my dimes went to it. I studied it, seated on the floor, my legs crossed in front of me. It sounded like a song about nothing, suggesting only that the Negroes had invented the blues, which was something, I guess, but a something that had already been proposed. Sinatra sang, "Oh, some people long ago," rather than "Negroes" long ago. And of course the word "southland" was in there.

It *had* to be Negro, but it didn't matter what it was or who had invented what. It was all in the brass, the voice, the diction, the glory of a head thrown back by an ebullient wail of disciplined singing. Sinatra's "Birth of the Blues" challenged the timid adult inside a composer's son. I bought drinks for the little group at Callahan's, thanking them for enduring one song for ten plays. One guy told me it was an old record. I argued that it couldn't be or I'd have heard it. Besides, Sinatra couldn't have sung like that a long time ago. The guy said, maybe two years. I said I'd find out.

Helfer's, on Eighty-sixth between Lexington and Third, didn't have it. They were out of it. "When was it released?" I asked. I was told that it had come out in 1953, two years earlier.

Tin Pan Alley, at Fiftieth and Broadway, would have it, or the Colony, someplace far away from any Liberty Music Shop, of which there were several scattered up and down Madison Avenue.

Tin Pan Alley was an overilluminated square of property next to the large Rivoli Theater. I approached a salesman, a snazzy dresser in a dark blue suit, black shirt, orange tie, and shiny black shoes with leather tassels. His black hair was swept back and held fast by Wildroot Cream-Oil.

"Do you have Frank Sinatra's 'Birth of the Blues'?"

"Do we have—of *course*. You're not goin' to believe it, you're not goin' to believe it!"

"I know, I know."

"Have you heard the new album?"

"What new album."

"You haven't—? You're not goin' to believe it!"

The guy was energized, agitated, dashing around the place, talking all the time.

" 'Birth of the Blues,' do we have it, *Jesus*, get me *Wee Small*," he snapped to a young attendant. And over his shoulder to me, from the far side of the store: "You're not goin' to *believe it*!" He was all Damon Runyon and hyped high by Sinatra. His punctuation was wanting; you couldn't get in there, he was too excited. First, "Birth of the Blues" on a 78 rpm. "Don't play it," I said. "I want to hear it by myself." "Right, right," he said, understanding. "Okay, listen to this."

Bobby Sherrick, age twenty-three, put the new Sinatra twelve-inch album on the turntable. "Hear that? Hear that?" he kept saying over the music. The sixth song was "I See Your Face Before Me." "My father wrote that," I said. "*What?* Naw. *What?* Naw." Sherrick was racing back and forth, up the aisle, back to the turntable. "You gotta be kidding. Schwartz? Dietz?" "Schwartz." "Jesus, come on. Naw. Really? Jesus!"

"Take it off, I'll buy it," I said. Sherrick's manic energy was interfering with Sinatra's amazing album.

"I'm Jonathan," I told him on the way out.

"Johnny, Johnny, don't bust my balls. Your father's Arthur Schwartz? Naw."

"I'll bring him in someday."

Which someday I did. Arthur, standing uneasily under the fluorescent lighting of Tin Pan Alley, appeared jaundiced, Bobby Sherrick all over him, talking nonstop, complimenting, *knowing* Arthur's work, playing records of his songs that Arthur had never heard. He bought them all from Sherrick, who finally saw us to the door.

We could still hear him from half a block away. "Would you believe that? Jesus, I mean—take care, Johnny, take care, Johnny."

In the Wee Small Hours was a work of art on a long-playing album. Quite honest, a document from the dark of the heart, its violins few and unsentimental, its voice at the center longing, pleading, devastated, an internal monologue of madness leaking out into the open, the singer an oblivious street mumbler so immersed in sorrow that he was unaware he was exposed.

Over and over I played *In the Wee Small Hours,* proud that its sixth song was mine, and Arthur's.

Over time, with an archaeologist's care, I dug through the earth for the bits and pieces of Sinatra from the past, putting them in some kind of chronological order, watching the progress move backward, as in a rewind, hearing the voice grow higher and sweeter until I reached the end, the very first recording, made when I was a year old.

"Birth of the Blues," it turned out, had been recorded on June 3, 1952, eleven months before my mother's death. It had been followed by a change of record label and two eight-song albums on ten-inch discs that had preceded *In the Wee Small Hours.* The brass of "Birth of the Blues" had Stravinskyed into a pleasant dissonance on the second of the two ten-inchers, the work of Sinatra's new arranger, Nelson Riddle. He was using eleven musicians—I tried to count them as I constantly listened to *Swing Easy.* Many years later, I learned from Riddle himself that there had been fourteen musicians. I had probably missed a couple of woodwinds in 1955. But I'd been close and had worked hard at it, isolating each instrument. Eight songs, wonderfully syncopated and touched with humor. Nelson and Sinatra were witty.

The album cover displayed a man at ease; tie loose, arms out, fingers ready for snapping, a pleasantly arrogant hat tilted a bit, bespeaking invulnerability in much the way the subdued figure on the cover of *In the Wee Small Hours* evoked despair: lingering in the night, a cigarette in hand, the blue setting in urban out-of-doors, the base of a lamplight a few feet away, a lit lamplight down the street, and still another in the distance illuminating, but just barely, a lonely town. A painting this time, and as the albums came out and the photos or drawings rolled by, they assumed the effect of a continuing story, sometimes joyful, sometimes less so. They worked collaboratively with Sinatra and carried great weight, even when glimpsed in a store window from a passing taxi. The singer, releasing only 78s for thirteen years, two songs at a time, had been a short-story writer whose work had been eagerly anticipated through the forties and into the fifties. Now he had become a novelist able to include sixteen songs at a shot (my beloved Beethoven quartets were enjoying the same luxury).

I played "I See Your Face Before Me" on the phone for Arthur on Cañon Drive in Beverly Hills. Although it was beautiful, he said, he took exception to the first note, on the word "I," which he had written as a string of identical notes to accommodate the title—in the key of C, for example, that note would be an E, the words "I see your face before me" all landing on that E, depending on it, before the melody ascended to F and G. Sinatra had begun by placing the word "I" on the low G before jumping up to the intended E. Arthur thought that the arrangement (by Nelson Riddle, who followed Sinatra's every step throughout the album and matched his candor and intelligence through and through) was "absolutely smashing" and asked who'd done it. I told him that Riddle was a staff writer at Capitol "who wrote the truth."

Poor Joanna Visher! Poor Mary Troy! Sinatra all over the apartment, loud.

"Could you turn it down a little bit?"

I could, but only a little bit.

I have always taken the unhappy measure of girlfriends. "Would you turn it down?" was a dark sign indeed, boding poorly for any future. "Would you turn it down a notch" was inflammatory, if not decisive. "Does it have to be so loud?" "A little softer, please." "I can't hear myself think!" "I'd appreciate it if you'd make the music softer." "Amy's trying to sleep, for Christ's sake." "Are you doing this to make me angry?"

The opposite. I was wooing, working, waiting. I was presenting myself in the music. That is who I am. I am those songs, those string quartets. I am Nelson Riddle's muted trumpet.

"I can't hear myself think," Mary Grey said in the ornate living room of 632 North Cañon Drive.

I was there for the Christmas holidays, half a year before high school graduation. Julie Andrews was no longer living in the house, but my father had the tapes of *High Tor*'s sound track. Julie and Crosby sang Arthur's beautiful melodies and Max Anderson's romantic lyrics. I followed with *Swing Easy* and *In the Wee Small Hours*.

Arthur and Mary Grey were giving a party the next night for the wrap of the filming of *High Tor.* The stars would come, and Hollywood folk—some of Arthur's old friends from the forties, from *Cover Girl* and *Night and Day.*

Here is what I'd learned to do: empty a Coke bottle, pour in some Scotch and then Canada Dry club soda, then hold the bottle in my hand. A cinch.

Julie Andrews showed up at the party, unerotically beautiful. She seemed to flow above the carpet, her long hair caught, somehow, in an indoor breeze. She accepted praise with gracious amusement. When, later, she sang to Arthur's playing, she appeared to turn the color of gold.

Bing Crosby, without his toupee, looked like an aging businessman. At first I had a bit of trouble digging Bing out from the strange fellow who was about to sing. When, a moment later, he emitted the very sound of earth, with Arthur still at the piano, he emerged as a complete Bing, casual of gesture, a chuckler rather than a laugher, and clearly above the fray.

Persuaded by my second Coke, I asked my father if I could accompany Bing on a song.

"Naturally, of course," Bing said, in his resonant, modulated, familiar way.

I replaced Arthur at the piano. Gene Kelly was leaning into the curve of the instrument. There he was, with Cary Grant, Orson Welles, Fred Astaire, Oscar Levant. Kelly was a congenial presence out there in the world, the absence of fury itself a guest at the affair.

I knew a song from *High Tor* that was Bing's. "When You're in Love" was cast in an Arthurian minor key, and I gave it an introduction that delayed Bing's entrance perhaps sixteen bars too long. Finally he leapt in, which I understood to mean that he was cutting me off. I had given him a winding Ravel slide into the tune, and I believe he was just making sure, as he entered, that I wouldn't decide to extend my introduction any further. My left hand was respectful to Arthur's harmonies, and Crosby was complimentary when we finished.

"I'd say your boy's got a future," he told Arthur, who was standing next to the piano bench. "Let's do another."

Another!

I took a long drink from my Coke, right down to the last drop. Waiting at the bottom of the bottle was Igor Stravinsky himself. With cape and cane, he had come to call.

" 'Mountain Greenery'?" I suggested.

"A dandy choice," Bing Crosby said to me.

"What's your key?" I said.

"Oh, I'd say, let me see, B flat."

I couldn't play in B flat. Never have.

"How about C? You can get up there, it's not too high." What confidence, joshing with der Bingle, picking his key even after he'd chosen one.

"Let's give it a try," Bing said.

The three of us began: Crosby, Jonno boy, and the great Russian composer Igor Stravinsky, in town just for the occasion, having arrived in a bottle of Coca-Cola.

I was hot, let me tell you, piping hot, dripping Igor and Nelson, a mixture of the two, my harmonies infused with musical double-talk, my tempos shifting from a jazz waltz to a medium fox-trot. I was swingin', I was movin', I was kickin' ass.

Crosby stopped singing at the bridge.

"You got Rachmaninoff here," he told Arthur, most pleasantly.

And I believed him, modulating into the key of D, and then, wildly and oh so wonderfully, finishing in G.

I was given a peculiar, muted applause.

Had I been brilliant?

Had I been terrible?

No one seemed to know except Arthur Schwartz, who shot a cold glance my way.

I graciously took a seat next to Mary Grey, a woman well into her cups.

"You were very good," she said.

I kissed her cheek. "Merry Christmas, Mary," I said, to discover that her eyes were closing, that she was about to doze off, just as Gene Kelly began "Long Ago and Far Away" by Jerome Kern, accompanied by Arthur Schwartz, the man who might have written it.

My father drove me to the airport with something he wanted to tell me. "Mary and I thought it best—" he began. I interrupted: "You and Mary thought it best to arrange a plane crash in which I would instantly be killed." Arthur, indignant, said, "How could you even *think* a thing like that?" I said something along the lines of "Can't you take a joke?"

He fumbled his way to his theme, which was that Mary was pregnant; that the baby was due in August; that in June we'd be moving from Ninety-fourth Street, for lack of space; that he had kept the penthouse so as not to disrupt my education by moving before the end of high school. We'd be staying temporarily in the Stanhope Hotel at Eighty-first and Fifth Avenue, then in a sublet at 300 Central Park West that the actor Louis Jourdan owned. I'd be going to college anyway, and I'd have a room on Central Park West.

I had a lot to think about on the plane, which stopped in Chicago for a long refueling.

Joanna Visher admitted that she'd been told all of it by Mary

Grey, who had sworn her to secrecy. "You didn't have to lie to me," I remember saying. "I didn't lie," Joanna said.

The last semester at the school set high upon a hill were months of college acceptances, rejections, maybes. Teddy into Dartmouth, Harry into Colgate, Kenny into Harvard.

I applied nowhere and slipped into Boston University during the summer, having failed Spanish, having to make it up in June and July as we moved away from Ninety-fourth Street.

Joanna, Mary Troy, and I had a final evening together. I played the piano, the two girls sat around me. I had begun, a year earlier, to sing, having learned Sinatra's songs and dozens of others. My style was his, but my voice was there, a young, emulative professional sound.

Joanna and Mary drank champagne from Arthur's liquor cabinet. I chose gin and orange juice, which led to dizziness and nausea. I got up from the piano bench and made my way to my mother's bathroom, the hall spinning, my regurgitation seconds away.

I sank to the familiar spot on the carpet and created quite a mess. Joanna and Mary cleaned me up and lay me on my mother's side of the bed. "You sing great," Mary told me soothingly.

I fell asleep to those words, awakening in the night, in the dark. I was alone, the girls asleep in other rooms.

This was like drowning, no question.

10

MY ROOM WAS ON THE SECOND FLOOR OF THE STANHOPE. MARY GREY, Madeleine, and Arthur shared a suite on the ninth floor. Madeleine, now seven, had become beautiful and a bit uncommunicative. The tensions between her mother and me hung heavily over the bizarre little family who lived in a hotel and promoted caution in the children. We were separated by more than eleven years and had been given no chance, really, to know each other. I saw us as two annoying shadows in the way of Mary Grey's and Arthur's "wild happiness," as they both constantly called what they felt in their marriage.

In the middle of my first night on the second floor, a loud crash, not vehicular, occurred outside my window. I opened the curtains and looked out. On the street directly below me lay a crumpled body of a fully dressed old person, most likely a woman, rivers of blood flowing out from beneath her.

Police arrived. An ambulance came. Eventually I drifted back to sleep.

In the morning there was no sign of the body, nothing to suggest what had happened.

I called upstairs. Mary Grey picked up the phone, and I told her.

"Bullshit," she said.

"Bullshit?" I said.

"Nothing you say is true."

"You are some sick cunt," I said, hanging up, causing Arthur to hurry downstairs for a talk.

"Ask the manager of the hotel," I said. "Wait. I will."

I put Arthur on the phone with the manager, who set him straight.

The suicide, for that's what it turned out to be, was secondary to my use of the word "cunt." Arthur was angry.

I looked him in the eye, and I spoke quietly. "Mary Grey is a cunt cunt cunt cunt cunt."

"I've tried to defend you," Arthur said, getting up to leave. Both of them, it seemed to me, were always leaving the room.

In about an hour, my father called to tell me that I was going to go to the Simons'.

The comedian Milton Berle used a piece of business on television that can tell you something about Andrea Simon that by 1956 had become, within her, a creative act.

Berle, after telling a joke, would extend his left arm out to the audience, palm out, saying stop, no applause, no applause. But down below his hip, the fingers of his *right* hand were wiggling back and forth, saying more, more, applause applause, more.

Andrea exactly. Welcome, but not so fast, pal. Maybe not. Come in, go home. We're all going to the movies on Friday, but Jonno will probably be gone.

Gone to where, I'd like to know.

I checked with the Stanhope. The room was still mine.

Andrea played best with paranoia. I had called all kinds of Stanhopes after talks with her. She had learned to abscond with your hope, and the summer of 1956 found her at the top of her game. You are loved, you are tolerated. You are welcome, but with severe reservations. "We all feel" was one of her especially toxic strategies. "We all feel" meant Lucy, too. No one ever spoke of it except Andrea, who was constantly on the watch. She lurked in the halls. She appeared suddenly at the kitchen door. Was I eating some of her food? The food was for *them,* for her, for Richard L. Simon, for Lucy. Had I slammed the screen door? Had I muddied the living room rug? That's where Richard would have to play the piano, in my mud.

And yet how voluptuous the summer was, fraught with dangers, flooded with longing, covered with the humidity of sex in the foggy early morning, in the quiet heat of the afternoon, in the summer dresses of cocktail hour. Friends from schools, neighborhood girls suddenly women, Lucy sixteen years old. Could she really have had a voice in "we all feel," whatever it was they all felt? She could sense your vulnerabilities and came to you with the medicine of unconditional love. She washed your wounds. She healed.

On August 20, Mary Grey gave birth to Paul Arthur Schwartz. I went with my father to the hospital. He was goofily joyful, throwing Mary Grey's words around in humor. "This is some fuckin' day," he said, in an elevator full of nurses. "Look at that doctor, a real pussy grabber."

When Lucy came to my room and sat on the side of my bed at midnight, I told her all about Arthur's behavior in the hospital. She laughed, saying it was so unlike him. Then she lay her palm on my bare belly for a moment or two before kissing my cheek and wishing me a good night.

The skin she had touched became red.

In the morning, the lovely evidence of Lucy's hand was gone, though I can feel it still, all these years later.

. . .

Robert Delvecchio moved his books and records into Miles Standish Hall in Kenmore Square early in September. He was to be a freshman at the School of Fine Arts of Boston University and used his pseudonym, Jonathan Schwartz, at school and in the dorm. Delvecchio, a young man of eighteen, had arrived two days early and had snagged the one private room in a six-student suite. The five others, mostly from New England, resented Delvecchio on sight, his private room, his music, his bookcases of four shelves, full to the top. Had they known the word "imperious," they would have used it to describe Delvecchio, a New York Jewish guy who kept to himself, coming and going through his own door. It was as if he wasn't a part of the suite, the gang, or even, for that matter, the freshman class. He'd announced from the start that he'd be there for only one semester. Then he'd transfer to Columbia. Irritating, too, was his knowledge of the Celtics and Red Sox. These kids were from Maine and Vermont and Dedham and Framingham, Red Sox and Celtic guys since infancy. This fuck-ass Jew was on some kind of other level, with all the stuff he knew. And the noise from his room! "Turn the fuckin' music down!"

Delvecchio wandered the streets of Boston. He spent late September afternoons at Fenway Park as the baseball season waned. Through Leonard Koppett, the sportswriter on the *New York Post,* he'd been granted a press pass by the Celtics under his pseudonym. When the schedule started up in November, he hung out at Boston Garden from late in the afternoon until the game was over at around ten. Then he joined the press and talked to the players. The Celtics' announcer, Johnny Most, became his friend. With Most, he used his pseudonym; with Arnold "Red" Auerbach, the coach of the team, he used his real name, Delvecchio.

Arnold Auerbach (he called him Arnold because the star of the team, Bob Cousy, called him Arnold) was a man from whom a smile was difficult to yank. His theater was basketball. Everything else held little interest except for Chinese food, which he ate, it seemed to Delvecchio, every few hours. There was no delicacy to Arnold. He ate his egg roll and talked basketball. He was gruff and loud and unafraid of the aberrationally tall young men who were his livelihood. He was *of* Brooklyn, had played the game in Brooklyn schools, but was too short to make it a career. Arnold was profane and arrogant, and with strangers he was glacial. His cigar was well known—he lit up on the Celtic bench when he felt a game was in the bag, sometimes prematurely. It struck Delvecchio that he had little information that didn't refer to his game and therefore to his life. He was devoid of irony but made of iron, so that his will became the fact of any moment. In his mind, even if there was no game at hand, he was three to four basketball moves ahead of an *imagined* game that was being played while he ate and sat and talked with other guys. Even while having sweet-and-sour pork, he might very well have been calling a time-out in his head to set up an inbound pass with but seconds left. Delvecchio adored him and still does.

In three months, I went to three or four classes at the School of Fine Arts. In an acting class was a tall girl with long brown hair like Mary Grey's. I spoke to Susan Harrison and invited her "to tea." At tea, she told me she was going to make a movie with Burt Lancaster and Tony Curtis and that she was leaving school in November. Although I saw her only fleetingly through the fall, there might have been a touch of truth between us.

Her film, *Sweet Smell of Success,* was released the following June. In it she was beautiful but baffled, almost numb. I saw it four times.

A year later, I went to a William Saroyan play in New York in which Susan Harrison played an important role, having received rave reviews from all the critics, particularly from *The New York Times.* After the show, I appeared backstage and gave my name to the man at the door, who went away and came back and told me that Miss Harrison wasn't seeing anyone.

An explanation.

Why Delvecchio?

Name: taken from a member of the Detroit Red Wings.

Motive: to have myself put on the press mailing lists of film companies that distributed foreign product and ran these movies in one of two screening rooms at 1600 Broadway prior to their release. I had decided on the name while lying in bed one morning at the Stanhope and put it to its first use in Boston.

As I had written to Janus, Kingsley International, and Embassy Pictures, Delvecchio was a freelance writer "on films and culture thought" whose mailing address was a post office box I'd set up. The films, many from Britain, Sweden, France, and Italy, were, for me, more honest than American things with Robert Wagner, the opposite of, let's say, Arthur's *Night and Day.*

Also, Delvecchio was a more alluring guy than I. As Delvecchio, I became as unafraid as Arnold.

My father had been able to maneuver me into Columbia's School of General Studies and found me an apartment near the university on a wide, clean street for $98 a month; three rooms, elevator, large kitchen in the only building on the street (120th) not owned by Columbia. We furnished it warmly, digging out some of Arthur's things from California that were still in storage and buying, for $150, a not terrible upright piano.

At the kitchen table, I began to write short stories, living off an allowance of $60 a month, and by selling books and records when I ran low.

In that apartment, there was no need to disguise whiskey. No Coke bottles or any other cloak to cuddle the secret. Harvey's Scotch, the least expensive authentic Scotch—that is, bottled in Scotland rather than sent to the United States in concentrated form with New Jersey water added in Newark—became the house brand. For the girls, Smirnoff vodka. One of them, Judy Robinson, drank only a glass of white wine to accompany her cigarettes. She would sit across from me at the kitchen table, her thick light brown hair falling into her face, and tell me about the play she was in. Judy was an actress in a big hit, William Inge's *The Dark at the Top of the Stairs*. Directed by Elia Kazan, it had become a glowing success, and Judy with it, as the sensitive young girl Reenie Flood. Tuesday Weld, Judy's understudy, resembled her, more classically beautiful, perhaps, but not more erotic, at least not to me. Judy was in love and pregnant. I assumed the sorry role of good friend, offering Judy any help of any kind at any time. Which she called for regularly, even sleeping overnight in bed with me, allowing kisses out through her thin theatrical lips; no clanking like Mary Troy. She wore pajamas. They were in her bag with cigarettes and notebooks and stockings and matches and loose M & Ms and occasionally a bra and panties, and once a condom.

For Judy, I sat at the piano.

"It's very enjoyable," she said after I'd performed an overblown version of "Soliloquy" from *Carousel*, its eight minutes extended to fifteen.

I prepared her late-night dinners.

Sinatra started up.

"Could you turn it down just a little?" Judy said.

. . .

Then she wasn't pregnant.

I spilled my love for her to her brother, Charlie, one of Joanna Visher's actors in the penthouse. It was, of course, meant to get back to Judy, but if it did it held no sway. She still wore pajamas.

Judy Robinson, unmusical and stymied in the face of metaphor, had stumbled upon a true obsessive who allowed her own rules and regulations the role of an organized government. I sexualized her beyond endurance and in so doing created a muse for the tentative fiction I was writing. Those short stories glorified this one twenty-two-year-old girl who, in the theater season of 1957–58, had become a celebrated actress.

At one of the screenings on the fourth floor of 1600 Broadway, Bob Delvecchio met a man named David Lewis, an American importer of delicate European films. Lewis was a quiet, portly guy with an ingratiating interest, not only in Delvecchio but in anyone who drifted into his line of conversation. He spoke in a clear, soft voice with a bit of Boston in it—he was from Plymouth. He always wore a suit and a dark tie. He was about fifty, and though his hair was receding, his warm eyes took years away. Delvecchio liked him and gravitated to him at every screening. Often they had drinks or dinner. On an April afternoon, they went to a Red Sox–Yankee game at the stadium.

Delvecchio, it turned out, had been married at nineteen and divorced at twenty. There were no children. Delvecchio, it turned out, lived on Thirty-sixth Street between Lexington and Third with a girl named Judy Robinson—"not the actress." He was from Los

Angeles, had gone to UCLA. His father was a lawyer, his mother had died when he was three. Delvecchio wrote for West Coast periodicals.

Lewis, who loved the movies, especially foreign movies, had been a distributor for five years. Before that, he had worked in advertising. He was divorced. His two children, seven and four, lived with their mother in Baltimore, her hometown. Lewis rented an apartment in the Village, on Sullivan Street.

Soon Delvecchio felt shame. Here, in David Lewis, was a man who spoke about books, the theater, all kinds of music, and, of course, films. Delvecchio felt that he was too far in to try and put things right. He understood that Lewis wasn't the kind of man who'd appreciate or even tolerate a hoax, not only of this size but of this duration. Delvecchio and Lewis were well into their second year of friendship.

Lewis had confided in him, telling him of his wife's "problem with alcohol" and how he constantly worried about his children in her house. He had told Delvecchio that his father had had a "problem with alcohol," which had taught Dave a thing or two about drinking.

Delvecchio had confided in Lewis, telling him that the Judy Robinson he lived with was indeed the actress and he'd just been covering up for her at first. He had also told Lewis that his father was an occasional archaeologist, currently in India.

At a cocktail party at the Four Seasons given by Joseph E. Levine, the head of Embassy Pictures, Delvecchio and Lewis were, as usual, standing together, this time by an enormous potted palm. They were looking over the crowd, spotting a movie star here or there, accepting caviar on small triangular slices of black bread.

Here came Leonard Lyons, the columnist, whom Delvecchio

had known all his life. Lyons looked happy to have discovered Delvecchio in the crowd, Arthur's son at a big-time event.

"Jonno!" Lyons said, and slid his arm around Jonno's back.

"Lenny, this is David Lewis. He's a film distributor."

"Not a day goes by that I don't read you," Lewis told Lyons. "And, you know, I think you're at your best when you're writing from abroad. I loved the *Porgy and Bess* period from Moscow."

Lyons was delighted to meet such a connoisseur. "People have told me that. Jonno, you told me that, didn't you?"

In fact I had, pointing out to Lyons, who was essentially a benign theater anecdotalist, that when he wrote descriptively, he was wonderful.

"Would you give my best to your father? Tell him I love his score for *A Tree Grows in Brooklyn.*"

"I will, Lenny."

"Great to see you, Jonno," said Leonard Lyons, leaving us to patrol his beat.

Lewis and Delvecchio stood together in silence.

"What is this all about?" Lewis asked finally.

"What is *what* all about?" Delvecchio said, ashamed and sad.

"Have you been dicking with me?"

"Would you let me try to explain?" I asked.

"By all means," Lewis said.

I laid it out for Lewis.

I've never forgotten what he said when, finally, I finished explaining.

"I'm dumbfounded."

"I'm sorry."

"I'm really dumbfounded."

David Lewis walked away. Halfway across the room, he reached for a traveling glass of champagne, the tray moving by at just that moment.

Then he turned toward me and raised his glass. I raised my Scotch and soda.

And so, I guess, we parted with no hard feelings, never to meet again.

11

PETER SCHWEITZER, FROM BRANT LAKE CAMP, WITH WHOM I'D KEPT casually in touch, told me on the phone that he had an uncle who owned a New York City radio station, and as Peter knew of my interest in radio, he thought it might be a good idea if I met Uncle Louis.

The Schweitzers, financially a part of Kimberly-Clark, the company that made Kleenex and other crucial products, had diversified business interests, including Uncle Louis's WBAI-FM in New York. It was a commercial station smack in the wilderness of what FM was at the time, mostly dial locations that duplicated the programming of their lucrative AM spots. There were modest interest and few listeners, but Louis Schweitzer enjoyed the occasional piece in the *Times* or *The New Yorker* about an odd signal at 99.5 FM that was doing some unusual stuff. Nat Hentoff and Günther Schuller played and talked about jazz. Cynthia Gooding and Theodore Bikel played and talked about folk music. Gideon Bachman did a program about film in the David Lewis sense. Henry Morgan dripped acidic comment on life in America. George Hamilton Combs stentorially addressed politics. Around it all ran classical music, formally presented by staff announcers in grave tones, their deep voices credible, distinguished, even comforting. The announcers loved their sound, the virility of it, the culture of it, the weight, the simple weight of it. On a Sunday afternoon, one of them got caught in his own resonant reflection. Presenting the music, he said, so beautifully, "We hear next a performance of Mozart's Symphony number 40 in G minor, Köchel listing number 550. The Philadelphia Orchestra is under the direction of Eugene Ormandy."

He was compelled to go on. "Mr. Ormandy," he said, "will conduct the Philadelphia Orchestra"—and there he paused, groping, finding—"with his baton."

Louis Schweitzer was a bald little man with an enormous office. There were two books on a shelf, both by Charles Goren. I recall a black carpet and a window that overlooked all of America's northeast. Could that be the Liberty Bell? Look, the White House!

"Any friend of Peter is a friend of mine," he literally said.

All I wanted was an hour a week on WBAI. I would program it, I'd do it for free, and I promised Uncle Louis a good show. Besides, my father, who had written "Dancing in the Dark," would be listening, so I couldn't just offer up some trash to the man who'd also written "That's Entertainment" and other songs, including . . .

"Of course not," Louis Schweitzer said. "I'll get back with you" (I remember the word "with").

Uncle Louis got back with me, offering the 11:00-P.M.-to-12:00-midnight hour every Saturday night.

Did I ever thank him! Did I ever promise him that I wouldn't let him down!

On February 1, 1958, I showed up at ten for my radio debut. My records were in a canvas bag in the order I'd present them. My father was tuned in to his exotic FM dial. I had taken no alcohol, on behalf of clarity. "I'm abstemious," I told Judy Robinson, who missed the show.

The Pierre hotel, at Sixty-first Street and Fifth Avenue, had allotted space for two FM stations in what I still think of as the attic. The elevator took you as high as it could, to the forty-first floor.

From there you walked through the grand ballroom and down a hall to a metal ladder perhaps twenty steps high. At the top of the ladder was another hall, dimly lit. At the end of it was a small room, off to the left, that housed WNCN-FM, an automated FM station that played tapes of classical music without comment. The station breaks were on tape. Everything was done by machine. One man, generally in short pants, sat alone, in charge.

To the right was WBAI, in a larger space than WNCN but still snug, at the very top of the hotel. There were a couple of desks, a tape machine, and a studio with a heavy wooden door, outside which was an AP machine for newscasts. In fact, there would be a newscast from 11:00 P.M. until 11:05 P.M., a big hunk of five minutes removed from my one hour before I even started.

I argued this point with the staff announcer-engineer, Les Davis, who appeared incredulous that I was actually suggesting he drop the news. "This is my first program," I said. "But Jonathan," he said, "I can't do that. Don't you see?"

I saw, all right. My program was to be fifty-five minutes long.

Lester was lean, mustachioed, and of modest height. Almost at once he told me about his childhood athleticism and that he might very well have gone on to play professional baseball. He was twenty-nine in 1958 and the one staff announcer undevoted to his speaking voice, which was reasonably strong; he could lower it opportunistically when he wanted to. While arguing about the newscast or talking about the station, he was about my speed, pitched a bit higher than the other guys.

Lester Davis, born Lester Deutsch, from the Bronx, aspired to a radio career. We shared the imagined inevitability of our arrivals at the renowned WNEW. It was just a matter of time before we'd be joining Martin Block, William B. Williams, Klavan and Finch, and Art Ford at the most sophisticated station in the country, "the home of sweet romance."

Lester wore glasses that he took off and put on with a humorous regularity. A cigarette frequently in hand, earphones dangling around his neck, Lester's eyes gleamed warmly as he defended the newscast. My absurdity, he suggested, wasn't irrational. What a terrific idea, to remove the newscast, one, two, three, just like that. Maybe another time we'd try it, as a team. Okay, I said, but I need my lighting.

I had brought a little lamp for atmosphere, and the studio's fluorescent lights had to be switched off entirely, leaving Lester, the man who would cue up my records and get them on the air, to work with a fifty-watt bulb, twenty feet away. "But *Jon*athan, I won't be able to *see,*" he protested with a witty delight.

Lester was a satirist, with attention to platitude, hypocrisy, and self-inflicted dismay. His italics, or partial italics, addressed grandiosities that he characterized as "*most* familiar." He was also a what-if guy, as in what if we actually *did* take the news off and announced a merger with WNCN. What if, as a *team,* we approached Theodore Bikel and told him that people all over the city were being oppressed by his grandeur, his bulk, and that he *had* to leave WBAI because he was ponderous.

We quickly became immersed in the hypothetical—what if we dropped the news *at the last minute.*

At the last minute, Lester realized that he *had* no news; that he hadn't gone out to the AP machine for copy.

"*Jon*athan!"

"*Les*ter!"

He stumbled to the door. Oh so slowly did it open. In the hall, he ripped a long piece of paper from the machine.

His classical music had ended. The needle had passed into after-groove. *Sha-kuh, sha-kuh,* all over town.

The microphone was on a long, flexible boom. I got up from my stool and swung it to the door. Lester, trying to get back into the studio before the door closed, made it halfway, enough to grab the mike while he was stretched across the carpet. "The red button," he said.

I pressed a red button. Lester's voice, in all the panic, could not assume a lower ground. From his position half in and half out of WBAI's one studio, the door holding his ankles captive, Lester delivered an abbreviated newscast in semidarkness. I again pressed the red button and went back to my stool in the corner, under the light, as Lester gathered himself to get me on the air.

"Good evening," I said, at 11:02, "this is Jonathan Schwartz with a new program that will be heard every Saturday night at this time. Ladies and gentlemen, here's Sinatra."

The menu I offered, in the event you'd like to take a quick look, began with Sinatra's "I've Got You Under My Skin"; Judy Garland's "Last Night When We Were Young" (with the Nelson Riddle arrangement, the second of her two recordings of the song); Jascha Heifetz's performance of the second movement of Bach's Concerto for Two Violins in D minor; Sinatra's "This Love of Mine" (from *In the Wee Small Hours*); Lester Young's "I Guess I'll Have to Change My Plan"; Fred Astaire's 1952 "Lovely to Look At"; Oscar Peterson's "Blue and Sentimental"; Mel Torme's "Keeping Myself for You"; and Sinatra's "My One and Only Love." "The Carousel Waltz" ended the program a few seconds after midnight.

Before the Bach, I told a story for which I hadn't made any notes. I felt then, and I still do, far more comfortable making stories up as I go along, which I'll try to do now in as close to the spirit I found for that Saturday night of long ago.

I wrote a letter the other day to a girl named Lucy at Bennington College, in the New England January of Vermont. I wrote that I missed her and that in the city without her, "the asphalt belches angry hoards of spite. The city is so lonly now."

I read and reread the letter any number of times until I was satisfied that it eloquently expressed my deepest feelings about Lucy being away. "The city is so lonly now." I liked that line a lot.

I mailed the letter at midnight from the corner of Ninety-second and Madison. I dropped it into the mailbox just as snow began to fall, and I walked home, confident that the letter was lovely and that Lucy would be moved by it.

In the middle of the night the wind rattled the windows, and I got up. There was no question about it, a blizzard was in progress. I turned on the light to read my letter to Lucy once again, the carbon copy I'd saved. Oh my God! I said out loud when I discovered that I had spelled "lonely" wrong. I had left out the "e"! *How could I have done that?* Lucy would catch the mistake, a mistake *in the most important word in the letter.*

I paced my room until six in the morning and watched the storm and listened to the wind grow ferocious with every passing minute. The snow was piled at least a foot high, but at 6:30, all bundled up, I left the house and struggled through the blizzard to the mailbox at Ninety-second and Madison.

I looked at the little square card on the front after brushing off the snow. The first pickup was at 7:20, the second at 10:18. Who were they kidding? Lies, lies, all of it lies! No mail truck had ever showed up at *exactly* 7:20 or at *exactly* 10:18. Even on perfect days, sunshine days.

I waited. 7:20 came and went. 8:15 came and went. Still no mail truck. There was no traffic on Madison. Everything was a sheet of white. I felt the stirring of tears in my stomach. At 8:30 I thought I saw it in the distance. Yes! Over an hour late, but it was coming.

At the mailbox, a Negro man stepped from the truck and scurried to the mailbox, holding a wet canvas bag. I ran up to him. I said, "Excuse me, sir, I mailed a letter to a girl and I've had second thoughts about it. I can identify anything *in* the letter. Could I please have it back?"

"Sonny," the mailman said (even when I'm thirty somebody is going to call me "sonny"), "I can't do that. You know that. It's against any regulation. I'm sorry."

He was really nice about it, but I kept at him, tears coming up from my stomach and into my eyes and onto my cheeks where they froze right there, on the spot.

"Go down to the Eighty-eighth Street post office between Second and Third. That's all I can tell you," the Negro said, safely back in the truck.

"Can I ride with you?" I asked.

"No, I'm sorry."

I stood under a nearby awning, crestfallen. My little crest was down around my knees. But I decided to go and to walk through the blizzard. Lucy would show that letter around Bennington. "You see the word 'lonly'? Ha ha. You'd think he'd know better."

Imagine what an ordeal it was to get from Ninety-second and Madison to Eighty-eighth between Second and Third. It's not a long walk under ordinary circumstances, but in a blizzard it is hell!

I arrived in a shambles. In the overheated post office, I began to sweat profusely. There was no place to sit, just to stand. There was no one else there. I stood between ropes on a nonexistent line to wait my hopeless turn.

I wasn't given any attention for about ten minutes. I called for help. A guy came out wearing a sign that said "O'Brien." I asked if the Negro had come in yet. He said no, I should wait. I thought he thought I looked like a madman.

Much much later I heard the Negro in the back. I approached O'Brien, who seemed to be standing in a cage. There were bars in front of him like a cashier at a bank.

I stated my case through still somewhat frozen lips. I told him that I could identify everything in the letter, that it was a love letter that I'd had second thoughts about, and that he, O'Brien, was welcome to open the letter and read it for himself. I told him the girl's name was Lucy, and I gave him my phone number and address and apartment number. I showed him my Social Security card and a check to me, signed by the composer Arthur Schwartz. "Do you know the song 'Dancing in the Dark'?" I asked. "My father, the man who signed this check, wrote that song."

"So?"

"Look, we are honest people. I'm a good young man who has made a mistake."

I held his interest, that's for sure. Now I could see the Negro in the back room.

O'Brien went back there. I could see the two of them talking. They were taking their time, that's for sure.

O'Brien came back with my letter to Lucy.

"Open it! Read it!" I shouted.

O'Brien actually opened the letter and read it. I know he would have done it only during a blizzard.

He kept reading. Then he looked up at me. "You misspelled 'lonely.' "

He gave the letter back to me. I shoved my father's check to him under the bars as a gift. He wouldn't take it. He told me there'd be no next time. I believed him, you know.

My father called at seven the next morning. He had loved the program. He had been surprised by the improvisational feeling it had. He had loved the music but wondered if "the Bach fit in." He thought the long story about the letter was "terrific." I asked him if it was too long, and he said no, because it was so interesting.

Who else had actually listened?

Through the 1950s, FM stations were but receptacles for their AM broadcasts. Do you recall the station IDs of that period? "This is WNBC, AM and FM in New York." "This is KNX, AM and FM in Los Angeles." There were few FM sets and little prescience in the radio community: the clearer sound, the wider band, the modest price tag, FM lying dormant under indifference, the oblivious owners championing their AM stations, four in New York affiliated with networks. The stand-alone stations carried popular music and ball games—the Giants on WMCA, the Yankees on WINS, the Dodgers on WMGM. On the last, Ted Husing, the well-known sportscaster, conducted a music show that was contractually called to the air at 5:00 P.M. If the Dodger game ran late (and Ebbets Field games, with scores like 12–10 or 14–11, often did), it was banished to the FM side at precisely 5:00 P.M. and, in effect, disappeared. I, however, went with the Dodgers to the FM side, which is how I had learned that it existed. Red Barber and Vin Scully and Connie Desmond were right there for the seventh, eighth, ninth, and often the extra innings of a Brooklyn Dodgers game. The Dodgers' presence on FM lent a luster, however modest, not only to WBAI but to (in my mind) the 11 P.M.–12 midnight Saturday show, which gradually gathered a small but ardent audience. "Fantastic." "Unusual." "Keep up the great work," my mail read. "You're a Jew fag." "You don't know shit." "Get off the fucking air," read my other mail.

WBAI was attracting advertisers: stores that sold stereo equipment, tennis rackets, magazines, expensive cameras, books were all finding us a good place to sell their stuff. I remember thinking—and telling Lester, who had started his own jazz show on Saturday afternoons from two until four—that "this thing will go on forever."

Or until 1961, when Louis Schweitzer, without fuss or fanfare, took a tax write-off and sold WBAI to the left-wing Pacifica Foundation, which owns the station (and its turbulence) to this day.

I called Louis Schweitzer to ask why he had sold us. He put me on hold, then disconnected. I called back. The secretary put me on hold. In about three minutes, she came back on the line. Mr. Schweitzer was in a meeting but would call back.

You think he called back at some point in these forty years?

You think?

12

ARTHUR AND HIS FAMILY SETTLED INTO AN APARTMENT AT NINETY-FIFTH and Fifth that he bought at a modest price. I rarely visited, wanting nothing to do with Mary Grey, afraid of a storm out of the blue, chaos without warning.

On Thanksgiving Day of 1959, I showed up, determined to leave unscathed. There'd be no other guests, partially because Mary Grey had alienated my father's lifetime friends, anyone who had known my mother. She wished, I'm sure, to wipe away Arthur's first marriage, to repopulate his life with her own limited picking. Her insecurity must have been painful to her. "The past," for that's what she called Arthur's oldest pals, would have no place in "Arthur's greatest years," as she saw the future reflected in their marriage. What a terrible burden I must have been, unbanishable, the one child of Arthur's nineteen years with Kay. "An aimless cocksucker" is how she had begun, repeatedly, to put it.

And so we gathered for the holiday and sat around the living room before a late-afternoon dinner.

Mary Grey had encouraged in Arthur the idea that he was not a songwriter but a composer. Songwriters were Sammy Cahn and Jimmy Van Heusen kind of guys, "cheap pop hacks," she often said, particularly that Thanksgiving Day.

"But what about 'The Second Time Around'?" I asked, referring to what I felt was an excellent new song from those very two men.

Derisively, Mary Grey spat out, "'Love is friendlier the second time you call.' What kind of crap is that?"

"That's not the right lyric line. Daddy, *please* help me."

"It's an okay song," he said, caught on the fence.

"It's just crap that your boy Sinatra does," she continued, holding her glass of red wine.

"Mary, you don't know what you're talking about," I said.

"You heard his record of 'Dancing in the Dark.' 'Dan*cin*' in the dark.' The cocksucker."

We were interrupted by Paul or Madeleine, but the air hung heavily in the gray November light from the picture windows across from Arthur's piano.

At the table, I brought up Judy Robinson's name. She now held a leading role on the soap opera *The Guiding Light*. Her character, Robin, had been the focus of the show for weeks.

"She's not very pretty," Mary Grey said.

"She's beautiful," I said.

"You're the only one who thinks so."

Maybe thirty seconds went by.

I got up from the table without a word.

"Where are you going?" Arthur asked, aware of something ominous.

"As it happens, Judy's favorite song is 'The Second Time Around,'" I said to Mary Grey, not knowing any such thing. I knew that Judy hadn't absorbed more than a handful of songs and couldn't possibly name a favorite, or any.

"I'm not coming back here," I said.

"Jonno boy, wait," Arthur said. "I'll talk to her."

"Too late," I said, taking the stairs down from the eleventh-floor landing to avoid Arthur's plea from the foyer.

At home, I typed a letter that listed Mary Grey's attacks. I told Arthur that I loved him but that I would see him only when he was somewhere other than at home. I wrote that if ever Mary Grey came near me again, I would "strangle her with my two bare hands."

My father wrote back and said that he understood my anger and that when things calmed down we all might reach some kind of understanding.

No understanding was reached.

"Mary feels you are constantly rude to her," Arthur wrote, around Christmas. "If you apologized to her, she thinks we could establish a family again that would include you."

My letter back, hand-delivered to the doorman of 1136 Fifth Avenue, shut down all communication with my father for three months. I recall it well.

> Once again, here is what your second wife has told me over and over since I met her: That I was 1. A scumbag. 2. An aimless cocksucker. 3. A fucking cocksucker. 4. A fucking liar. 5. A lazy no-talent cocksucker.
>
> When she came into the house she was an adult in her thirties. I was going on sixteen. And you are asking for an apology from *me*? I want both of you OUT OF MY LIFE.

For the first time, my father and I fell to silence. His monthly check didn't show up; out of my life meant out of my life, is how I took it. I began to sell lots of record albums; in fact, many of the albums from the Liberty at Seventy-sixth and Madison wound up in a tiny shop at Third Avenue and Fourteenth called Used Music.

I was told of an agent who booked pianist-singers into small restaurants and cafés in New Jersey, on Long Island, and in Westchester. His name was King Broder, and I would never meet him—remarkable, in that he booked me at least a hundred times. In a light blue VW that Arthur had given me for my twenty-first birthday, I drove to Great Neck, Rye, Huntington, West Orange, Tarrytown.

For the most part, these places were restaurants with lounges somewhere in the front or the back. I played popular songs, and when I revealed myself as an acceptable singer, I was asked to sing. I received $50 a night, but with the singing and the large repertoire, I was often tipped another fifty or so. A Thursday, Friday, Saturday in the same place amounted to about $300 a weekend. My bar bills during each evening substantially reduced my income, even though the drinks "for the entertainer" were priced at a minimum.

The waiter would bring me a small glass that was filled to the top with Scotch. One ice cube floated in the whiskey.

This was the drink that I found least visible and the most efficient to receive and consume at a piano. The waiter got a five-dollar bill from me at the start of every night, when I described what I wanted. "Fill it up," I always said, "and I want only one ice cube. You dig?"

I had taken to "You dig," "Yeah, man," "It's a gas," partially from Sinatra and more generally for shortcuts through uncomfortable social settings, which meant every social setting imaginable, particularly those with me right out there in public.

The evenings were long and the breaks were short. The clientele was married couples who were generally clamorous, the more so in later hours. Occasionally voices were raised in anger. My Rodgers and Hart tinkle, vulgar and sad, created a dichotomous hell.

Now and then an unattached younger woman (or older woman) would follow me home in a Buick and spend the night at 120th Street. More often, I drove slowly into the city alone, aware of whiskey and my own anger soaked in Scotch.

I would add a couple of drinks in my apartment while I made dinner. Then I would listen to Jim Gordon on WABC.

Gordon, in the early 1950s, had been the voice of the NBA's Syracuse Nationals. I'd heard him often at night through radio static and admired his unhysterical description of the hysterical games. Now here he was in a quirky role, taking phone calls from listeners whose questions couldn't be heard on the air. He had to re-create those questions and convey the nature of each call while he listened on the phone. He began at 3:00 A.M., taking over for "Big Joe" Rosenfield on *The Happiness Exchange*. Rosenfield paraded needy people before the microphone who spilled their sorry stories of destitution and despair to Big Joe's large audience—WABC was a nighttime powerhouse up and down the East Coast—and, taking pity on this one or that one, the audience would respond financially. Rosenfield, whose wife, Choo Choo, hustled her own line of perfume, had bought the midnight-to-six A.M. time from WABC but found that his audience dwindled after three A.M. He had hired Gordon to take over for the last three hours and do whatever he wanted with the time; the result was the first phone talk show in America.

I'd call from bed a couple of times a week to talk basketball. I became a sort of character on the show, a Vinnie from Queens or a Morty from the Bronx, though my voice was never heard. I was Jonathan from Glen Ridge, New Jersey (Judy Robinson's hometown). "The Celtics have had four bad third quarters in a row," I said to Jim Gordon. "The Celtics have had four bad third quarters in a row," he repeated for the listeners. "Why the letdown?" "Why the letdown?"

One call of length had to do with a 173–139 Celtic win over Minneapolis, a record 312 total points. We went over the other high-scoring games and low-scoring games in the NBA's history and the Celtics' double-overtime game seven win over St. Louis in the finals of March 1957, all of this taking quite a bit of time on *The Jim Gordon Show.*

An hour after the call, still awake with the lights off, I heard Jim Gordon repeating a listener's comments: "You're saying that ASCAP songs are being prevented from being heard on the air because BMI is owned and was created by the networks themselves, who have a vested interest in promoting their own tunes. Is that right?"

A silence.

Then Gordon again: "The public should be aware that all the great songwriters are ASCAP members and BMI is putting their music in peril."

It was clear to me. Over at 1136 Fifth Avenue, Arthur Schwartz, a board member of the American Society of Composers, Authors and Publishers, ASCAP, had taken to the phone in the middle of the night to address an audience anonymously, in fact, to inform an audience that something wasn't cricket in the music business.

It could have been someone else.

I called Jim Gordon again.

"I think that was my father on the ASCAP call," I said.

"You think that was your father on the ASCAP call," he said.

"If it was, would you ask him to phone his son, me, Jonathan."

"ASCAP caller, if you have a son named Jonathan, he wants you to call him."

In seconds Arthur called.

We talked until daybreak, expressing regrets, love, devotion to each other. He offered to send me money. I told him I was doing okay, that I was playing piano in clubs around the area. He told me that he needed Mary to keep him going, that she really took care of him. "I'll be sixty, you know," he said.

"A young sixty," I said.

"Oh, Jonno boy," he said, sadly.

"Really, truly."

"I want you to know something," he said. "I wish I had written 'The Second Time Around.'"

I thanked him for saying that. I told him we could work things out if I didn't have to come over to the house. He agreed. We set lunch for one o'clock that day at the Hamburger Heaven at Sixty-second and Madison, where we sat at the counter. I put my arm around his waist. With tears in his eyes, he kissed me on the cheek. For a quick moment I saw my father as utterly lost, and I vowed to conquer the world for him, to bring him pride in his son. To make him happy.

In 1960, Peter Dean's office, just west of Fifth Avenue on Fifty-fifth Street, occupied two rooms on the first floor in the back of a residential apartment building. Telephones rang all the time, and music played constantly. Uncle Dutch was there a lot, and one of the Simon girls, Joanna, would use the smaller room to shower or rest during an afternoon or early evening. The pianist Buddy Weed, affixed to a couch along the left wall of the front office, chain-smoked cigarettes and toyed with a tuna-fish sandwich that was often on the coffee table in front of him. The rooms, facing brick walls, were dark.

What made the young singer Lynn Taylor so striking when she appeared was the colors of her presence. Her hair was curly blond, her eyes were green, her thin white arms were in constant action. She wore blues and purples that, in their quiet, italicized the lighter strokes. She was wide awake, ready to laugh, and always eager to sing. As a singer (she was one of Peter Dean's "people"), she'd traveled with a small Benny Goodman group and had played clubs on her own, mostly in the West. In her music, I knew her to be the master of unfalsified emotion. When she wandered away from the written passage, she never insulted the melody. With Buddy Weed playing for her on the upright piano across from the couch, her ballads did not flatter a technique. Instead, they warranted attention for their simplicity. I listened, occasionally catching a warm glance from the singer, a twenty-four-year-old woman from Philadelphia who had changed her name from Pat Fowdy to Lynn Taylor. Peter Dean, her agent-manager, thought her to be "one of the best alive." She was part of his "long-range plan."

I offered Lynny wine and dinner and songs when she came to dinner at 120th Street. Oh, did she make me laugh. She called car racing "one long left turn" and told jokes about deaf midgets. In my apartment, she sat on the floor by the piano and sang, the first night for four hours. I knew more songs than she. I taught her some of my father's lesser-known things. She was able to listen to a melody and a lyric and sing them right back to me with only an occasional stumble in the lyric. The second time she was so sure of the tune that she was able to take off from it, buzzing in and out, landing dependably when the melody beckoned. She sang softly and without vibrato in an unremarkable range that she filled with inventions—a flattened note here, a blues arc there, a flirtatious touch of a high F—all surprises that complemented her minimalism.

She told me that she had an infant daughter named Gia, that she was getting divorced from a drummer named Johnny, and that she liked to speak what she felt by singing. She said that she loved my radio show because of its "unusualness."

She came up to 120th Street a few times before, and at last, permitting intimacy.

She was a scholar. I called her Professor Fowdy. We became involved with each other without falling in love. We were not fragile, uncommunicative, furious, or petty. We were musical friends who lived without the weaponry of obsession. She would sit with me during my program. Les Davis recalls that when she did, there was *finally* light in the room.

At night Lynny and I haunted hotels where pianos sat silently in dark ballrooms: the Pierre itself, its ballroom just below the radio attic; the Manhattan Hotel, at Forty-fifth and Eighth; the Sherry Netherland, a few blocks from the Pierre; and three or four others, most with Steinway or Baldwin grands. I would bring whiskey and wine in a canvas bag. While she sang, Lynny would stand in the curve of the piano, sometimes wandering around in the candlelight that we would often set up. Occasionally we were asked to leave. Once we performed for two security men who had come to throw us out but stayed instead. Mostly we were left alone. We set our own hours and would, every now and then, go until daybreak.

Lynny learned a number of Arthur's songs, and I told her that the material would be great for an album. Peter Dean made it happen on a label called Grand Award. He put Buddy Weed at the piano with a small group of jazz musicians. I titled the album *I See Your Face Before Me*. The cover, a hideous drawing of a busty, chewing-gum blonde, thoroughly missed the point. Despite the cover, I spread the album around WBAI, leaving it in everyone's mailbox. Skip Weshner, an early Bob Dylan "expert" with a program called *Accent on Sound* that emanated from his Greenwich Village apartment, was attracted to the inaccurate album cover and sought out the singer.

Weshner, it must be said, was a flabby egotist who easily bore the weight of grandiosity. In his apartment, he was surrounded by as many record albums as had been made in the 1950s, though his special interest lay in folk music. Dylan, edging into view, had caught Weshner's passion. Skip would become his "discoverer," as he often said on the air, even though the job had already been done. "I control Dylan," he said to me when I took Lynny over to his disorganized pad. She called him "Dad" a couple of times, "as a joke," she explained later, when I asked her about it.

Weshner was a moralizer, a monologuist, a talky interviewer, a self-praiser out of nowhere, and a sound expert fond of the word "components." He was thirty, or younger, or older. It was rumored around WBAI that he had "real money."

Lynn Taylor slipped into the whole messy thing, entangling herself in Weshner's disorganized life. She moved in with him, Gia and all. She met his friends and, with two of them, formed a group called the Rooftop Singers, at the suggestion of Vanguard Records, which needed a new name to record but one song.

"Walk Right In" became a number one hit in no time at all, an old country blues brought up to date with a sixties folk arrangement using twelve-string guitars.

For a brief time in 1961, Weshner, bringing in his own sponsors, conducted a program on WABC from the very studio in which Jim Gordon had asked the ASCAP caller to contact his son. Lester, too, brought his jazz program to the same call letters and preceded Weshner on the air. Lynny sat with him now and then as Weshner prepared, heavier than the year before and noticeably sloppier, his shirttails disengaged, his belt buckle undone to allow space for girth, his collar frayed, his shoes, as Lester said, "mucky."

Lynny, alert and chirpy, gave no sense of dissatisfaction, though "Dad's" papers flew every which way. His car, which Lester noticed on the street each night, "a big clumsy American thing," was filled with piles of magazines and newspapers, candy wrappers and empty Pepsi bottles, record albums and boxes of stereo components. Cigarette butts littered the floors, and Weshner's laundry was shoved halfheartedly under the front seats. The car itself was sometimes awkwardly parked, either too far from the curb or partially upon it. It occurred to me that they might, one day, wind up living in that car, Dad, Lynny, and Gia. I suspected that soon Weshner would be unemployable and that I, too, had that potential. Just some crazy guys with records.

"You're your own worst enemy," Mary Grey had once told me.

Skip Weshner, encamped in sloth, did not go unnoticed. I felt that I would have to negotiate the politics of nuttiness with care or implode into the utter failure Mary Grey had predicted for me.

In one of our last middle-of-the-nights together, in the ballroom at the Pierre under the radio attic, I told Lynny that I felt that Skip and I were somewhat alike, in that we believed far too intractably that we were right, though we probably were. I said that I had been thinking that Skip's boat was sinking far too quickly; that I had noticed the water on the floor.

"There's no water on the floor," she said calmly. "Dad loves Gia and he loves me, and he'll take care of us."

I said that I didn't doubt that for a minute and that I was wrong to have brought the whole thing up.

We did some more songs. We even kissed.

At home by myself at five in the morning, I listened to Lynny's album of Arthur's songs.

After a few hours of sleep, I wrote a short story called "Annie's Trouble" in which ocean waves capsized a sailboat.

Everybody on board drowned.

Arthur was writing beautiful melodies for a new show, and he came up to 120th Street a few times to play me the score as it progressed. He had chosen the Arthur Schnitzler play *Anatol* to adapt with Howard Dietz. Barbara Cook, the sought-after ingenue of the day, would costar with some kind of "comic foreigner," as the producer, Kermit Bloomgarden, said. To that end, Bloomgarden contacted Walter Chiari, known as "the Italian Danny Kaye," who asked that the composer come to Italy to play his songs.

Arthur set out alone, and what he found in the hills of Tuscany was an excitable, flamboyant leading man who drove Arthur through the mountains with ferocious speed in an Italian sports car, shouting at him happily in speedy Italian. My father hired him, I've always thought, just to get out of Italy alive, only to find in New York that Chiari's singing voice was grating, unmusical, and deadly. Coaches arrived and huddled with Chiari for hours, improving Chiari's instrument only slightly. Why, how, please tell me, did Arthur, one of the better melodists in the United States, engage this guy without hearing so much as a note of his singing?

Gradually, on the road, when it became obvious that Walter Chiari was, at best, a distressing singer, more and more songs were given to Barbara Cook, even one last-minute enormous production number called "The Label on the Bottle."

The show opened on a Saturday night, which meant a delay until Monday for the reviews. The party, unusually relaxed, was warmly anticipatory. The score was gorgeous, Chiari had elicited some unexpected laughs, and Barbara had brought down the house with her magnificent singing. Maybe a smash hit at last.

I played piano for anyone who wanted to sing, and that meant Barbara. I took my Scotch straight up in a little glass with one ice cube, as if I were working in Huntington, Long Island. Eventually I fell asleep, my head in Barbara's lap.

"Colorful, cheerful and leisurely," wrote the *Times* man on Monday. And three or four other reviews were pleasant and cheerful. Arthur saw the hit he always had wanted. "We've got a smash," he told me several times in taxis and on the phone, "and I'm going to send you around the world."

"Am I so terrible?" I joked.

No, of course not. Arthur wanted to give me a present. A trip abroad, which he could now afford, what with *The Gay Life* selling out every night.

By January 1962, two months later, it was apparent that my father's smash was doomed. Walter Chiari, who, as Howard Dietz said, "couldn't act, dance, sing, or speak English, which was a handicap," was bringing down the event, even though the show had become a sort of Barbara Cook concert. It closed after its 113th performance, winning the words "short-lived."

"Daddy, if you hire Chiari, your show will be short-lived."

"Arthur, you've got a short-lived show on your hands."

My father, ashamed and desperate, took to his couch, which I never visited. During one of our many phone talks, I told him that I was going to Paris on my own; that I wanted to put myself in an environment without English so that I would have to live internally and "at least try and be a writer." After all, I had written twenty-three short stories and sent five of them around to various magazines without success but with some encouraging notes in the return envelopes.

Arthur offered $1,000 for the trip, and so, as a matter of fact, did one of the women who had followed me home in her car from a Long Island gig. At twenty-six, she was divorced, childless, and wealthy, though she had at first presented herself as married, the mother of two children, and the wife of a garment district executive who was "hardly making ends meet." The truth came out in the dead of our third night together. She had made everything up. "It's my tendency," she said. She was attractive, still a young girl, as I can see now, an aspiring writer herself who showed me two graceful stories that she had written—sketches, really—that she hadn't let anyone read. I asked for proof of her solvency, of her assets, not really knowing what to believe about her and thinking of accepting a loan. Irrefutable documents were placed before me, and I accepted her "advance," as I called it, at Downey's restaurant, an actor's hangout at Forty-fifth and Eighth in which, as an envelope of cash was handed to me across the table by Susan, not by the Karen she had initially allowed me to believe, I saw Judy Robinson sitting at a table nearby with three men. She had her back to me, and I didn't go over to her and didn't see her again for thirty-two years.

"You don't have to pay me back," Susan said after dinner.

"But I will," I told her, and did, three years later. Her postcard acknowledging receipt, a voluptuous Renoir print that will always remind me of her, told, in small print, what I assumed to be the truth: "I am married with a son named Ben. We are broke. Your gift is very welcome." I thought to insist, through the mail, that it wasn't a gift but a return of her loan. But in the end, I did nothing.

13

"I KNEW YOUR MOTHER."

Drew Bradley, my seatmate on Air France, had, during several drinks together, identified me. A self-described "philanthropist," he had been an investor in *A Tree Grows in Brooklyn.* "I give to the theater," he said. At parties and functions, he had observed that Kay was a "vivid character." He recalled that my mother had been well informed on the Alger Hiss case. He told me gaily that my father was well known for being "a man-about-town."

A wrist toucher clearly on the make, Bradley drank bourbon on the rocks and spoke conspiratorially with a flaky intimacy that suggested we'd known each other all along.

"I'll give you a lift into town. I have a car and driver."

Morning light. We had flown through the night and were now greeted by a Paris rush hour. Through customs, French mingled with Italian and German. Deprived of language, reduced to visual impressions, I regressed into a sort of bubbly adolescence. "Well, well, well," I said to anyone who placed himself before me.

In Bradley's car, he returned to his conspiracy. "I'm from Atlanta, you know, as I told you. But I live here now," he said, gesturing at the passing scene. "I'm an expatriate, and I love every minute of it."

I asked if he lived in an apartment, a house, or what.

"A beautiful residence, with a fireplace the size of Norway, and a country home," he replied, with the first annoying impurities in his voice. The fireplace, the country home, a juicy kid from New York.

As we drove, I noticed a consistent flow of Sinatra posters attached to telephone poles by the sides of the road. L'OLYMPIA, JUNE 5, ONE PERFORMANCE ONLY, SINATRA! All in French, but I got through it.

"Sinatra?" I said to Bradley.

"It's a charity thing," he said, not particularly interested.

I remember thinking that Bradley was a concocted man, maybe seventy years old, a Georgia peach with a British accent, up to here in inherited funds, a persistent gull circling his prey. A prey, I might add, carrying six Sinatra albums, ten classical albums, Miles Davis's *Sketches of Spain,* a thirteen-pound record player, an Olivetti typewriter, and one bulky suitcase.

How would I get an apartment?

The offer of his own residence was officially made.

I thanked him and demurred on behalf of my desire to "go it alone."

If Drew Bradley felt regret, he didn't show it. Instead, he piped right up with solutions. First, a modestly priced hotel near Place de Clichy. Then, and just by chance, he knew a sergeant at SHAPE who was going back to the States. I asked about SHAPE.

He told me it was the NATO base outside Paris. SHAPE stood for Supreme Headquarters Allied Powers Europe. He told me that Sergeant Harry Furgeson had a great little pad on rue Nollet, near Place de Clichy, and, if it was still available, it was mine. Drew would get on it as soon as he got home.

The least I could do was hug the guy and thank him and thank him. He lingered in the hug, but I let him. Everyone is so needy.

. . .

A stove, a sink, a humming little refrigerator, a tub, a bidet, a single bed, a window facing the street.

How to get food.

On the street in a drizzle, I found a *charcuterie*. "Cheese?" I asked, unknowingly standing by a large Brie.

Two steamed artichokes, a pound of rare sliced roast beef, a quarter of the Brie. I produced French currency. Though I'd been instructed on the new and old francs, I forgot everything and splashed paper and coins all over the place.

Down the street was a liquor store, a tiny place that looked to be a Johnnie Walker showroom. More bills of a hundred thousand francs, coins slipping to the floor, all for one quart of Johnnie Walker Red Label Scotch.

After half a bottle, I took out my letter of introduction and corresponding phone number. Arthur hadn't known anyone in Paris, but the theater critic Richard Watts, who had often invited me to parties of journalists and showpeople in his Dickensian apartment at Seventy-third and Fifth, had suggested I contact a man named Tom Curtiss at the *Paris Herald Tribune*. Which I thought to do, what with my Scotch flowing and Sinatra singing "Pick Yourself Up" from a brand-new album that Arthur had somehow come up with before its release (I suspect Sammy Cahn).

I tested my sobriety by rehearsing a phone call. "Mr. Curtiss, my name is Jonathan Schwartz, and Richard Watts told me to get in touch with you when I got into town. I've never been to Paris, and Dick suggested . . ."

I was slurring, sliding, exaggerating, and obvious.

I finished the bottle that night and spent the next day unable to move, except to crawl to the bidet to vomit. Not knowing its real function, thinking it a peculiar European elegance, I fell upon the idea that the bidet was precisely for my kind of problem; Europeans being who they were, a sophisticated receptacle for the consequences (I was right, of course). After a midafternoon episode, I fell asleep on the floor with my arms around the bowl and awoke in the evening to the sound of thunder and heavy rain. I held tightly to the bowl and watched the sky turn black. I don't think I'd ever been more frightened, though I'd surely been more alone.

Sergeant Harry Furgeson's apartment would be available in two days. He was returning to Cleveland, his hometown. He was an American made of iron, with a crew cut and icy blue eyes, suggesting the New York Yankee Hank Bauer. I'd never realized how American-looking Americans were until I'd been outside the country. Furgeson was an ethnic blank, whereas I looked more like an Arab. Other Americans I'd identified on the boulevards resembled Los Angeleans. They were versions of Ozzie Nelson—goofy, sincere, and woefully naive, just big strolling boxes of Cracker Jacks.

My rent would be $200 a month for an L-shaped room overlooking rue Nollet on the fourth floor. The bed was somewhere between a single and a double, not an American size. The pillows, it seemed, were made of metal. The floor was of gray linoleum with little yellow triangles scattered about.

From the window, I began to notice the colors of the city: the white of bottled milk on doorsteps; the fine silk threads of green asparagus in baskets of yellow straw surrounded by glowing red plum tomatoes. The flowers in the shops, violet, yellow, red, gold. The tan bare arms of women confident with opportunity, arrogant in the face of longing.

Thomas Quinn Curtiss was a powerhouse at the *Paris Trib.* He wrote from most anywhere about everything. His byline had already become familiar to me in the few days I'd been in town. I realized, when I phoned him, that he was a real hotshot, unlikely to pay attention to a kid with a letter of introduction.

Not so. Dick Watts had *called* him on my behalf. "Watts is one of my closest buddies," Curtiss said, and invited me to a cocktail reception that very night in honor of Abel Green, the founder and editor of *Variety*, the weekly paper that had become known as the "show business Bible."

In my one blue suit, I set out for La Tour d'Argent in a roaring taxi that knew no New York equal for maniacal speed. Jangled and dizzy, I left the cab at Notre-Dame and sat down on a bench to calm down, almost (but not entirely) oblivious.

Notre-Dame.

The restaurant's fourth floor overlooked the cathedral through spectacular picture windows. In front of a long tableclothed bar was a white-carpeted reception room, a king's chamber, with roving trays of Beluga caviar and velvety white asparagus tips. The trays of food, artfully on the move, were served by young women in uniforms of red and white stripes. A pianist, a Negro at a Steinway grand at the far end of the room, was playing "Where or When." I was aware of his awareness of one of the guests, Oscar Peterson.

Roger Vadim, Yves Montand, Jeanne Moreau, Gerry Mulligan, Fredric March, and Abel Green, whom I knew. Why hadn't Arthur thought to call him?

When we met, Tom Curtiss, a smiling, disheveled man, lavished me with enthusiasm. He took me to Abel Green, who warmly extended his hand. We spoke of the failure of *The Gay Life* and of its beautiful score.

We were joined by Gene Moskowitz, *Variety*'s man in Paris, in Europe; the crucial film, cabaret, theater reviewer for the continent under the name Mosk, in *Variety.* I had long admired him, and here he was with a woman I recognized as Betsy Blair, the red-haired actress who had, in the 1940s, been married to Gene Kelly. She remembered me as Arthur's very young son around the set of *Cover Girl.* Like Drew Bradley, she had known my "gorgeous mom."

All the attention I was getting was not lost on Gene Moskowitz. Nor was my detailed praise of many of his reviews. Not a handsome man, Mosk, who was from Brooklyn, perfectly turned out in a gray suit and yellow tie, cut a masculine figure, dipping into and out of French or Italian when well-wishers drifted by. He had inherited Art Buchwald's position at *Variety* and would keep it for the rest of his life. Betsy Blair, who had played Ernest Borgnine's girl in the film *Marty,* was, I imagined, Mosk's romantic connection, though there seemed to be no tacit current between them; rather, they were two Americans abroad, linked by profession, buddies around town.

"Look," Mosk said, gesturing with his hand.

In the entrance, under a high arch, stood Sinatra. He was unaccompanied, vulnerably so. Abel Green instantly materialized to greet him. He escorted Sinatra into the room, handed him a drink from out of nowhere, placed him before appropriate guests, all of whom he appeared to know.

Oscar Peterson stepped forward and gracefully embraced Sinatra. They spoke with warm smiles, preventing intrusive new greetings.

"Oscar and Sinatra," I said in amazement.

In a bit Sinatra headed toward our little group.

He was forty-six years old, effortlessly imperial, shyly suspicious, dangerously iconic. With us he was somewhat charming, greeting Betsy warmly, Mosk with a handshake. When he was introduced to me, I threw Arthur at him. "He's a good friend of mine," Sinatra said with a strong squeeze of my hand, though my father had met him once and spoken to him on the phone twice about ASCAP business.

"Why are there two different versions of 'To Love and Be Loved'?" is what came out of my mouth.

"I don't know," Sinatra said, correctly sensing one of the music lunatics.

"There's one with the high note and the other is shorter with the same arrangement by Riddle but it's a different take and it doesn't have the high note so I was wondering why the two versions were released and also recorded on two different dates because . . ."

Sinatra turned away.

Mosk asked me what that was all about.

I told him that I had simply lost it.

He said that he had an extra ticket for the concert that very night, and would I like to come with Betsy and him.

I had forgotten, in my excitement, that this was Tuesday, June 5, 1962. Sinatra at L'Olympia. In fact, he was leaving now. Abel Green was seeing him out.

Betsy Blair told us to meet her at an address that Mosk committed to memory. 7:30. An hour from then. She left, saying to us as she moved away, "Don't wait too long. I'm having trouble with him."

In Paris, one wrong digit of an address could mean a million miles away. Mosk hadn't gotten it right. In early dusk, in courtyard after courtyard, we scrambled out of the taxi and shouted her name. "Betsy Blair! Betsy Blair!" And again in some other courtyard or on some street corner: "Betsy Blair!"

Mosk, not an excitable guy, took his time. We went on, beseeching Betsy Blair to appear. At last she did, in tears. She spoke in English. The gist of it was, a lover's turbulence. She couldn't come. How sorry she was. Please, you two go, have a great time.

As we settled back in the taxi on the drive to the theater, Mosk said, looking out the window, "Don't ever get involved."

Charles Aznavour was on the stage, introducing Sinatra. As we found our seats and sat down, he said, "*Frank Sinatra, Paris c'est à vous!*" "Frank Sinatra, Paris is yours," Mosk told me.

The concert Sinatra gave that night, accompanied by only six musicians, was terrific. There was little chatter from the singer, just those Sinatra songs tumbling into the history of the Olympia. Sinatra, right up there in the center of all of Europe, was throwing vocal caution to the wind with improvisational flashes that were new even to me, who had heard Sinatra do all kinds of things. He didn't speak or sing in French but was intimately understood and received—after every song, a wave of standing applause. Later on, sitting on a stool, Sinatra addressed the audience. "We'd like to do one of the great Cole Porter songs, one of the best songs ever written in the world, in the past hundred years, you might say." He sang "Night and Day" with passion and depth. He took it slowly and included the verse. His performance was uninflated and honest. A guitarist was all he had, yet a symphonic height had been reached. I noticed that there were tears in Mosk's eyes, as there were in mine. Even before the ovation had acceptably waned, the sextet took up the opening riff of "I Could Have Danced All Night" as Sinatra was about to speak. He looked over his shoulder with a pleasant, if confused, smile. "Oh, you're sure in a hurry tonight," he told the band, which, although quieted, continued to play. "I wanted to say something about Mr. Al Viola," Sinatra announced. "That he is really one of the world's greatest guitarists, and we're happy that he came on this trip because usually he's so busy all the time, but I'm pleased that he's with us, and I think he plays beautifully. As a matter of fact, if you weren't looking at him, you'd swear he was an octopus." A puzzled audience gave a modest chuckle that Sinatra found necessary to help. "Whatever happened to those jokes?" he said. Warm laughter. The band picked up steam. Sinatra clapped his hands in rhythm and joined the happy fracas, kicking "I Could Have Danced All Night" to a higher level than the record of it I had recently played. I turned to Mosk at the end and told him in a full speaking voice, so that I was able to penetrate the applause, that the ten minutes of "Night and Day" and "I Could Have Danced All Night" had been "significant." Mosk's face was still wet with tears, though his eyes had become limpid and loving. "I'm not the same," I told Mosk. "I understand you," Mosk replied. Soon there came a superb "One for My Baby," then "Foggy Day" with the new Johnny Mandel arrangement, next a piano-voice "Ol' Man River" followed by a loose "The Lady Is a Tramp" with the Nelson Riddle arrangement sounding a bit skimpy with just six guys playing. After an intro I'd never heard before, he sang a jumping "I Love Paris" with an obviously Riddle arrangement. "There's no recording of that," I told Mosk above the applause. "First time I ever heard it!" "It's a fine little thing," Mosk said. Sinatra easily made it through his familiar cigarette cough during "Nancy" and "Come Fly with Me," the last two songs of the evening. During "Nancy" Sinatra joked, "I'll have to stop sleeping in the park." But despite that, his voice was lubricated and beautiful. He wasn't struggling, just clearing his throat. The crowd stood in the aisles, pressing forward to express their thanks, their joy, people shouting to each other in German and Swedish and French and English, shouting at Sinatra as he stood before them, finished. All those faces looking up at him reverentially, twenty-two years of those faces facing him, shouting his name the world over.

"Let's go backstage," Mosk said.

Ushers, police, private security, nothing stopped Gene Moskowitz. Everyone said hello as we passed into the back; everyone knew Mosk of *Variety.* A little path opened up for us, and we were in Sinatra's dressing room, a small windowless space ablaze with flowers and candles, crammed with cookies and candies and trays of sandwiches, bowls of fruit, bottles of liquor and champagne, buckets of ice, and one table of extravagant toiletries. The air was alive with international effusion.

Sinatra was seated on a white couch next to a man whom I recognized as the Los Angeles restaurateur Mike Romanoff. Sinatra held a crystal glass in his left hand, and with his other, and from a sitting position, he accepted the fluttering, adoring fingers that longed for his touch.

He was told a number of things in different languages. He reacted warmly throughout, nodding graciously, even to a lengthy tribute in Chinese.

"Gene, how the hell are you!" he said, when he spotted Moskowitz, even though they'd met a few hours earlier. "Holy Christ, the inspector," he added when he took a look at me.

"I'm sorry, I really am," I said.

Sinatra took my hand for the second time that night. I realized, as I stood beside him, how short he was for so noisy a guy. Frank Sinatra was a little fellow.

Sensing the right moment, Mosk whisked me away.

We walked for a while, and I talked passionately about Sinatra's music. My own ambitions spilled out. I was a writer, but I was also a pianist-singer. How good was I? Mosk wanted to know. I said, "More than acceptable." He asked if I *really* wanted a job in Paris, playing and singing. "My God, *yes,*" I said.

"Come with me," Moskowitz said. "Let's see if we have any luck."

The Blue Note was a jazz joint on the Right Bank run by an American named Ben Benjamin. I remember him only as a very tall man packing a good deal of weight. He was delighted to see Mosk. I was introduced as a New York musician looking for a gig. Benjamin invited me to play and sing right then and there, despite the fact that Ella Fitzgerald's record of "Easy to Love" filled the room.

Unannounced, I took the stage, supplied with Sinatra's confidence. I felt calm and operatic. When Ella finished and the lights were turned down, I performed "I See Your Face Before Me" with just a little tempo, rather than as a straight ballad. I did Rodgers and Hart's "I Like to Recognize the Tune" in the spirit of Mel Torme, where I'd found it, and "Don't Ever Leave Me" as a closing ballad, just one chorus and out. The reception, I've got to say, was munificent.

I found Mosk and Benjamin in the back. They were both pleased. I glanced around the room, once again almost fully lit, and spotted the pianist Erroll Garner in a large group at the far side. I knew that he had seen right through me.

Benjamin said that he'd love to use me sometime during the summer, but right then he knew of a place that would snap me up.

Le Calvados, a long, narrow club with a piano in the back, was across the street from the George V hotel. Mosk knew a man named Polumbo, who ran the place. Apparently he was awaiting the return of the blues singer Joe Turner, who was in jail in Sweden. Temporarily.

My Cinderella gift from Sinatra was still in command, though the crowd was lethargic and only polite in its response. But Mosk and Polumbo had cut a deal while I was singing: $200 a week, six nights from 8 P.M. until closing. A half hour on, a half hour off, starting the next Monday, June 11.

To celebrate, Mosk took me to the Crazy Horse Saloon down the street, where he was welcomed with the usual enthusiasm. I was euphoric, and during the stroll over I bellowed out Cole Porter's "I Love Paris" in Sinatra's style earlier that night, which didn't discourage Mosk from friendship. He was *Variety*'s man in Paris. Think of the loony characters he'd dealt with.

In June, a job with a week to kill, in Paris. I would be twenty-four on the twenty-eighth, Richard Rodgers's birthday. I should have done more Rodgers at the Blue Note and at Le Calvados. What was I thinking?

Drew Bradley's companion turned out to be a man named Roy Short. Having called Drew to tell him of the job at Le Calvados and to thank him for everything under the sun, I was invited to his country home for the weekend and given directions by train.

"What a glowing place," I said, when I arrived at the house in Chantilly, forty kilometers north of Paris.

The living room and dining room were one, all the floors a shining dark oak partially covered by two small oriental rugs, one under a round pine dining table on which a large Camembert, in the midst of dark blue porcelain bowls of cherries and grapes and smaller wooden bowls of cashews and walnuts, was presented on a mahogany lazy Susan set at dead center. Bottles of local red wine on a nearby coffee table were illuminated by the sun from a window that looked out on a perfectly manicured lawn that swept down to the edge of a black stone swimming pool at the far end of the property.

Roy Short, his gray hair in a crew cut, was dressed, though the day was sultry, in a white cashmere turtleneck, blue blazer, and light woolen gray slacks. His only acknowledgment of the beginning of summer was the red sneakers that he wore without socks.

He appeared subdued, as if after a nasty confrontation, though his approach to Drew was droll, warm, and not at all exclusionary.

I asked if I could see the rest of the house.

On cue, a manservant named Charles appeared with a tray of gravlax and pumpernickel bread. A Laotian, he spoke little English or French but clearly intuited the desired rhythms of the house.

The aesthetics were all Charles's: the roses, daisies, chrysanthemums; the light green candles on the dining room table; the silver cigarette cases placed strategically around the living room; the two glass bowls of deep red tomatoes on a table by the beige couch and on the wide windowsill next to the front door.

At my request, he took me through the kitchen: chopping blocks at different levels, various sizes of hanging copper pans around a beautiful battered wok, flowing green plants in brick pots on either side of the pans and wok, two large wooden salad bowls on a small table by the one window in the room.

Drew preceded me upstairs.

The two bedrooms on the second floor were small, immaculate, and sunny, both without books or any reading matter. The master bedroom, shared by Drew and Roy, was of a very modest size, its carpeting the only luxury.

After martinis and gravlax, lunch was served: artichokes at room temperature, Dover sole, wild rice, steamed asparagus, all served flawlessly by Charles.

In the late afternoon I took a nap in the guest room above the kitchen. I was awakened in an hour by a recording of a solo cello downstairs. I lay on my back with my eyes closed and soon was brought to tears by the single instrument, which evoked the alleys of Beverly Hills, my mother's dark bedroom, my own stillness behind a curtain in someone else's house as I listened to the concert of an actual family. I ground the heels of my palms into my eyes, wanting to cry out but afraid that my cry would be mistaken for need; Drew and Roy Short would hover above me, offering unbefitting solace that most terribly would commit injury to the music by soiling my introduction to it. So I wept in silence and stilled myself, and later on I appeared downstairs for drinks.

At the stereo, I learned of the Bach unaccompanied cello suites. I had come to Chantilly, I strongly believed, for this astonishing discovery. Sinatra to Ben Benjamin to Le Calvados, all of it orchestrated by *Variety*'s man in Paris.

Several years later, while listening to the Bach at home, I wrote Gene Moskowitz to thank him for the trail that had led to the essential cello suites. He never replied. In time I heard that he had died, still holding his position.

A half hour on, a half hour off.

I alternated with two fellows, one with a guitar, who moved from table to table singing "Granada." Whenever possible, I crossed the avenue Pierre-1er-de-Serbie to rest my eyes on a couch in the lobby of the George V, sometimes shooting beyond my half hour off.

On most nights, I worked until six A.M. Then I'd make the quiet early-morning walk to the Étoile for the metro to Place de Clichy, picking up breakfast from the shops that were opening at seven.

One night, Frederick Loewe came into Le Calvados alone. A formal, undemonstrative man whom I'd known around Alan Lerner and my father, he seemed happy to find me as entertainer. I created a Fritz Loewe medley, "a suite," as he called it later. I remember thinking, after the composer left, after he bought me a drink and praised me and allowed me to sit with him during my half hour off, that I didn't love his songs. Something had to be *made* of them in order for them to breathe. One had to undo the vast cummerbund around the music to get to the emotions in the melodies. They were perfectly made little things that applied themselves to Lerner's belief that a good song in a musical show could take the place of twelve pages of dialogue. The trouble for me was, and is, that in Loewe one can hear the craftsman hammering the schmaltz into shape. The music lacks beauty but achieves charm, froth, and mischief, made mischief by Lerner. It is possible that Lerner's invitation to Arthur had something to do with boredom, irritation, entrapment.

"I'm Wally Ridley. Would you like to make a record in London?"

"Wally Ridley?" I repeated, trying to recall the name.

Ridley, a tough little Cockney, was an A and R man at EMI Records, working under Norrie Paramor, a record producer who also made sloppy albums of great songs, performed by more violins than you'd care to hear but harmonically a step above Mantovani or Gordon Jenkins.

Ridley—now get this—wanted to fly me to London to record as a singer at the Abbey Road Studios, where Elisabeth Schwarzkopf frequently worked. "You've got a hip sound," he said.

This on the evening of August 11, after two months of 8 P.M. to 6 A.M., too much alcohol, too little sleep, and a "Granada" overkill.

True to his word, letters were sent, a thousand-dollar check was cut, and a recording date was set for September 16.

I gave Le Calvados two weeks' notice and then slept for much of the second half of August. I had enough money for at least four months of quiet, and in three weeks I wrote two short stories, rewrote an earlier story, and sent them all off to an editor at *The New Yorker* I'd met a few times. He turned down everything and returned the manuscripts with an unencouraging note, among other things telling me that my stories were "incomplete, sentimental, and not credible."

A couple of days later, while speaking with, *persuading* a young film actress whom Gene Moskowitz knew, I was surprised by one of her questions. It was "Why you?"

"Because I'm incomplete, sentimental, and not credible."

"That's what you look like to me," she replied before ambivalently agreeing to go to the Blue Note to "take in some jazz," as I had put it.

Ah, English! I hadn't realized how suffocated I'd felt in Paris, grasping for the air of vocabulary, deprived of nuance, clarity, wit. In London, in an almost constant rain, I could overhear and understand, and ask and tell and emphasize and suggest.

I rented a room on West Cromwell Road in the Earl's Court neighborhood, in a three-story house otherwise occupied entirely by courteous Indians who never complained when Sinatra records went on for hours, repeated and repeated at top volume. I was studying up, thinking to add illumination to that which was already illuminated.

I learned the subways, walked for miles, haunted bookstores, and built a bit of a library in my bleak West Cromwell Road rented room. I ate at Wimpy's and drank in pubs that disappointedly closed in midafternoon for a couple of hours, and then for good too early in the evening. My first English brew caused diarrhea, which I fought through to the happy moment of realizing that this warm ale in a glass in a drinking room centuries old was far better than anything American. My God, Rheingold was reduced to putrid water.

I hiked through the British Museum and thought of Ira Gershwin's lyric in "A Foggy Day": "The British Museum had lost its charm."

My father, from London years earlier, had sent Ira a postcard that pictured the building and had anonymously written, "On the contrary." I did the same to Arthur, signing my name in full and adding, "of EMI Records."

Wally Ridley, who took me to lunches and dinners, picked the musicians for my two songs. They included Jack Parnell, well known on British television, and Eddie Blair, an excellent trumpet player, who I insisted use a mute on my things, as Harry "Sweets" Edison was doing for Sinatra.

Ridley, a true record guy, was enthusiastic and lively, and delighted to talk records and music. After his three martinis, I learned why I'd been beckoned. Ridley, now expansive, told me that American "artists," for that's what anyone who recorded was considered, were hard to get into a studio in London and would seldom fly over to perform in the United Kingdom. In Le Calvados, Ridley had come upon an available young Yank, an ersatz Sinatra who might move some product. Give him a shot, it's summer, what the hell, what's to lose, a couple of quid?

The Yank knew his music and kept Ridley drinking until close, and then somewhere else that Ridley knew about in an available living room posing as a pub. Sinatra details held Ridley spellbound. Did Wally know that there had been a sixteenth song recorded but not released at the *Swingin' Lovers* sessions? Did he know that *Close to You* was missing three titles? Did he know that there were two released versions of "To Love and Be Loved"? No, he did not. He didn't know any of these things and sat there, across a little table, soaking up every word. I told him that in Paris, after the concert, I'd gone out drinking with Sinatra and his crowd.

"Christ!" is what Wally Ridley said, stunned. That's all he said.

I picked two songs that Sinatra had never touched, Arthur's "Oh, but I Do" and the Gershwins' "Soon." A ballad and a swinger.

On the sunny, warm day when I was to record, I took the tube to St. John's Wood several hours before I was due and roamed around Lord's watching cricket, which struck me as balletic and lovely, the game, like baseball, offering time for reflection as it leisurely leaned forward. The sun was almost hot, having been hidden for so long, and I stood by a white fence and fell into reverie. I would bring home a recording and a few more dollars than I'd had when I'd left. I'd written another short story in London and had sent it to *The New Yorker,* to the very same editor. I'd get back on the radio, I'd fall in love, I'd write a novel. Here I was at Lord's on a superb afternoon, waiting to make a record. The available Yank, a couple of quid, there were no losers here.

The studio, a vast auditorium for symphony orchestras and enormous choruses, had been primitively partitioned to produce a small space at one end that created the illusion of intimacy.

All business, I strode in, wearing my blue suit, which had become a bit shiny through the summer. I was introduced to the six musicians and listened as they ran down the two arrangements that Jack Parnell had done. I suggested a slower tempo for "Oh, but I Do" and little else. The whole thing seemed glorious to me, and I realized how relaxed I was. I believe I said out loud to someone, perhaps to the control booth, "I'm in my element."

We did the songs in an hour, and soon after, I was back in my room on West Cromwell Road, having taken a cab in celebration. I'd been given no evidence of what I'd done, though I was promised a demo in a few days, a record that is still unreleased.

I slept for a while, then went out for Scotch and ale. The whole thing had happened so quickly, with the minimum of talk, bandy, laughter. I had sung well, if emulatively. I was happy with the playbacks and thanked everyone in mid-dispersal.

Then nothing, just Scotch and ale. No piano, no blond singer Lynn Taylor (she had married Weshner as a pregnant girl). No novel to write, no job, no marriage. Just courteous Indians on the stairs and Graham Greene, Peter DeVries, E. B. White, and some ghastly British porn—all that white skin, all those glazed eyes.

When the demos arrived a week later, I packed up and left London in a foggy drizzle and waited at the airport for five hours for takeoff. On a postcard I wrote Lester a pack of lies but discarded it at the gate. If not Lester, who?

14

I SAW PRESIDENT JOHN F. KENNEDY ON A LATE JULY AFTERNOON IN 1963. He was leaving the *New York Times* building as I happened to pass by. The crowd, mysteriously large—the visit to the paper had not been publicized—surrounded the President, touching him if possible, shouting admiration as he moved slowly to his limo. His eyes flicked from face to face. He took hands and wrists into his own two hands, which I found unusual. He accepted a hug from a boy half my age, which was then twenty-five. He said something to an assistant I recognized as Ted Sorensen. Then he raised his eyes, as if to seek out what I imagined to be a skyline or a horizon or, I remember thinking, the spectacle of history. (I later wrote it down.) I thought, what if a gifted novelist assumed the presidency for one year and then, after leaving office, captured the horizon, the skyline, the spectacle of history, while identifying and caressing the details: a child in a Kansas field; a mother with her infant in a crowd; the acoustics in the East Room of the White House; the yellow tie on a senator from the South; the smell of mustard near the ocean; rain in a cemetery; inflicted solitude. I wondered, standing across the street, if the gifted novelist as President could withstand the technicalities, the documents, the climate of decision, the odor of aspiration.

On the subway, returning home to 120th Street, I settled on the author of *The Adventures of Augie March*. Now, *there* was the skyline, *there* was the spectacle of history, all of it in a voice that I knew would stay alert, eyes unteary, stomach settled; the voice not of Augie, mind you, but of Saul Bellow himself, short, lean, lucid, brittle, cerebral beyond the task, and hilarious!

Less hilarious was Arthur Schwartz, though at first the acquisition of Mary Martin for a show called *Jennie* had made him positively giddy. Dick Rodgers's favorite gal was now Arthur's. So sure was he that a smash was at hand that he had taken whatever savings he'd accumulated and had invested in *Jennie*. This was to be his moment, his Mary Martin time of life.

With Howard Dietz, Arthur wrote what I consider to be a perfectly reasonable but uninspired score for a show that, when I saw it in Boston in September 1963, looked utterly doomed. As I remember the show (not well), there was a staged fire, noisily moving scenery, false emotion, songs in the wrong places, and a heaviness of spirit in every moment of its overlength. The whole misadventure, it seems to me, spoke of Arthur's imagining, needing, a favorable comparison to Rodgers through the connection of *Jennie*'s star. I saw that connection as but two paper cups and a string. Rodgers at one end, Arthur at the other. "Hello, Dick, can you hear me?" "Who is it? Who's calling?" "Arthur Schwartz! Have you seen *Jennie*?" "What?" "Have you seen *Jennie*? Mary Martin is in it." "I'm sorry, I can't hear you."

The *Boston Globe* reviewer, Kevin Kelly, in his pan, accused my father of plagiarism. Arthur sued him.

Mary Martin's husband, Richard Halliday, battled Arthur at every turn. Their communication ceased after a nasty confrontation in the lobby of the Ritz-Carlton Hotel following a particularly dreadful performance of *Jennie* at the Shubert Theatre.

Near the end of it all, a week or so before the New York opening, my father played me a song that was going into the show that night. He sat at the piano, dragging energy and hope out of nowhere. I remember him as so tired, the circles under his eyes looking like bedeviling makeup. At Mary Grey's insistence, he had, a few years earlier, begun to color his hair a shoeshine black, which gave him a dishonest youth, transparent at a glance.

He was an old man, or so he said to me one day in a taxi. I asked him to come out from under his hair. He replied, "Mary won't let me."

His song, the last written for *Jennie,* was called "See Seattle."

Mary Grey loved it.

I heard it as a desperate concoction that Arthur delusionally thought "would save the show."

I told him it was perfect for its spot and that it was "a real rouser."

I watched the opening-night curtain go up, sitting on the stairs that ran down the side of the orchestra seats. Maybe I was on the sixth or seventh stair, close enough to feel the sweat of failure.

Midway through the first act, I slipped into the lobby, which was empty except for an usher.

On the concrete steps outside the theater, I spotted my father, his elbows resting on his knees, as he faced Forty-fourth Street.

I left the lobby and sat down next to him in the cold.

For a while we didn't say a thing. When, finally, he spoke, he barely whispered.

"We're not getting over," he said. That was all he said.

Before I left him, I kissed his temple.

Jennie opened in October 1963, and remained at the Majestic Theatre for eighty-three performances, not even making it through the holidays. Its closing was Arthur's closing on Broadway, though in the next two decades he would write two complete scores, one for a projected show called *Nicholas Nickelby,* the second for a show called *Casablanca,* based on the movie. For *Nicholas Nickelby* he and Mary Grey wrote the lyrics. For *Casablanca,* Leo Robin, whose words to "Thanks for the Memory" are a small part of American popular culture, collaborated with Arthur. (Howard Dietz had left the theater because of Parkinson's disease.) There were no workshop performances of either show, no readings or tryouts or out-of-town reviews or opening nights. It is fair, then, to point out that a high percentage of Arthur's success, and most of his best and enduring music, came from the early and mid-1930s and followed him through the years like a heroic hitting streak from an ancient season. His ambition never collapsed, and his energy could rise to any occasion that would honor the hitting streak, but his nights were spent with a radio on his chest, seeking out his glorified melodies.

A little note appeared in *Variety* announcing that "a search" was under way at Boston's WNAC for "a fresh new voice" for its Saturday-afternoon programming. I went up to meet the general manager, with a three-year-old *Variety* review that praised my WBAI-FM show. I also brought authenticating tapes, playlists, and a couple of letters of recommendation, one by Richard Rodgers.

WNAC was owned by RKO General and appealed primarily to an older audience, like WOR, its sister station in New York. Women dispensed advice to women, horticulturists appeared frequently, chefs gave out recipes.

The station carried the Metropolitan Opera on Saturday afternoons, but the program would leave the air in April, and that's where I came in. WNAC was hoping for a younger sound for the thousands of college students in the area. "We've made an exhaustive search, you know," I was told at the moment I was hired. I began on April 25, 1964, from 2 P.M. to 7 P.M., having flown up from New York with heavy bags of albums.

Joanna Visher called me after Mary Troy told her that I'd gotten a job on a Boston radio station. She expressed delight and told me that she had a married girlfriend from years back who would show me the town. Her name was Anna Gold.

The program was an immediate success, made so in part by a warm editorial in *The Christian Science Monitor.* The station added Sunday afternoon to my schedule and put me up at the nearby Kenmore Hotel for Saturday nights.

In the autumn I was offered the evening hours, from 7 P.M. to the station sign-off at 1 A.M. Monday to Friday, and the Sunday show. I rented an apartment on Beacon Street with the help of Anna Gold.

Quite a little dancer she must have been at age sixteen, seventeen, eighteen. Three years of the Ballet Russe de Monte Carlo, a girl with an improbably large bosom, and all the rest was dancing muscle. Anna in London, bathing and taping her feet. Anna in some hostel in Vienna, alone, weeping, so young, straight from Framingham, insisting on her long brown hair, not a favorite of the other girls, this American Jewish dancer who could rise from the stage, her thin white arms over her head, and sail high into the sky and graze the moon with her fingertips; there was always one of these girls, better leave her alone, she thinks she's too good, which wasn't true, of course. Anna had her doubts, that's for sure: her brown eyes were far too large, her oval face offered no lovely peculiarities; not a student, not a linguist, not much of a talker—it took her Joanna Visher time to get started—and then she had to stop, find words, what was the word! What was the idea to start with? For heaven's sake, I am useless.

Now she was a housewife in Brookline, Massachusetts, married to a man named Robert Stein, who was "in produce." It had taken her a little while, during a walk with me up Commonwealth Avenue, to find the words "in produce." "Cabbage?" I asked, and she laughed and slipped her arm through mine.

She was thirty-five, nine years older than I, and the mother of two young girls, nine and eleven. People stared at her on the street, sometimes stopping, just to get a longer look. I was proud to be seen with her. We went to Locke-Ober for lunch. Josh Logan was there and came over to me to say hello and to fix his eyes on Anna Gold. We went to the Exeter Theater to see *The Man in the White Suit.* I slipped my hand between her legs and found her receptive.

Two hours before my first evening program, I ate alone in the dining room of the Kenmore Hotel. By 6:30 I was severely food poisoned, barely able to walk.

WNAC, in the rickety old Buckminster Hotel, about seventy-five yards behind Fenway Park's left field wall on Brookline Avenue, was a rambling basement installation, a maze of hallways, locked closets, stairs to nowhere. Both the radio station and the television station (Channel 7) were settled along the murky corridors. If it could be found, there was a men's room that I had chanced upon, unlit and out of use, with a shower, never used. I stumbled my way to that men's room, undressing along the way, thinking that a shower would clear my head. There was no hot water, but I took the cold, retching and excreting. When I finally jumped out onto the tiles of the lavatory, with only the dimmest light from the hall to work with, I thought, for the first time, of a towel. There was only toilet paper, and for a moment I didn't know where to begin.

The program director appeared in the doorway with a clipboard under his arm, taking in the scene. Not often do radio men see each other undressed, but what Joe Duby came upon was a shivering, naked guy, urinating, defecating, vomiting, and dripping ice water. Unfazed, Duby, whose features have flown far away, said, "Be sure to get the national anthem on at 12:58:30." Then he left without further comment.

That I made it to the studio was remarkable. That I did half the show sitting on a wastebasket before being relieved by the television booth man ("This is Channel 7, Boston") was, I suppose, admirable.

In bed on Beacon Street, I phoned Anna Gold. She came over to help out.

Did you know that you can run a really high fever with food poisoning?

Anna, the mother of two, brought a thermometer to Beacon Street. And aspirin, two of which she gave me with a glass of water.

Then she sat down in a puffy old chair, after dragging it close to the bed. She wore a dark turtleneck sweater, black slacks, and light blue moccasins.

I fell asleep and awoke in an hour. Anna was working the small fireplace, and soon the room was filled with crackle and light. All the lamps were dark.

I told Anna about Mary Troy and Joanna Visher in the penthouse, and Mary Grey; and I told her about Luke and the records from the Liberty Music Shop at Seventy-sixth and Madison.

Then I fell asleep again for three hours.

Anna gave me a glass of ginger ale, though I hadn't had any in the apartment. I took one more aspirin, at her urging. Then she sat in her chair. The first thing she said was that I was "keeping the liquid down." Then she told me about her marriage to Robert Stein. Anna had "figured" in 1952 that he would be her "last chance." She smiled when she told me, meaning no harm to anyone.

I asked where Robert Stein thought she was right now.

She told me that he went to bed very early and that frequently she slept in another room.

"What about the kids?"

"They're okay."

I was feeling better, but I was really weak.

Anna asked, "Music?"

"Yeah," I said.

She chose John Coltrane's *Ballads* album from my organized shelf.

Then Anna began minimally to dance; a shuffle, an arm held head high, a sway. Off came the turtleneck, then the black slacks. A bra and panties were tossed near the fireplace. It turned out she was already barefoot.

Right then, as she approached the bed, I instantly recovered, so that I could healthily fall in love.

The Boston winter of 1964–65 was dire. Severe cold, constant snow, and a New England gray that I'd never seen in New York. Even when the sun was out, it cast no shadow, or so it seemed; the blanket of the dark winter held the light back.

Anna called herself "a warm-weather girl" and bundled up into a bulky heap for each trip out-of-doors. Her nose turned a bright red, and her teeth chattered until my fireplace warmed her. I gave her Scotch and played her music during many a morning and afternoon. When Robert was away, and he was often away, I would go to her house after my program at 1:15. She would rise from sleep, find her way downstairs, and eventually make me dinner. I would leave just before dawn. Her children liked me, the new friend of the family, Joanna Visher's friend with a radio show on WNAC. When I met Robert, he was courteous, with an actual "How do you do."

I loved his wife; I wanted to marry her. She wanted to dance; I wanted her to dance.

On the Channel 7 side of the building, a local entertainment show made only decorative use of a large sturdy birdcage that hung above the usual talk-show set. It was someone's idea to do a program with a dancer in it, wiggling and wagging. In an orange birdcage.

Anna wanted that job.

"Isn't it demeaning?" I asked.

"Nothing's demeaning," she said.

Wearing a tight yellow sleeveless dress, Anna stole the show, dancing the twist, so at ease, so sexy. At one point, she was on camera for three minutes straight.

The show used a trio—piano, bass, and drums. I have no recollection of the host. The pianist, called the music director, was Joe Raposo, who became my friend.

Joe, a Harvard man, was a heavy, round-faced guy with wide-open brown eyes, puffy cheeks and jowls, and appetites more numerous than stars in a desert sky. He was carnivorous, alcoholic, anecdotal, hyperbolic, ambitious. He was Portuguese through and through and ingeniously musical, classically trained. He played the piano in a popular mode as well as anyone I had ever heard. He was simply a wunderkind in his twenties.

Joe was the father of an infant boy. His wife, Sue, who often joined him at "the drinking table," as she called it, oversaw their Somerville apartment, not far from Harvard Square. The place was jammed with the literature of music—opera scores, record albums,

Broadway songs, biographies, articles and films and photos were everywhere in the dark apartment. Could there have been four rooms? The living room, devoured by a grand piano that left only slivers of space for a couch and chairs; the child's bedroom, appropriately tiny; the kitchen in the back, in which, at five in the morning, we would gather over blood-rare steaks, still with our whiskeys, the three of us, and once or twice with Anna Gold, who had, during each visit, fallen asleep, curled up in a corner of the living room on the floor, almost under Joe's music.

His first invitation to me was extended after meeting Anna in her yellow dress. I came alone in Joe's car. Caught in a Storrow Drive traffic jam and so new to each other that we had yet to find a workable punctuation, he told me the following story, in about the same language I will use here. He spoke conversationally and without inflection, like a newsreader.

"Recently, a man got on the shuttle flight from New York to Boston and took a seat next to a prim, middle-aged woman who was wearing a gray suit. From his briefcase, the man took out a copy of *Playboy,* unzipped his fly, and opened the magazine to the centerfold. Holding *Playboy* in his left hand, he masturbated to completion with his right hand. When he finished, he dropped the magazine, removed a handkerchief from his jacket's inside pocket, and cleaned up. When he was done, he folded the handkerchief and put it back in his pocket, before returning the magazine to his briefcase under his seat. He then turned to the woman next to him and said, 'Pardon me, do you mind if I smoke?' "

The happy furor that followed established our line of credit together and determined our flexible boundaries. It moved us quickly into music, where Joe had never been challenged but now had found an equal, sitting right there next to him, inching along Storrow Drive. *And* the son of a famous man, which was most important to Joe Raposo.

I have found that when people say, recalling years gone by, "we used to hang out together at Tom's place on Friday nights and listen to Miles Davis records," the truth is, really, that on *one* Friday evening, twenty years earlier, they went over to Tom's, and he played them a Miles Davis album.

In Joe's case, in my case, we did indeed hang out, night after night, drink after drink, song after song. I sang, he played. He played and sang, I listened. I never played—what was the point?

He was a terrific accompanist. His modesty made its impact only when he played for a singer.

After the singer, he was ready with a new tune he'd composed, a new lyric he'd written, or a new idea he'd found for a Rodgers and Hart piece. He'd rope you into his amusing narcissism with alcohol tears. I wanted him to go on and on. I told him to "play forever." One night he replied, "I will. You can bet on it."

Joe made a bit of money playing in the bar near the Charles Street Playhouse in Boston, where, as a singer, I joined him once or twice. I began to learn a few of his own songs, which were high-level things, both words and music. I remember saying to Anna late at night that Joe "better take his ass to New York." Anna said that she'd already thought the same thing.

She and I were caught up together, arms around each other all the time, her plans for leaving Robert in the making.

A meeting with Arthur in my apartment on Beacon Street became inevitable.

Later he told me to move slowly; that she was nine years older; that she had two daughters. Was I sure I wanted to take on all of this? Of *course* I was sure; what was the *matter* with him, goddamn it! Why did he always take a *negative* position, goddamn it! Arthur said, "She certainly is beautiful." I said, "And unlike Mary Grey, she is kind."

At WNAC, we all received a memo in April. The station was going to gradually switch (beginning in the evening) to an "all-talk format," which was attracting listeners in other parts of the country.

The Boston Globe ran a story. Channel 7 carried the news.

I would be replaced on June 7, 1965.

Someone organized a rally in Harvard Square that protested my departure.

Anna and I stepped back a bit from our future but clung together during the spring's melancholy birth.

On a sunny afternoon, Joe and I sat by the Charles River and made plans. This was his moment, I pointed out. He could live with me in my apartment on 120th Street until he found something for his family. Anna would divide her time between New York and Boston. "She'll be bicoastal," I said.

I finished out my time on the air as gracefully as I could, embarrassed as a lame duck and as a "terminated DJ." That's what Anna called me for a little while, in the best of spirits.

I biked around Boston, sat by the river, and lay awake at night, either alone or next to Anna.

I had failed at the first big opportunity on the air and was being replaced by a guy who would talk to listeners on the phone. Who in the world would tune in to such crap? "Would you call some guy on the air?" I asked Anna. "No way," she said. "You see what I mean?" I said. "Nobody's going to call anybody like that. It's ridiculous." "Maybe lurid people," Anna said. "You wouldn't get on the air with lurid," I said.

The large picture: I had $5,000, my New York apartment, Anna Gold, a fair number of short stories waiting to be expanded, rewritten, edited, reconsidered, renounced. The whole process excited me, with the additional exhilaration at the thought of writing *more;* better, longer, shorter, deeper, wider, slower, faster.

I would read more, everything away from the USA: Chekhov stories, Henry James, Proust to the end, all of Kafka.

“I may not be brilliant, but I’m not ghastly,” I said to Anna.

“Who said anything about ghastly?” she asked.

“I did,” I said.

15

HERE ARE SOME OF THE THINGS YOU MIGHT WANT TO KNOW ABOUT A stretch of time culminating with and including the Labor Day weekend of 1967.

The Raposos came to New York in June 1965 and stayed with me for about a month, until they found their own place on West End Avenue. Our time together was pleasantly chaotic: an infant crying, the piano going, the kitchen crammed with "three chefs," as Joe called us. Anna came down from Boston, newly separated from Robert, her children away, I think at camp. More than once she curled up on the living room floor by Joe's feet on the piano pedals and fell asleep. More than once I picked her up and carried her to bed before a middle-of-the-night dinner at the kitchen table.

Awake in the morning, energized, feeling little grief at Robert's departure from their house in Brookline, she would disappear into the city, to dance classes, music festivals, and, surprising me, to spiritual gatherings. With formal instruction, she began to learn the Alexander technique of massage, from which I benefited.

At the World's Fair, late in the summer, it struck me, as we walked around without holding hands, that Anna was slipping away into the Lovin' Spoonful, the Byrds, gatherings of strangers, questionable therapies, ideologies, and phony benevolence.

I sat at home, the Raposos gone. I wrote for several hours each morning; I napped; I drank vodka; I made lunch. I read at length.

Far too frequently I wrote love letters to Anna. I have a copy of one. It's mercifully brief, but uncomfortable for me to review:

Darling Anna,

I'm a-missing you down here amongst my futile manuscripts and empty bottles of Scotch. I even went to a shrink to sort out, as he said, "Your feelings." I went with my little record player and *Wee Small Hours* and spent a session playing him the album. I actually paid him 50 dollars to listen to a Sinatra album, *which he did,* at 53 Park Avenue South, all 16 songs, after which he said, "I'm sorry, our time is up for today." I guess I was sorting out my feelings. He's a nice man who somewhat resembles the pictures I've seen of Philip Roth, the writer. I was trying to tell him that I loved a girl and missed her, and I felt that she was starting to move away from me, and this was making me feel lonely and tearful and suicidal and angry and cowardly and all the things that come from being in love with someone like you. I see you blossoming in front of my eyes, but without my help. What do you mean exactly by spiritual? You say it's not religious. You say it's a presence of mind. Anna, could I ask you this? Do you have another lover? Or have you been—sorry to be so gross—laid? If so, just tell me. I'm a big boy, I can take it, believe me I can. Maybe it's someone more successful than I, my failed terminated self, and my unsold short stories that are becoming more and more about you, and then of course there's my dwindling funds. All kinds of my funds are dwindling these days. My energy, my desire to actually live. I live on music and Scotch and Antonioni and avocados and mental photos of your naked body in the kitchen making coffee. Now it turns out that this naked body likes Jefferson Airplane. I'm a big boy, I can take it. And the Beatles. They're right about one thing: I want to hold your hand. Simple and temporary as the Beatles may be, they touch upon truth. Good for them. You've never seemed happier, and I like to think I'm a part of it. Maybe it's just the removal of Robert. It's painful to imagine you naked in another kitchen with a guy watching you reach for the coffee way up there in the cabinet, your body stretched to its limit, the Ballet Russe de Anna Gold, the ribs, the breasts. How did you get around the stage with those breasts of yours? Suzy Strasberg had to rope in hers to play Anne Frank. I've been meaning to ask you.

Love, the Truly Terminated

Her answers to that letter and to the others were gentle, simply written. No, she hadn't been laid. Yes, she'd be coming to New York.

And she did, in boots, leotards, and turquoise jewelry.

In bed, I would search her eyes for clues: *What is going to happen to me?*

What if? How? When?

It became clear that the weight of even mild conundrums simply puzzled her to pieces.

In late 1965, I was taken on by a literary agent, a self-described "tough old dame" even though she was probably in her early forties. She sent my stories around and mailed me the rejection slips. On one thrilling morning in March 1966, she phoned, her gruff cigarette voice a bit lighter than usual. She told me I'd sold a story to *Redbook* for a thousand dollars. It was called "A Singular Honor," and *Redbook* had "adored it." The fiction editor of *Red-*

book phoned to tell me that she "adored" "A Singular Honor" and asked if I had any other stories to show her. Of course I did, I said, and I would, "very soon."

You can imagine the Sinatra albums that got charged up on 120th Street; and champagne in a beer mug; and calls to Anna and Lester and to my father, and to many people I hardly knew.

The "tough old dame" didn't like the story I'd chosen to submit after "A Singular Honor." Okay, I said, I'll give you something else. I, on the other hand, rather admired "A Fine Silk Thread," and sent it to *Redbook* pseudonymously, under the name Steve Safion, a radio engineer at WINS I knew.

Two weeks went by, and I assumed that *Redbook* had simply thrown "A Fine Silk Thread" into the garbage. It had come in as a part of the "slush pile"; that is, manuscripts sent in without agents.

Another morning call from the "tough old dame," a bit testy this time. She told me that she'd gotten a call from the fiction editor at *Redbook,* asking if Jonathan Schwartz knew someone named Steve Safion, with a Bronx address. They'd received a story that was stylistically so much like "A Singular Honor," and they "adored it," but they were wondering about this Steve Safion.

I told the "tough old dame" the truth, which threw her into an ambivalent tizzy: angry and hurt that I'd gone around her but happy that the story had sold, for another thousand dollars.

As things turned out, "A Fine Silk Thread" was published first, in the September 1966 issue of *Redbook* magazine. "A Singular Honor" followed in November. I told Anna on the phone that I felt "overexposed."

The letters to Anna by this now-published, or soon-to-be-published, writer got fancier, but it was as good as done. What I had written to Lucy at Bennington years earlier—"The asphalt belches angry hoards of spite"—became, for Anna Gold, "The manipulation of the soul often occurs obliviously, but more frequently it's a malicious product, like razors in marshmallows." To which, Anna replied, on a postcard with a photo of Boston's Symphony Hall, "What do you mean by razors?"

Though she came to New York only now and again, she did read my stories, though she objected to her presence in their pages. "My private life is my private life," she said. "So is mine," I answered.

She was now "disinclined to meat," "allergic to dairy," and, most severely, she was "alcohol free."

She was quick to undress and enthusiastically intimate. In the morning, one rainy Monday morning, she told me that she would like to talk with me about "spiritual matters" but she knew that for now, I wouldn't be interested. I protested and eventually got her to say that "the ego should be stripped away. That's what I'm working on." "With whom?" "With the enlightened." "Enlightened?" "I guess you could say that I am a seeker of truth."

As a seeker of truth, and therefore a speaker of truth, she confessed that she had become "close to" a musician named Israels.

"Is that his first or last name?" I asked, quaking.

"That's what I call him," Anna said, in a holy hush.

"What does 'close' mean?"

"I've been with him," she said, as a truth speaker. "He's in a little group."

"A band."

"Yes."

"How the fuck do these rock scumbags dare to call themselves bands! *Basie*'s a band! But you *know* that!"

"It's a trio. He's in a trio."

"*Bill Evans* is a trio! But you *know* that!"

"That's the one."

"What the fuck are you talking about!"

"He's in the Bill Evans trio."

"Chuck Israels, the bass player?"

Another holy hush. "Yes."

"Oh, Jesus," I said. "Oh God."

"A band is what you make of it," Anna said.

"Bill Evans" is all I could say.

A letter she sent to me a few days later was but one line, written in red ink: "You have come with me this far, and now it is time for me to travel the rest of the way alone."

Then Anna fell silent. She didn't answer my letters. She changed her phone into an unlisted jumble of unattainable numbers, and on the two occasions when I went to her house, her actual house, I found it dark, the lock changed, the grounds unkempt.

Anna was out in the world, egoless, happy with Bill Evans and the Beatles, traveling the rest of the way alone.

It was a true termination, no doubt about it, and it spun me around. I was lost in what I wasn't, the list complete, finished off by Anna, my focus. I began to understand that she hadn't left Robert for me but for a chance at a carbonated existence. I had been but a catalyst with whom she had fallen kind of in love, a big shot in Boston on WNAC, but no longer. My value had diminished, my future a question mark. A writer, maybe, but the verdict was out; an underfunded (I'll say) out-of-work disc jockey without spiritual inclination or any sign of enlightenment whatsoever. It was now time for Anna to travel the rest of the way alone. I told Lester that she was off to see the wizard. He replied, after thinking it over, "That very well may be, but you might want to warn her not to pull the curtain open."

Joanna Visher told me that Anna loved me dearly and would always love me dearly, but that "in her heart of hearts, she knows she will eventually fall behind you."

"What does that mean?" I asked.

A Joanna pause. In fact, an Anna pause.

"I think she thinks you'd outgrow her."

"What bullshit!"

"Couldn't it be seen as generous on her part?"

"By whom?"

To which there was no response.

What a hot summer!

Do you remember 1967 in the East? The humidity was demoralizing, the constant blare of the hazy sun was treacherous. *Sgt. Pepper* and "Light My Fire" floated out of many open windows. The searing southern heat of "Ode to Billy Joe," so popular in those months, sounded to me like an implied murder or suicide. I focused on suicide and began to contemplate what it might be like; how best to go about it; where to accomplish it; who to tell about it beforehand. I chose my, by then, closest friend, WBAI's announcer-engineer on my first night.

"Lester, I am entertaining the idea of suicide."

"But just an entertainment, I gather."

We'd spoken for hours on the phone, wandering from sex and rejection to baseball, literary movement, jazz, and Sinatra. Lester, at once satirical and sobering, was often reflective on the themes of lost opportunities and hidden feelings. He was truthful but sly and receptive to any finger-pointing at his accountability. He was profoundly aware that he had, as a very young man, devised a merry countenance with which to woo the world. He might have been too fearful to pursue what Lenny Bruce had started. He wouldn't have been as harsh and certainly not as obscene, but a comedic ramble made of human truth was, I know, his aspiration, though as a radio personality he chose, for the most part, an undisruptive course, presenting an amiable self with no explosives in his repertoire. As a citizen named Lester Davis, off the air and on the phone, at a restaurant table, or as a seatmate on an airplane, he was introspective, mischievous, annoyed. In the privacy of friendship he emerged from beneath his immaculate pleasantness and still continues as adviser, bosom buddy, and critic forty-five years later. A casual fellow, just a fellow, Lester, strolling through the days without fuss or fanfare; "glancing" at magazines, "chuckling" at jokes, "skimming" movie reviews, "wandering" by a new restaurant, "scanning" the menu in the restaurant's window, speaking "sotto voce" to a hotel clerk, "suggesting" or "indicating" or "remarking," nothing declarative, mind you, often starting up with "It occurs to me that . . ." He would take a "bite" of a piece of pie, a "sip" of clam chowder, a "sample" of chocolate soufflé. He mused, considered, dipped into, dropped by, whispered briefly, thought to (but didn't say), mulled it over, and was baffled by.

I, on the other hand, caromed off the walls, howled with laughter, ate the whole soufflé, studied the magazines, took the whole pie and shoved it into my mouth so that it dripped down onto my face and onto my hands and shirt and pants. I also dived into the pool so that the water splashed people on their chaise longues.

How, then, this friendship?

It seems to me, as Lester might say, that we flourished in each other's company, bearing no malice, with the shared recognition of the vaudeville of melancholy.

Lester, nestled in a sunny little apartment at Seventy-fifth and Lexington with an attractive new wife, did not take my suicide talk seriously. "I'd likely advise against it," he concluded at the end of our call.

From the phone in the living room, I went to the medicine cabinet in the bathroom, and from a bottle of liquid cough suppressant, I removed the true ingredients, which I had stashed in the emptied-out, washed, and dried container. I shook thirty Nembutal sleeping pills into my left palm, took them into the bedroom, and lined them up, one by one, on the clear surface of the bureau.

It was noon on the Tuesday before the long Labor Day weekend, which would invite an autumn and winter without Anna, without hope. "I am dying," I said out loud, sitting at the foot of the bed, aware that I would become thirty years old in ten months, the son of the composer Arthur Schwartz, an unaccomplished kid, almost middle-aged.

Anna was now a preposterous hippie, fucking a famous bass player (who had left the Bill Evans trio—I saw it in two jazz magazines). Maybe leaving Bill Evans for Anna. I mean, Christ, anything was possible. She would stay up late, listening to long bass solos just for her. And to think, she'd had one of the world's best pianists at her disposal. Joe Raposo, goddamn it! And she had fallen asleep over and over. But she stayed awake for Israels, I'll bet you.

I lay back and fell asleep for an hour and awoke with the idea that I would simply marry a girl I'd met named Sara, a *Boston Globe* reporter. In fact, she alone was the New York bureau of the *Globe,* operating out of her apartment. She was a Berkeley graduate, five years younger than my grim thirty-in-ten-months. I'd show Anna a thing or two by picking up fourteen years, from thirty-eight to twenty-four, with this Sara, no hippie ex-dancer but a journalist for an important newspaper, the paper that had been delivered each morning to the Steins' front door in Brookline.

I would marry the New York bureau of *The Boston Globe*! How about *that,* Anna Gold!

I imagined that I would enter into this marriage to a woman I found unbecoming, self-pitying (unlike, of course, myself), and coldly judgmental. As she had said more than once, she was "disgusted" by my father's music, calling it "sentimental and passé." Not just Arthur's music but, as Sara put it, "the entire genre." She used words like "genre" a lot. "Oeuvre," "track record," "portfolio," "credentials," "text," "résumé." Cold language, somehow dismissive. She was, as I see it now, a young woman I didn't like a great deal, though frequently what she said flowed interestingly through the numerous threads of her ambition. "I don't mind if you lag behind," she told me a couple of times.

Anna's scrambled notions had taken their time emerging, finding shape, order. "Come on now, spill it out," I'd told her gently, now and then. Sara needed no such encouragement. Hers was a fluent and informed presentation that floated on journalistic curiosity and, as she said, during a drive to Bridgehampton, "a search for myself."

"Is that what I really want?" I asked Lester on the phone. "A search for herself while I lag behind?"

"How far behind?" he asked. "Can she at least hear you shouting that you want a divorce?"

I asked him if he felt that's what the outcome would be.

"With your oeuvre?" he asked.

Lester didn't care for Sara, sharing my father's antipathy. But I hung in there. "At least she's not a go-go girl," I said, referring to Anna's birdcage in Boston.

"Anna has guts," Lester said. "To me, this Sara seems a bit condescending," he said when I called him again, this time with suicide off the agenda.

Almost as soon as I hung up from Lester, Anna called, wanting to stay at my place starting the very next day, "but just for two nights," Wednesday and Thursday. "I've got some business in town."

"Sure," I said.

"Remember, we're just friends now."

"Sure. There'll be no problems. Really."

"I'm coming to New York to see a publisher Thursday morning."

"A publisher?"

"I'm going to write a book about what real enlightenment can mean."

"Wow," I actually said.

"But don't forget, no miracles."

"Of course."

I had about sixteen hours to work with. There was so much to do: rugs to be cleaned; flowers to be bought and arranged around the apartment; refrigerator to be stocked with fruit, shrimp, brownies, orange juice, coffee, lettuce, avocados, tomatoes.

I bought four throw pillows for the living room couch and a beige ottoman as an extra chair near the piano.

I wanted my weight at exactly 180 and fasted overnight, pulling out a 178½ at 6 A.M.

I called Brian, the man who lived next door on the sixth floor. I asked if he would accept my bathroom scale "just for two days," so I wouldn't have it around to bother me. He said that he'd slide it under his living room couch and that I could pick it up Friday.

I took the scale over to Brian, a high school teacher, a single man who often traveled to the Orient with other single men. He was a short fellow about forty years old. I remember imagining, in the shower a half hour later, that Brian secretly attempted to make himself taller by the use of a stretching apparatus in some other man's apartment. He would tie himself into or onto the machine and activate a device that would pull at his limbs and his head and feet, so that, in time, with repeated visits to the other man's apartment, he would become taller.

An hour before Anna's announced arrival—5 P.M.—it became important to me to know my weight at the exact time of her entrance. I phoned Brian but got no answer. I knocked on his door. No reply. I went downstairs to the lobby and rang his buzzer. No one rang back. I went out onto the street and looked up at his sixth-floor windows. The living room window was open ever so slightly. I pulled myself up to the fire escape and began the climb. On the third floor, I stumbled on a solitary brick placed in front of a plant. The brick fell to the street, narrowly missing an old woman wearing a black hat and veil. She burst into a trot as the brick slammed onto the sidewalk a foot or two to her left. "I'm so sorry!" I yelled down. "No harm done!" The woman really had some speed going.

I entered Brian's apartment through the living room window.

To my surprise, a large crucifix lay over the couch. I pulled the Detecto scale out from under the crucifix and couch and took it to the linoleumed hallway, knowing that the white carpet in the living room would distort my actual weight. I stood on the scale naked, knowing that even underwear weighed something (about a quarter of a pound, generally).

The front door opened. In a moment I faced a stranger, a man resembling Brian but with a full head of red hair. He wore a plaid scarf around his neck. When he saw me, he let out a moan of fright that built to a siren wail.

"I'm Brian's neighbor," I said over and over again.

The siren wail turned to tears.

"I swear to you I'm Brian's neighbor. I asked him to hide my scale, but here I am, weighing my options." (I couldn't hold it back.)

The red-haired man sobbed.

"Everything's okay," I said, grabbing my clothes and the Detecto scale.

"Brian, oh Brian," the red-haired man moaned.

"It's not what you think," I said, running down the hall to the door, naked and now sweaty.

On the sixth-floor landing, I slipped on the very recently mopped tile. The scale fell from beneath my right arm and shot away toward the elevator, as if lubricated. It landed, catching Anna Gold's left ankle.

A bruise, but that was it, nothing serious.

What was I doing naked in the hall?

Well, I had been about to take a shower, had weighed myself, found that the scale was way off kilter, and right then and there decided to throw it out into the garbage can on the landing that had been temporarily left by the elevator. So I went real quick, in and out of the apartment.

I dressed and poured a Pepsi for Anna and a Scotch for myself. We sat and talked in the living room, Anna on the new ottoman. I can recall the conversation verbatim.

"What do you truly mean by enlightenment?" I asked.

"You take the ego away, and you have truth. It's about learning to live in a whole different way. Enlightenment means being awake and in a certain kind of harmony and in direct touch with yourself. It's being in complement."

I asked what that meant.

"It means knowing your role in a group and being aware of the dynamics of the group. The eyes of the heart are always open. There's a school of enlightenment on the West Coast called the Arica Institute that's going to have an impact all over the world. In fact, it does now. Arica is close to being a great domination."

I had always been wary of great dominations. The Germans, the Japanese, the Russians, polio, drought, the moon falling down on the earth, rodents coming out of the walls to eat toes. To me, enlightenment and harmony meant suppression of personality and individual spirit, a ridicule of ideas, and a condemnation of everything I'd ever done or thought about doing. Here it was, represented by Anna Gold, wearing a turquoise necklace, tie-dyed T-shirt, red jeans, and green moccasins. She was in New York to discuss a book deal. She thought she was going to write a book. Released from the birdcage and from a silent marriage and from a convenient affair with a much younger man, she was in direct touch with herself. Sara, the journalist, dribbled similar stuff.

The Russians are coming, the Russians are coming, so love me tonight.

Anna asked for a massage, and I gave her one. She lay nude on her belly on the living room floor.

She asked for dinner, and I made it—wild rice, bluefish, and salad.

She asked to sleep, and I put her in my bed and took the living room couch for myself.

In the morning, she was up early, readying herself for her meeting. She had decided to stay with a friend that night, but she was grateful "for your hospitality."

I asked with whom she'd be staying.

She said, "No one in particular."

I asked her to let me know the developments.

She told me that she'd call me from Boston.

At the front door, we shared an unequally distributed kiss. I noticed that the garbage can was gone.

The elevator took a while. We stood without talking, until finally she was able to leave completely.

Through the little square window in the elevator door, I was able to see, as she descended, that she was taking a look at her ankle.

Suicide.

I dressed in a suit and tie before spreading the Nembutals out again, this time on my desk. I poured four ounces of Scotch into a plastic bathroom glass, sat down at my typewriter, and wrote a letter to my father on double-spaced pages.

Thursday August 31, 1967

Daddy:

I think the colon after Daddy goes along better with the Daddy. It kind of toughens it up, takes away just the right amount of baby fat. "Dearest Dad" and a colon is hypocritical, and maybe even belligerent, despite the "dearest." The "dearest" in that case is just softening you up for the kill. I'm going to hit you for money, or accuse you of something or other, or the absolute worst, confront you with your altogether stinko performance in life, towards me, towards my mother when she was alive, and of course your inflicting your sick wife on me and everybody. So the colon renders the "dearest" sarcastic. In other words, dearest my foot. How about Hey Pa. But the trouble is the period. It makes the Hey Pa declarative, thus shutting off the flow of sad information. The letter ends right there. Hey Pa. Bye Pa. Hey Pa, you old son of a gun, how you doin'? Bye Pa. You see? Hey Pa with a comma is silly. And besides, Pa is not a word ever used between us, especially followed by a dimestore comma. If I were you, I wouldn't even read such a letter. Then there's the issue of Arthur. Calling you Arthur under these circumstances reminds me of eight-year-old boys who wear grown-up hats, like guys making sales calls in their late forties. Did Miller have Willy Loman in a hat? Would that have been up to Kazan, or what? Then there's Father, which isn't even on our desk. It's like having breakfast in a cummerbund. So I'm stuck with Daddy, which has served me pretty well through these years and seems to get the best out of you. It keeps us both young. I won't burden you here with a new paragraph, knowing what I have to say. It would be cheap with calculation, in its attention to literature. I don't think I'm going to go on living much longer. I'm considering calling my life a day. The politics of it, the moment by moment of it, the rejections, loving someone deeply, wisdom gone awry, sudden changes of the microscopic variety that turn up the heat of panic. For the fun of it I just looked up politic—singular. Listen to this: "Sagacious in promoting policy." That's exactly what I mean by the moment to moment of it. The policy of personal conduct, the sagacious promotion of the way one combs one's hair, the way one accepts an invitation, or clouds an issue, or drives a car, or holds a woman, or writes a letter. That's policy being, perhaps, sagaciously promoted. Now the word sagacious comes into play. Let me look it up. Listen to this: "Of keen and farsighted penetration and judgment." Also: "Caused by or indicating acute discernment." IN WHOSE OPINION? The policy holder's, of course. HIS OWN POLICIES. What we're all busy doing is sitting back with our own policies in our pockets and at the same time judging the sagaciousness of the other guy's policies. And their promotion mechanisms. If they dance persuasively, or if they come and sit at the lip of the stage to sing "Over the Rainbow" or dangle loot before our eyes if we'll only see it their way, so that we can then buy (or take) that loot and buy food, or buy jewelry to give to a woman so that we can promote sagaciously our policy that reads: Sexual Intercourse is a good thing right now. What is our private reaction to accepting the dangled loot? Do we think less of ourselves? A good policy may be to earn the loot on your own. Why is it that the single most common human impulse is to do things for their personal disadvantage? What I'm writing to you about, it seems clear to me after all this babble, is the death of a salesman. Me. I am out of sagaciousness. I'm trying to sell basketballs to midgets. It's a case of everything breaking down so utterly completely that there is very little sense in keeping the life support system working, despite baseball, music, artichokes, clams, Bob and Ray, Bellow, girls in their summer dresses, Bob Cousy, you, your music especially over all other music, over everything else, even Anna.

Love, Jonno

When I finished writing, I took a sip of Scotch, leaving the pills in a yellow pile. Then I lay down and slept for two hours. When I woke up I called Arthur Seligmann, the doctor who had married Richard L. Simon's sister and who had become my quite reachable physician. He asked me to come to his office on East Fifty-seventh. There he suggested I enter Paine Whitney, the psychiatric ward of New York Hospital, with which he was affiliated. We took a taxi over to Sixty-eighth and York Avenue, where I was interviewed and accepted. I was permitted to go home to pick up clothing and toiletries. Seligmann stayed with me during the Paine Whitney process, though his was one of the busiest practices in town—his office, when I'd stopped by, had been jammed.

What to do with my light blue VW Beetle?

Lester's wife told me he was having a shave and a haircut "somewhere around Seventy-fourth and Third."

I found the spot, double-parked, and ran into the barbershop. Lester, foam-faced and apron-covered, said, "Jonno!"

I said, "Lester!"

"What does this mean?"

I explained, without shame, to one and all, perhaps eight men and one woman, the manicurist. I urged Lester to come outside to see where the car was.

"But *Jonno*!" he said.

"You've *got* to do this for me!"

Lester rose from his shave, dripping and wild-eyed, and came out onto Third Avenue.

"Here are the keys. I don't know how long I'll be in there."

"But Jonno!"

"Thank you."

In Paine Whitney, during registration, I was asked to display the books I'd brought with me. A male nurse, perhaps thirty years old, considered *The Magus* acceptable, but not *Lilith.* I objected to its removal.

"We don't encourage books about insanity," I was told.

"But *Lilith* is about the 1948 election from Henry Wallace's point of view," I said.

"You'll just have to adhere here."

"Ad*here* here?" I said nuttily.

I was given a bed in a two-patient room on the locked ward that was the seventh floor, the floor where all "newcomers" began their "recovery."

My roommate was asleep on his back, a bald, much older man who looked dead. The room was fluorescently lit, which I found embarrassing, cruel. Even under the covers, where I immediately fled, I felt revealed and ashamed.

I read *The Magus* for a while and then got up to go to the bathroom. A male attendant in the hall insisted on accompanying me. I don't believe we said a word to each other as I stood at the urinal, staring at gray and black octagonal tiles. While I did so, the attendant lingered at the door and passed the time.

Back in bed, I could hear "Ode to Billy Joe" from somewhere on the seventh floor. It brought tears that I rubbed away with the pages of *The Magus*.

"Good evening to one and all."

My roommate was up, wearing a yellow sweatshirt and black jeans. Taking a seat on the side of his own bed, he produced, from under the bed, a Slinky, which he maneuvered like an accordion.

"How did you sneak that in here?" I asked. "Couldn't you hurt yourself with that?"

"You're a nitwit," the man said.

"That may very well be," I said.

"Ode to Billy Joe" became "Summer in the City," which became "Ruby Tuesday," which became something else, way in the distance. All except "Billy Joe" were unfamiliar to me, though I would identify them eventually and remember them shockingly.

The very early dinner, I believe at five, was institutional, right down to the Del Monte sliced peaches. Women from the west wing joined the men from the east wing. One of the women, barely a postteen, named Holly, was alluring and silent as she picked at her food. I asked how she was doing. She answered by nodding her blond head in the affirmative.

My roommate ate with his hands, fingers pressing stubby canned string beans into his mouth. He sat at the other end of the table, at the far end of what I remember imagining as his very existence. Oh, the setbacks!

At bedtime (I think at eleven, which that night was too late for me) I was given a liquid sedation. The lights were mercifully clicked off, and only the city's nighttime illumination from beyond the barred windows prevented an absolute darkness. The music, which I now knew had come from the recreation area, had shut down, allowing a whisper or an occasional moan to drift down the hall. "Nellie! Nellie!" It was howled from one of the rooms, with, oh God, so much longing. I thought to reply with Anna's name but didn't.

I awoke during that first night to realize that if my rent wasn't paid by Wednesday, there'd be a good deal of trouble—I'd been running behind.

After breakfast, I phoned Joanna Simon from a hall pay phone. Would she lend me $600 by taking care of the rent directly by mailing it to Pearce, Mayer, and Greer, the landlords of my building on 120th Street? Of course she would. I told her where I was. I told her that Seligmann had helped me. I told her I'd be out soon. I told her that the seventh floor was "like a fucking Alcatraz."

I was overheard by an attendant, who asked, later on, if I was planning an escape. He had escorted me into a room to talk privately, a cubicle at the end of a long hallway with only a mattress on the floor.

I assured the attendant that I wasn't going anywhere. "I put myself in here," I pointed out reasonably, which closed the issue.

I learned late in the day Friday that, because of the Labor Day weekend, there'd be no consultations until Tuesday, no "evaluations for arrivals." Meaning me. No one would professionally consider my case until Tuesday, September 5.

This news made me cry, until I fell asleep.

"Why does dinner have to be served at three in the afternoon, or something?" I asked Holly at the table, who, surprisingly, responded with a British accent.

"I know, it's awful, isn't it."

"The Spanish would go crazy," I continued, escorting her to a couch in the recreation area after our chocolate pudding. She came along agreeably and sat facing me, her legs tucked beneath her. Though she was hardly gabby, she listened well enough as I wove a lunatic tale.

"In Spain," I began, "dinner is served at ten o'clock. But a Spanish person here in Paine Whitney would have to eat dinner at five. But if they had a snack before going to bed at, let's say, ten-thirty, it could be looked upon as breakfast, kind of, and the following morning's actual breakfast could be considered lunch, and so on and so on, until Paine Whitney would begin to pick up time on Spain, gradually cutting down the time difference, which I believe is five hours, maybe six, until finally there'd be *no* time difference between downtown Manhattan and downtown Madrid, and then soon we'd move ahead, which would begin to upset the political balance of the globe, and at some point, with climate and other earthly circumstances coming into play, like gravity, orbiting, stuff like that—at some point the galactic pressure would build to the bursting point, and there'd be a calamitous explosion that would result in millions of years of spatial realignment, a new planet capable of supporting life, or even many planets, for all we know, and of course the sophistication of the species, the eventual emergence of language and history, and surely archaeology, which would lead to the discovery of artifacts from *our* period, and then the capturing of things in orbit, and then, bit by bit, the understanding by the new species, or more than one species, of the cause of *our* destruction, which was, quite simply, the serving of dinner at five P.M. in an insane asylum at Sixty-eighth and York in the city of New York, in the United States of America. Do you see what I mean?"

Not my *exact* little rap, but close enough.

Holly had followed me closely, her eyes engaged. She was a pretty girl with alabaster skin, green eyes, and short blond hair. She now looked frightened, as if she'd been following a horror film.

I apologized for scaring her. I told her that everything I'd said was ridiculous.

"It's ghastly," she said, perhaps angry.

I told her again how sorry I was.

"The ghastly logic of it," she said.

Something interrupted us. Someone came over to us or music started up on the radio or someone shouted something—I'm not sure. Holly left the room, that's for certain. I noticed that she had dancer's legs, like Anna's.

We never exchanged another word.

After the lights went out, my roommate spoke.

"She showed me her twat," he said affably, a chunky, crew-cut man in late middle age.

"Who did?"

"Holly Long."

"When? That's her name, Long?"

"Many times. Yesterday."

"Bullshit."

"Bullshit yourself."

"How old are you?"

"Seventy on October third."

"Why would she show you her twat?"

"Because I'm handsome, and unlike certain people I know I'm not a fag."

"What certain people?"

"It's all agreed on the floor. You're a fag."

"You're telling me there's been a discussion about this?"

"I'm telling you there was a meeting of the minds," old affable Slinky said.

"Well, if that's the case I'm not in any danger," I said, affably.

"What exactly is that supposed to mean?" Slinky asked.

"Nothing."

"Fag."

"Shut up."

"*You* shut up, fag."

Slinky left his bed and went to the door. "Fag attack!" he yelled into the hall.

An attendant showed up in seconds.

"He went down on me," Slinky told him, returning to bed.

"And you let him?"

"He overpowered me with a knife."

"Where's the knife?"

"He shoved it in that drawer," Slinky said, pointing to the bureau close to my bed.

From the drawer, the attendant removed an open pocketknife. All of this by flashlight. I held the covers to my chin.

"This yours?" he asked me.

"Clearly it's not," I said. "This asshole belongs in a loony bin. I can't see a doctor until Tuesday?"

"Dr. Emerson will be here then."

"Will you take the knife away, please?" I asked the attendant.

When he was gone, silence settled into the room.

I had learned that the attendant's last name was Mercury and was, in fact, about to tell Slinky, when he spoke out.

"Fag," he said, ending our evening.

Dr. Emerson, with clipboard, consulted with me at 9 A.M. on Tuesday. I was careful with my sanity and dispensed no humor.

By noon I was told that I'd be moving to the fifth floor, having been evaluated as "not psychotic."

The fifth floor, far less restrictive, even festive, with its television aglow in the recreation area, was no match for what I had in mind.

Leaving everything behind, I took a flight of stairs down to the lobby and ran out of the building with Jackie Robinson, Jr.'s speed, and kept on running up York to Seventy-ninth, cutting west and continuing over to Fifth Avenue. On the park side of the avenue, I sat down on a bench, breathing heavily, on the alert for any pursuer. A few minutes later, Robert F. Kennedy, wearing a pin-striped suit, walked by with a man I didn't recognize. "Hi, Senator," I said. "You've caught me at a weak moment."

Kennedy said, "Thanks, and good luck."

About fifteen minutes later, I crossed the park to Amsterdam Avenue and walked all the way home to 120th Street.

On the desk was the letter I'd written to my father. I read it, folded it (my idea of filing was—is—to slip documents into record album jackets; this particular document, so very personal and, after rereading it, so embarrassing, found a home in the jacket of Sinatra's *Ring-a-Ding Ding*).

I drank through the evening, letting the phone ring and ring, ordering up Chinese food, listening to music, all kinds. I didn't get to sleep until late. I got up early Wednesday morning, went downstairs, and bought all the newspapers, to read about the Red Sox, who were involved in a five-team pennant race, which they would win. I fell asleep at about ten in the morning as I was charting the Red Sox pitching rotation through the end of the year, Sunday, October 1. I stayed asleep for fourteen hours.

16

IN 1966, THE FEDERAL COMMUNICATIONS COMMISSION RULED THAT owners of both AM and FM stations were no longer permitted to simulcast twenty-four hours a day. The idea was to open up the FM dial, to create new stations, to expand the industry.

Many station owners turned to loopholes: tape the AM and play it back twenty-four hours later on FM, thus circumventing the ruling. Or: purchase hundreds of hours of classical music and play it robotically around the clock.

Or, and here is where things picked up a bit: start with a new idea, a different entity from the AM. Get André Kostelanetz records, employ one announcer to tape station breaks in a reassuring if disembodied voice, add to Kostelanetz all the instrumental music of popular songs, violins in the thousands. This is what became known as "elevator music."

Or: hire women (it had never been done) to announce Johnny Mathis records, give the weather and headlines, have them acknowledge who they were, and return to the music. "Back now to the romantic sounds of Tom Jones."

Exactly WNEW's scheme, which failed in less than a year. The women were obsequious, the "beautiful" music was crummy, especially so in the national tensions of 1967. I heard it as an anachronism, even though an occasional Arthur Schwartz song dribbled out. Anna Gold dangled turquoise, and Sara, the reporter, owned

Sgt. Pepper and *Blonde on Blonde* and dozens of other brand-new albums that made her apartment shake at full volume.

In September, my father ran into William B. Williams, WNEW-AM's star personality, at a party. They had encountered each other through the years but had never spoken at any length.

William B. was a slim, white-haired man with a big following in the New York area. He was inevitably cordial, and comfortable among the many Jewish comedians who gathered every day at the Friars Club. It seemed that anyone in the world named Joey or Jackie knew William B. Williams. And the singers, of course, their music slipping away under *Sgt. Pepper* and *Blonde on Blonde,* were beholden to William B. but embraced him with more honest affection than their need for him dictated. Sinatra allowed him access, Judy Garland gave him interviews, and Steve Lawrence and Eydie Gorme were tried-and-true friends.

Williams was gifted with an amazing speaking voice, pitched down into the deep valley of masculinity. My father told me that he had asked how things were at WNEW, pursuing his own concerns over at the one station that continued, as he had begun to occasionally put it, with his "style of work." Williams had spoken of the new FM that was going into some sort of new music—he might have said rock 'n' roll. My father had then asked him whom his son Jonathan might call to interview for a job on the new WNEW-FM. William B. Williams told him, and Arthur, with a twenty-nine-year-old just escaped from a loony bin, was, to put it quietly, anxious to help. He phoned me with the name of the man to call at WNEW-FM and warned me that the music "might not fit your temperament."

On Monday, September 25, I showed up at noon for a talk with Nat Asch, who had told me on the phone that he was the general manager, the very head of WNEW-FM, and that William B. had mentioned that I might call.

Asch was a muscular little guy, wearing a blue shirt and an orange vest, his jacket on a hanger on the inside of his office door. He immediately turned anecdotal: affectionate William B. Williams stories, WNEW lore, all of it interrupted by constant phone callers, to whom he gave his interminable attention. To the interview, I'd worn the blue suit I'd retained since Paris, for perhaps the first time since 1962. A thunderstorm had soaked me as I'd dashed from the subway at Fiftieth and Broadway to the station at Forty-sixth and Fifth. Drenched and oily, my eyes ablaze with need, I saw myself, as Nat Asch spoke on the phone, as an unemployable geek, dripping water and sweat onto Asch's light brown carpet.

The fact that my father was Arthur Schwartz impressed Asch, who spoke of his music with respect. I didn't correct him when he said that his favorite Schwartz-Dietz song was "Old Devil Moon" (by Yip Harburg and Burton Lane). Nor did I question his "long-time friendship with Frank Loesser."

"*This* station is a whole different ball game," he eventually told me. "Do you know the new music?"

I told him I did, on a one to ten scale, eight.

"Make us a tape," he said, "doing what you did in Boston."

He was skimming my modest résumé, which included the two stories sold to *Redbook*. In fact, here they were in large manila envelopes, the actual magazines themselves.

"I'm a writer," Asch said.

"I didn't know," I said.

A couple of days later, after midnight, I joined the living Steve Safion at WINS, bringing with me albums by the Mamas and the Papas, the Lovin' Spoonful, the Rolling Stones, the Beatles, and the Doors. From these albums, which I had bought and memorized, Safion created a demo tape, working tape machines under the cloud of his constant cigarette smoke. He used only the beginnings and endings of songs—"the tips and tails"—cutting them professionally, smoothly. Between the songs, I spoke of the music and the groups—I had read everything available—and told fairly brief stories, including the letter-to-Lucy story from my first show on WBAI, nine years earlier; this time it was only a sketch. Safion, quietly, brilliantly, crafted a fourteen-minute, reel-to-reel demonstration tape that made me sound like a rock expert with a feel for intimate radio.

I gave him fifty of the two hundred dollars I had and took a taxi home to listen.

In the morning, I hand-delivered the tape to the WNEW-FM (and AM) switchboard operator (always hand-deliver *anything*), returned to 120th Street, and disappeared into vodka and music.

"Guess what," Nat Asch said on the phone two days later. "You've got a job."

We met again in his office at 2:30 that afternoon.

Here, as he laid it out, was the plan: the women would be phased out; the music would change to "the new music"; a man named Rosko would begin on October 30; I would start on November 16; and Scott Muni, a fabled top forty guy whom I'd actually heard of, would join the station on December 18. My slot would be 2–7 in the afternoon; Rosko would follow; and when Muni arrived, I'd be moved to 10 A.M.–2 P.M. and Muni would take over the 2–7 P.M. I should tell *no one;* it was all a big secret; nobody knew *anything,* including "the chicks," Nat Asch said.

A man entered the office, dressed in a suit and navy blue overcoat that a sudden cold spell had required.

Nat Asch introduced me to George Duncan.

Merriment abounded; irreverence between Asch and Duncan. Obviously Duncan was Asch's assistant. I became irreverent, casually wisecracky. I asked Duncan, after a while, if he actually did work with Asch.

"Occasionally," he replied, with a big grin.

"In what capacity?" I continued, happily.

Duncan laughed. "I'm his boss," he said.

"You're not the general manager?" I asked Nat.

"He told you that?" Duncan asked.

"Not really," Nat Asch said, unembarrassed.

"Who's who?" I asked.

"Who's whom," said the writer Nat Asch, the program director Nat Asch, a second banana in a vest.

George Duncan, a successful salesman for WNEW-AM and FM, had, I learned later, taken a big financial gamble, which had cut his salary significantly, to become the GM of the new FM, starting first with the women and now, and most seriously indeed, with the new music of the land, "presented without pretension," Duncan said. "The jocks will make it up as they go along. I know you come from theater music and the AM songs. Are you sure you're up to this?"

I was up to it.

"AFTRA scale, $175 a week?"

"Fine."

"Six days a week?"

"Fine."

"And don't let Nat screw you around."

I wouldn't.

"Just take care of business."

I would.

"I loved your tape."

"Really?"

"It's not phony."

"Wonderful. Thanks."

"He's right," Nat said.

"You're only the program director," I said.

And we all laughed.

In the busy sixty days that followed, before I began at WNEW-FM, the Sara connection took on some sort of urgency. I know that Anna had a lot to do with it, having relegated me to the industry of despair. Sara's greatest attraction: she was the entire New York bureau for the newspaper I'd been combing for Red Sox stuff since my late teens. The connection excited me.

I listened to her albums, blues and folk music, Cream, John Mayall, Jefferson Airplane, the Doors, the Paul Butterfield Blues Band, Jimi Hendrix, and, with the greatest difficulty, the Stones, hearing their music as a disorganized rumble, vulgar, and androgynized. Hendrix, on the other hand, struck me as a brilliant jazz musician. I realized, while listening to him, that rock was jazz under pressure, to which Hendrix brought an improvisational talent and droopy-lid singing that created menace.

My father's music was being displaced.

The Red Sox won the pennant. Yes, they did.

I went to the last two must-win games at Fenway Park against the Minnesota Twins, having gained single seats to each game, with help.

In 1965, a Red Sox radio guy, Ned Martin, had called me with praise during one of my programs on WNAC, and soon we'd become friends. It was Ned who found me seats behind home plate for the September 30 and October 1 games of 1967.

I loved what he did on the air game after game, through years of planes touching down in the Midwest, of hotel rooms at four in the morning, of steaks with sliced tomatoes after whiskey midnights and long conversational extensions of the game that night, or afternoon, or yesterday, or ten years ago, groups of men standing at bars, their stories filed, drinking themselves toward dinner, toward the well-done meat and the hardball rolls, toward the 2 A.M. phone calls to women asleep far away.

Ned Martin on the air had a feel for all of it and often spoke like a writer, though he never jotted anything down. Listen to this: "The rim of a black lake of summer rain way in the distance is inching towards Fenway Park, threatening this afternoon's episode." *I* jotted it down.

"Episode" defined the game as a fragment and satirized it with soap opera jargon. "Rim" glamorized the coming storm and promoted exciting concern, like Jimi Hendrix. The fragile center would not hold, as it's been said, but not about a field of green or the lazy, harmless flow of baseball only a few miles from the rim itself.

As it turned out, Ned was a determined recluse, an almost anonymous figure in a very public environment.

We drank Scotch in his house on the Saturday night between the two Minnesota games, the Red Sox having won the first that afternoon. His was no bar in Cleveland. On this night, emboldened by anticipation, we drank ourselves through Sinatra, Basie, and Ned's particular favorite, Helen Merrill. We stood, we sat, we got beer to help out the Scotch. We ate God knows what in the middle of the night and were still what-ifing as Ned went upstairs to sleep.

Our what-ifing had a lot to do with the Detroit Tigers, who were still in the race and, on this last day of the season, were scheduled for a doubleheader against the California Angels. The Tigers would have to sweep their games, if the Red Sox won their single game, in order to finish in a tie and create a play-off game with Boston.

That the Red Sox *did* win, and how they won, is, of course, legendary stuff. That they, and all of us, would have to wait around until sunset, standing above or crouched down by radios tuned to Boston's WHDH, which was pumping in the second Tiger game, Detroit having won the first, was a plotline unexamined. Now, back at Ned's, I lay on the floor with my eyes closed until the Angels' agonizing win, which made the Red Sox a World Series team.

Put it all together now: Anna Gold (who'd begun to sniff around again), Paine Whitney, Nat Asch, Jimi Hendrix, Ned Martin, and each and every member of the 1967 American League Champion Boston Red Sox, and what you have is a crazy, young guy determined to complete some kind of picture. Marrying Sara, the reporter, would surely rock Anna to her very being. And let's face it, Sara was amusing and smart, lucid and literate. For every conceivable wrong reason, I entered into an inappropriate marriage, my nights around the actual date (January 26, 1968, in Lester's apartment) spent with a by then torrentially returned Anna Gold. Anna, her kind and open self, was right back in the midst of things.

It must be said that Sara had not endeared herself to my friends or to my father. She regarded everything about him, especially his music, as "irrelevant" and allowed him to see as much of a sneer as she could get away with. My father's remark, while walking with me on Madison Avenue, was stark. "She is not a pleasant person, I can say that."

Had I married Mary Grey?

A psychiatrist posed that question in his overheated little office on Fifty-seventh and Second.

I replied angrily, "Why would I do *that*?"

Silence.

"Well?" I demanded.

Silence.

"Fuckhead," I said.

If there was an annoyance in the "presentation without pretension," it was the man named Rosko. He was, in fact, Bill Mercer, a cantankerous journeyman DJ with a trail of disputes, threats, terminations, volatile on-the-air quittings, personal abuses in both his private and professional lives, and a general contempt for "human hypocrisy." A slim, attractive black man, who'd been working, like Scott Muni, at WOR-FM, Rosko carried himself stealthily, athletically, crisscrossing the country, a radio transient, a psychological arsonist who would leave the town in flames on the last bus out. His life was littered with wives and children, a field of inaccountabilities; weeping women, often white, forgotten sons and daughters, and mayhem planted in far more noble lives—paranoia so easily sown—he could do it with a raised eyebrow, a puzzling grin, a small gesture of his hand. I thought at the time that all of it, the vast weaponry, was locked in place simply on behalf of his own survival: a black guy in white radio through the fifties and sixties, a musically sophisticated guy with a creative programming talent, a skill with records his one integrity. I came to understand that survival was the least of it. The fellow was fierce, duplicitous, mean, wildly stupidly mean, while he preached, through his readings on the air of Kahlil Gibran or during his own oily raps, about love and tenderness, and at his nightly sign-off: "That's it. Gotta go. And remember, I love you so."

We are talking here, if you'll forgive me, of a punk.

He took to the air on Monday, October 30, 1967, at 7:00 P.M., and stayed until midnight. In those seventeen days before my debut, I must have heard almost all of what he did. "This is Rosko on WNEW-FM, the new groove," he would tell us in quiet triumph after a wild rock piece. The sound of his voice, however, was so compelling, so declarative, that it allowed for an entirely different and more reflective music to follow without sounding anemic. It was exactly what I'd been doing in Boston and on WBAI in New York. Rosko, working with a different musical vocabulary, was able to teach me the language. Because of him, I was able to latch onto the new idea: the evocation of personal identity, the music shorn of its beauty, its craft. What was left on the recordings was unrefined desire awash in conflicting possibilities. Sex and war empowered groups in outrage, who gathered everywhere under four or five electrified guitar chords at deafening levels. Furious graffiti were splattered in the streets by the authors of the vast, improvisational moment. A master key had opened the armor of chastity, which had already begun to rust. If the American popular song had applauded "the great big moon above," it was now finding its romance from the dark side, the unseen, unimaginable side of that "crazy," "silvery," "gorgeous," "smiling," "friendly" moon "up there above."

The Rolling Stones surfaced in full. My opacity melted away almost overnight, as I discovered their genius. And genius it was; the heartbeat of contempt, authorized disorder, lurid danger. I now heard the superb music as thrilling, as, dare I say it, Basie. Two years later, it would throw me into a frenzy at Madison Square Garden, during back-to-back numbers at the end of a Stones concert, "Honky Tonk Woman," "Jumpin' Jack Flash," and "Street Fighting Man." Jodi, my guest, a painter, quiet and guileless, seized upon the unfathomable impulse to bare her breasts and scratch at my face, leaving nail marks on my right cheek. Stunned and wild and only a bit high on Jodi's grass, I shouted, "Stones!"

Later, in Jodi's tiny East Village apartment, the ambivalence of our intercourse, our festering sorrow, put an end to whatever it was we'd become.

In a 4 A.M. taxi, at a red light at Fiftieth and Third, I realized that my slow separation from Sara, the reporter, had to be accelerated. I believe I said out loud: Swab the decks.

WNEW FM took about fifteen months to explode into a wild success. Rosko, Scott Muni, and I were so harmonious on the air, so different in voice and content around the music that had overwhelmed the streets, dorms, bedrooms, cars, and beaches, that we came to stand for the 1960s. Woodstock was but an extravagant extension of our FM signal.

Keep in mind, if you will, that Muni's success had been solidly built in top forty radio. One of "the Good Guys" on WMCA-AM in the early sixties, his gravelly voice was as familiar to adolescent boys and girls in the New York area as the records he'd played.

And play them he had, over and over again. Top forty radio is, of course, just that: a repetition of the best-selling, most desired, most *needed* singles as assessed by charts and graphs. Scott had spent years surrounded by an infinitesimal group of recordings, mostly preadolescent things that were themselves repeating musical phrases of three or fewer notes, topped off by semiliterate declarations of endless devotion in lyric form. To report to work for that amount of time; to proceed each day to the taxi (or limo); to drive down the avenues; to ride the elevator; to walk down the hall and into the studio; to sit for four or five hours, perhaps six times a week, for *years,* required, it seems to me, a mind at rest.

This particular mind at rest was a dear thing; childishly romantic, playful, sweet, pickled. I quickly became fond of Scott Muni and envied his absence. How immune he was to paper cuts in the heart, to the twirl of metaphor, to the sting of parody. He was, instead, not there but with his records, now expanded into albums and personal choices. That he fixed on Bob Dylan was, to be honest, amusing. That he took my side, even when I lacked credibility, was an important part of my survival.

Rosko, hearing me on the air and understanding that I was nipping at his heels, created a detestation. He froze me out. I wasn't there, that's all, like Scott, only different.

Standing by the elevator, I chanced, one day, on Bill Mercer himself. Anxious to improve things, I told him that I'd heard his wife was pregnant. To my surprise, to my relief, he replied.

"It's gonna be a cesarean section."

My God, a link!

"Rosko, that's incredible! *I* was born Caucasian."

Invisible again, I disappeared from Rosko's life until, basking in self-regard, he resigned from the station to live "in God's country," the South of France.

His time slot, 6–10 P.M., had become the key commercial time for the station, the star spot on the daily clock. Who would inherit it?

Scott might move into it, this by now iconic figure at the peak of his powers. There were others, too, even a woman named Allison Steele, a holdover from the all-girl community.

And there was me, to whom the assignment fell.

That was not to Rosko's liking, you can be sure. I was later told he'd had a lot to say about it after the fact—raging phone calls from God's country. His departure, it seemed, had lightened everyone up a bit. The swelling subsided.

Stations around the country popped up in our image, all of them getting right down into the whole of the music, using albums not for hit records but for literate theater. KSAN in San Francisco. WBCN in Boston. KMET in Los Angeles.

The best radio performers, and Rosko was surely one of them, could arrive onstage with a hundred albums, which meant dozens and dozens of songs—let's call them words—and, as writers laboriously do, arrange those words into sentences, paragraphs, pages, and eventually books. Because one's time on the air was expansive—four, five, or six hours—the arrangement of words in the right hands could build into a moody work of fiction, often autobiographical, frequently alive with joy. The stories spun from words on the album, the connections made, the rearrangements achieved. From Joan Baez at the start, her long hair streaming down her back, blowing in the wind, her acoustic guitar a hollowed angel in her hands; to Tom Paxton and the implication of strings and argument; to Arthur Lee's Love Group, the tension mounting, the strings restless and prodding. A punctuation: "This is Rosko on WNEW-FM, the new groove." Then Jefferson Airplane, "White Rabbit," psychedelic, sinister; Hendrix, "All Along the Watch Tower"; Led Zeppelin; then the Beatles, "Why Don't We Do It in the Road?"; Buddy Miles, eighteen minutes of red-blue lava; then pulling back: the Stones, "As Tears Go By," with strings; Dylan, "It Ain't Me, Babe"; and Judy Collins, "A Maid of Constant Sorrow." Back to Baez, you see?

All of it taken in through the night, ingested through the prism of grass or through trickier disguises; dorm rooms lit by candles and perfumed by incense while sleet tapped on the windows. A hall phone rang in the distance, mellowing into rearranged words.

Anything was possible.

A secret ambivalence: Carly Simon's unanticipated ascension. A national star. An international star. Her recordings flowed from both AM and FM radios, besieging her siblings at every turn, her musical, aspiring sisters, her high school and college friends, and me, on the air, promoting her, playing her albums, leaning on the hit records and digging deep into the albums, my own little career dwarfed by the world's embrace of Carly Elizabeth Simon.

Joanna Simon, when recently asked, said that she had rationalized Carly's success in the early 1970s by viewing herself as "a serious singer; a mezzo-soprano above the fray of Carly's pop things."

My dear Carly, malapropistic in my mother's way: "Let's get down to brass tactics," she had said to me conversationally once or twice. There remained a bit of a stutter that accompanied a stage fright that got some press as the years went by. And a marriage to James Taylor amid the tumult of paparazzi and *Rolling Stone*.

I stood between Carly and James one day in an empty room in their new apartment, bare except for stereo equipment and three sets of headphones, and a demo of a record they'd just made together. On came "Mockingbird," played over and over, the room silent, as if in oblivious calm.

A few years later, as I waited for my car in the middle of the night near the bottom of a New York City garage, the radio in the cashier's booth presented "Mockingbird" with surprising volume. The music attached itself to the acoustics of the cavernous space, as I stood alone, the cashier off to get my Volkswagen. Carly, gone now from our intimate childhoods, I remember thinking, carrying all of us in a slightly diminished cabinet within her heart, would have to travel a tricky road, fraught with doubt and pride, wrapped in complications both petty and authentic, occasionally thrillingly happy, but most often, less so. Her voice rang out as my car came up the ramp with unnecessary speed. To me, James sounded secondary, like one of the Pied Pipers doing a brief solo. It was Carly's show, reducing all of us to vocal groups.

I got in the car, and found the end of the record on the radio.

I have seldom loved anyone as I loved Carly that night.

George Duncan ascended within Metro Media on the winds of the smash hit WNEW-FM. He became the general manager of WNEW-AM, and at the right time I approached him with an idea: Why not an AM Sunday-morning show, without station jingles, weather forecasts, or promotional announcements? Just me and the music—Sinatra, Basie, Fred Astaire, Ella Fitzgerald, Billie Holiday, *and* whatever I saw fit to play from the rock world or from the classical catalog. "And who knows, George, I might talk for twenty minutes now and then. Books, movies, theater. But it's got to be four or five hours. The thing needs space."

In October 1971, I began, against every piece of advice that Sara, the reporter, could muster. I jotted down one or two things she said: "You'll lose your credibility with the FM listeners when they hear you play that old stuff." And: "All you're doing is scraping the past for those little tunes like your father puts out."

My real credibility had gained some unexpected strength that had vitalized my presence in the radio community and, I'm sure, had molded George Duncan into an agreeable recipient of any wild scheme I might have put before him.

It seems that at some party in town, a friend of mine, George Vecsey, then and now a writer for *The New York Times,* had engaged a Doubleday editor in conversation. The editor, John Ware, had apparently asked Vecsey if I was a writer, after hearing Vecsey mention my name. "Yes, he's a writer," Vecsey had apparently replied. "He sounds like a writer," Ware had said. "Do you think he has anything to show Doubleday? A novel? Short stories?"

I called John Ware moments after Vecsey told me about their talk. I told him I'd written a number of short stories and that I would gather them together and bring them to his office.

When, in a week or so, we sat together at his desk, I found, in a Doubleday editor, a radio fan of mine with a literary tilt. I put before him fifty-five manuscripts, including "A Singular Honor," "A Fine Silk Thread," and six others that had appeared in small periodicals, including *The Paris Review.*

Ware was white-skinned in the extreme, with very light blond hair that had all but disappeared from his head. Perhaps he was a bit overweight, but his manner was energetic, even forceful, on my behalf. As I now see it, he was youthful, ambitious, and, perhaps, smitten by the celebrity he imagined I was. Radio, after all, is seductive and romantic, and occasionally convincing. If Ware could pass the idea of a collection of short stories, written by an unknown author, through the high rung of Doubleday editors, he'd clearly enhance himself, especially if the book had any kind of a sale, which seemed to me unlikely.

Almost Home, a collection of thirteen of the fifty-five stories, was published in the summer of 1970, sanctioned by Sam Vaughan, the actual "publisher" at Doubleday; a man whose laughter, to this day, I cherish, whose advice I almost automatically take, whose adultness I envy.

Almost Home paid him back a bit, with unusually strong sales for short stories and national reviews that Arthur Schwartz couldn't have written for me.

George Duncan received an autographed copy and actually read *Almost Home,* commenting with specificity and pride, though it did take him eight months. I've got to think that the AM program I proposed, not long after, was helped along by the book's success; that a clearing materialized in the "format" of WNEW-AM for an anarchistic Sunday morning partially because of it.

"You're wasting your time," Sara said. "The music is *old.* They'll probably take you off in a few weeks."

The program grew steadily, if not quickly. The ratings increased consistently over the first five years and remained elevated for the next twenty-seven years.

In March 1968, Anna came to Philadelphia with me for a radio conference that I'd been asked to speak to—music, the advent of FM, so on. I had taken a private compartment on a train from New York for just the brief ninety-minute ride. The ruin we made of the compartment left us beyond disheveled when we arrived at the conference and encouraged George Duncan, who was present, to jokingly suggest that "you must have had a rough ride down." Anna replied, "Rougher than that."

We were driven back to New York late at night by someone I can't recall. Anna fell asleep, her head in my lap in the backseat.

I told Sara that the conference had been "dull dull dull" and that I would never attend another.

About a month later, Anna asked if I could lend her $1,500. She wanted to go to a "spiritual gathering" in Jakarta but didn't have "that kind of money." I gave her $2,000 as a gift during my program in the FM studio. She sat on the floor next to the turntables in what she told me was "the lotus position." In that position, she fell asleep.

Later, I rode with her in the elevator to the lobby. We walked down the street with our arms around each other. The drizzle that we hadn't felt turned to rain. I hailed a cab at the corner of Forty-eighth and Madison. Anna got in, took my hand through the open window, put it to her cheek, and held it there. Then she said, "Good-bye, dearest boy."

Joanna Visher told me a month later that in Jakarta Anna had met and married her "spiritual partner."

I have never seen or spoken with her since, though I know she's in California. I think she's in California.

A woman now in her seventies.

Somewhere.

Jac Holzman, the founder of Elektra Records, called his country home Tranquility Base and had hung out any number of stereo speakers that faced the pool, the sides of the house, and possibly what I recall as a back lawn. Elektra had treaded water through the sixties, holding only Judy Collins as its big-time own. Then the company had signed the Doors and released a single, "Light My Fire," and the top executive found himself viewed as an industry wunderkind. HOLZMAN SAVES ELEKTRA is a headline I remember.

He was a tall, red-haired man, without (and believe me, I got down on my hands and knees to search the floors) a modicum of wit or a feeling for any single kind of humor, from the Three Stooges to James Thurber. He seemed to be married to a woman named Nina while escorting a young rock critic, who had bravely convinced *The Saturday Review* of its need for such a writer.

Ellen Sander at Tranquility Base, during my one visit, was something to see: naked, voluptuous, her long hair a signature of the moment, flowing down her back as she ran across the lawn for a dive into the pool, the Doors at top volume. She lolled naked, wandered naked, retrieved a Frisbee naked, and naked, on Holzman's kingly bed, placed the wunderkind inside herself as I lay beside them attentively. I remember thinking how perfect Holzman would be for Sara the reporter, consummating themselves under the churning of Elektra albums. Indeed, after Sara and I separated, Holzman lavished her with goods, the savviest a BMW, that must have thrown the two, both by then living in California, constantly into each other's arms.

Mel Karmazin, a speedy little guy who conducted crucial talks while practically trotting down streets or hallways, had become the general manager of WNEW-FM. His ascent from salesman to big cheese had taken only a moment, it seemed to many of us. All that racing around had twirled Mel into a blur, a peculiar contortionist.

As my new boss, he was congenial when cornered. I told him I wanted to leave both stations on May 1, 1976, a year down the road. I told him I'd come back at some point for the Sunday show on WNEW-AM if I was wanted but that I'd been working seven days a week as both radio guy and writer and I wanted to concentrate on a novel, move to the desert, and be quiet, "be still."

"What do you mean by still?" he asked.

"You know, silent," I said.

The "still" part was not something that Mel understood. To him, language was only utilitarian; it slipped from his lips as he hurried through his days, while clumps of financial declarations dribbled down onto his lapels during flurries of cost-cutting meetings and memos and phone calls and one-paragraph letters, a few of which I read upside down on his desk when he left the room for a minute.

All of it served the dismal fact that Mel had no interest in music, news, sports, books, theater. It mattered not what a station proffered, only how it profited. He went about his business with false joviality, clearly inherited from George Duncan, who'd moved into the hierarchy of Metro Media.

That Mel Karmazin would eventually create and champion Howard Stern (especially on television); that he would rise to the presidency of CBS in its imposing entirety; and that he would amass a personal fortune to flow through the Karmazin progeny, makes him appear, somehow, gifted. It is hard, however, to avert one's eye from his sad conquest as a radio and television mogul: the abolition of shame.

17

"I WAS FLYING BACK FROM NEW YORK IN MY LOCKHEED ELECTRA—must have been 1942—and I was low on fuel, so I looked down in the fucking desert and spotted a landing strip. I sat on a bench while they fucked with the plane, and suddenly I realized that I was in fucking paradise. Hot, dry, and the fucking mountains. I felt like I was *home*."

The words of an untidy, internationally respected composer driving from Yucca Valley, California, to Rancho Mirage, hitting eighty miles an hour for long stretches, the fly of his pale green Bermuda shorts half open; a Hawaiian shirt, badly torn near the left armpit, catching the wind; fingernails uncut for a while; a two-day growth asking for a shave; a bald head, white and smooth, not yet in fashion; a plop of belly nudging the steering wheel; sandaled toenails turning prehensile.

"Swingin' on a Star," "But Beautiful," "Moonlight Becomes You," "Nancy," "Here's That Rainy Day," "Love and Marriage," "Come Fly with Me," "Imagination," "All the Way," "Call Me Irresponsible," "The Second Time Around."

All melodies by James Van Heusen, now hitting eighty-five on Route 62. A fabled bachelor for many years; a Sinatra pal; a titanic drinker, when he'd had his health; an avocational aviator in the forties who had flown pals around the country, Van Heusen was answering a question from me, the only passenger in the car. "How did you discover the desert?"

"That night in L.A. I told Sinatra about it. The fuckin' dago wanted to fly down right then, right then and there, fuckin' crazy motherfucker. We were bombed, but we made it. We got there when the sun came up. He got the picture right away. First thing you know, he's building a fuckin' house, around the clock. Guys working under lights at night. It was done in a couple of weeks. The desert is the most beautiful place in the whole fuckin' world, and believe me, I should know, I've been laid in the South of France."

As Arthur Schwartz's son, I'd been welcomed when I'd first called a year earlier, in 1970, after a couple of visits to the desert on my own. I had experienced it in the same way—with immediate, unqualified love.

Oh, the colors!

The rose purple of the sand verbena; the magenta blossoms of the barrel cactus; the white desert lilies; the yellow blossoms of the creosote bush; the violet bougainvillea; the white or pink oleander; the lavender jacaranda.

The great expanse of the desert that stretched east, a whipping wind in late afternoon blowing dust and sand across Dillon Road, simmering down for the purple-orange sunset in Banning Pass in the northwest, where the mountains diminished and finished or began; a perfect oval sun in rapid disappearance, leaving behind a purple haze.

Jurgenson's market displayed their large green artichokes in pyramids. The corn, local from May to early July, was white or yellow, and was set out across from the artichokes and next to the local asparagus, zucchini, and Hass avocados from nearby Nemit. Trees in many backyards bore oranges, grapefruit, lemons, and limes. Swipe one if you wanted, or a barrel, uncourteously. The local dates were adored if you liked dates (I didn't). The beer, the really good beer, was Mexican, the California-Mexico border 150 miles south.

There was about Palm Springs a special nudity, the natural result of arid days and hot nights. Skin turned quickly to brown, skipping red (except for the Irish). The nudity was not as condescending as the European exhibitions in Nice or Saint-Tropez, or on Mykonos or Naxos. The bare bodies of the desert were accessible, unwily. Swipe one if you wanted, or more, uncourteously. There were no regrets. Often there was music.

For me, with a typewriter, there was work through the late-morning hours, the beginnings of a novel. A table in a wickered room; an equipped kitchen; a private patio (small); a working air conditioner; record albums and cassettes—I stored them in a friend's garage.

Oh, the canyons!

The dream of hikers before the full sun bore down. Iguanas and rabbits were there and gone, scurrying across the flat rocks by the, yes, rolling stream, which was crossable on logs, or thick tree limbs, or gravel and stone, or through the cold water itself, melting snow well into June; then up an ancient trail, cleared by the Indians of another century, an uncomplicated climb until a boulder interfered—too high, too wide, too slick, reasons for pause. The only choice was to recross the stream, now a bit tougher, deeper, rockier, with no logs, no thick tree limbs on which to slowly negotiate a passing. Waist-high in the water was your only option; sneakers, shorts, soaked from the earlier crossing, now soggy, on, finally, the far trail. But no boulder. A rattler lay in the sun in the sand. *If you don't bother him, he won't bother you.* Yeah, yeah.

Finally, the waterfall you'd heard about. Not Hawaiian spectacular and Kodak ready. Even better: noisy, dense, dropping down from a high white stone as smooth as the boulder. Then, under the sun splitting the palm trees, an icy swim in a rock bowl filled to the brim with the end of snow. Nude young girls dove from the sides, squealing and laughing, finding male arms in which to surface. Then they yelped and squiggled away, like the iguanas and rabbits. From a cassette machine perched on a safe tree limb, George Harrison's "My Sweet Lord" looped over and over.

You became a part of them, you and your unreluctant girlfriend Sally. You were as old as or older than the others, seldom younger.

For a while, you sunbathed on the rocks by the pool. Perhaps, just perhaps, Sally sat upon you. The skin of her knees tore on the rock, but still she moved, altering her position, lying on her back with her legs by your sides, her feet at your shoulders. You pulled her feet toward you, then pushed her back, rowing her successfully to shore.

No regrets, my sweet Lord.

The great western horses were there to ride at sunset, at the base of the mountains, into the face of the hot wind, the purple haze. Jackrabbits bounced into the bush. Bobcats and coyotes veered off to the left and right of the trail. Iguanas, the color of earth, stayed still, frozen under smoke trees, motionless in the sand. Families of quail made efficient excursions across the brush, suggesting a destination.

The gallop, the Cadillac of gaits—full speed, faster!

I wore black jeans and a T-shirt and rode barefoot with confidence. Sally wore dungarees and a small bikini top. Barefoot too, she was the better horse rider. As I rode, my father traveled across my mind, hailing a cab on a humid afternoon. Anna, too, on the train to Philadelphia, fogging the windowpane.

Nothing ever goes away.

Back at the stable, the dogs took over, the Queensland heelers who corralled and guided the horses to and from their stalls. Sally, from the West, brought forth a carrot from inside her pants. She rode horses a lot. She extended her gift and caressed the nostrils of her frothing animal.

Jimmy Van Heusen became an almost nightly occasion once I settled into the Ocotillo Lodge in the early spring of 1976 and began making real progress on a novel.

And an occasion he was! Profane, anecdotal, and ever the host—I think he saw himself as a guy with Sinatra largesse—Van Heusen had chosen to remain an eighteen-year-old boy: a boozer, an eccentric child with immediate needs. *Eight* fried eggs. *Three* women at the very same time, four maybe. A *quart* of whiskey in three hours. *Two* apple pies, all for himself. Chester Babcock, "a fuckin' Baptist from Syracuse," is how he put it. His real name had been used in one of the Crosby-Hope road pictures. Bob Hope had played Chester Babcock.

What had failed to remain eighteen years of age, what had grown into adulthood, was Van Heusen's ability to write beautiful melodies. He played the piano floridly but sang youthfully, liltingly. "You are loveliness itself," I once said to him, sitting on the piano bench next to him as he played, at my request, my favorite song of his, "Suddenly It's Spring."

Van Heusen, at fifty-six, had married a tiny little woman twelve years older than he who packed heat in her handbag, a gift from Van Heusen, a gold-plated, glittering Derringer. Bobbe Van Heusen, once married to the Hollywood producer William Perlberg, had been, in her youth, one of three singing siblings known as the Brox sisters, all of whom, in 1976, lived in Palm Springs and still came together for a cappella concerts at private parties. All three, tiny gals in their seventies, would shoot you dead in a second if even modestly provoked. Bobbe, possibly the oldest, had taken on the job of Chester Babcock: the pills, the liquids, the insulin shots, the trips to the doctors, for which I commended her. Their house, on a golf course (neither played), was tidy, carpeted, wax-flowered, and Academy Awarded. Five statues stood on Jimmy's upright Yamaha in his messy studio. He had won them for "Swingin' on a Star," "All the Way," "Call Me Irresponsible," and "High Hopes," and an Emmy for "Love and Marriage."

Piled in the corners of the room were cassettes, reel-to-reels, some of them marked "FS." In time I went through them all, to find that I'd already discovered and owned many of the tapes that Van Heusen had tossed to the floor: Sinatra in nightclubs, recorded "off the line," meaning off his microphone, rather than tapes made by someone in the audience, of which there were hundreds.

Jimmy was Sinatra's crony, probably the closest thing to an absolute friend, the friend with the music in his head. He served as Sinatra's rehearsal pianist, confidant, a buddy from the start, before the war, the only other guy in the room during, God knows, three thousand hours. Sinatra recorded seventy-seven of his songs, far more than any other composer (Richard Rodgers holds the second position at forty-one).

Yes, there was Mickey Rudin, Sinatra's lawyer, always on the phone, spending half his life trying, as he told Van Heusen, "to keep the Sinatras quiet."

The Sinatras weren't the Sinatras until the summer of 1976, until their marriage in July at the home of Walter Annenberg, whose vast estate was nearby, a side of it running along Frank Sinatra Drive. The former wife of the very least of the Marx Brothers,

Zeppo, Barbara Blakely, a tall, white-skinned, blond woman of an appropriate age (Mia Farrow had preceded her), was a ubiquitous social figure in desert circles, now and then alone at a party or function, dynamic in a slightly chilling way that might have had something to do with Sinatra's absent shadow but more accurately, perhaps, because of its own strength, its satiated ambition, its cool command of what might or might not occur. I was aware that Barbara Marx was swabbing Sinatra's deck, amputating old friends, running his accessibility. In this suddenly strange new world, James Van Heusen survived, flourished.

On the afternoon of June 9, I answered the private phone in my room at the Ocotillo. I remember that I had just written down a line from a Smokey Robinson song: "If good looks is a minute / You is a hour." I was prepared to repeat the line to anyone who called.

"Hello, John, this is Ol' Blue Eyes."

"Hi, Frank," I said, standing below the four hanging potted plants I'd affixed to the rafter.

"Tell you what," Sinatra said, "meet us at Lord Fletcher's tonight at eight. Then we'll go back and watch a movie."

"I'll be there. Thanks for asking me."

Lester heard from me, and perhaps a dozen others heard from me. *Sinatra called.*

Ah, clothes. I owned nothing but shorts, T-shirts, bathing trunks, and sneakers. And one pair of jeans that I thought about wearing.

"Jonno."

"Lester."

"Jeans to Sinatra?"

In downtown Palm Springs, a store called Desmond's had presentable if cheesy stuff. A dress shirt with little green triangles on each shoulder. Black slacks with white piping running down each leg. Brown shoes with tassels. Gray cotton socks that reached ever upward to the calf.

That is what I wore to Lord Fletcher's, a commodious roast beef house with a British motif, Yorkshire pudding, fish and chips, ale from the United Kingdom, and a fine oak bar just inside the front door, where I spotted Van Heusen in his usual Hawaiian shirt, Bermuda shorts, and sandals, though I noticed that his fingernails and toenails had been cut, manicured.

He put his arm around me. "How the fuck are you?" he sort of asked.

Frequently, some of Sinatra's dinner guests were people he'd never met; girlfriends of cronies, business partners of business associates, relatives of small-time desert entertainers, whom he charitably included.

I, however, was no stranger. Although, I assume, Sinatra had forgotten our encounters in Paris, he'd been made aware of and had heard my program on WNEW-AM, which, to a degree, focused on his music but with greater depth than was ordinarily found on the air.

Ten years earlier, Sinatra had become friends with the cofounder of Random House, Bennett Cerf, possibly having seen in him a gateway to the literati, a group who might have authenticated something within Sinatra in need of nourishment. Cerf, a star on the weekly TV program *What's My Line?*, enjoyed the celebrity of his position and must have been delighted to take in Sinatra after the two of them met.

Bennett Cerf's voice had been one of several that had pointed Sinatra toward my radio show. Another was that of Joe Raposo, who had made an enormous success through the songs he'd written for *Sesame Street*. His Harvard friend Christopher Cerf, one of

Bennett's two sons, had led him to the publisher and to the social hierarchy of New York, precisely what Joe had aspired to from the start.

Waiting, of course, was Frank Sinatra, a songwriter's dream, who fell in love with "Raposo at the piano," considering Joe a true *paisan,* or, as Van Heusen said, "Dago the Second." Joe, who, as I've mentioned, was Portuguese down to his toes, never said a word, leaving the "Dago the Second" thing to mature.

Oddly, without his input, Sinatra had discovered one of Joe's *Sesame Street* songs, "Bein' Green," that had been written for Kermit the Frog. Sinatra had lovingly recorded it and liked to sing it while Joe played the piano at parties around the city. In fact, he loved to be accompanied on *anything* by Joe.

A scheme was hatched. Raposo and Chris Cerf would arrange for me to meet Sinatra (who was in on it).

The eventual evening, finalized late on a Tuesday, is worth recounting for that very night at the Cerfs'.

"I'm on the air until ten," I told Joe.

"Come then," he said. "It's just a little gathering. Just Chris and some of his friends."

"I'm dressed informally," I said.

"It's informal," Joe assured me.

No mention of Sinatra. Just Chris and some of his friends.

After my FM show, after Led Zeppelin, the Grateful Dead, the Who, the Stones, Buddy Miles, Earth Opera, Country Joe and the Fish, Jimi Hendrix, Creedence Clearwater Revival, Mountain, MC5, Santana—after my four-hour show—I drove my VW Beetle (with a stick shift) to the Cerfs' Sixty-second Street town house, dressed in a black T-shirt, jeans, and sneakers without socks. I was abnormally tan from a recent desert trip, but at least I'd had my hair cut a few days earlier.

Joe opened the door with a radiant smile. "Let's go upstairs," he said.

On the second floor landing, leaning over the banister, were Alan Jay Lerner, Betty Comden, Gene Kelly, and Adolph Green. And, how wonderful! Irwin Shaw.

What were they expecting? All of them dressed for a gala.

Behind them, in the living room, Sinatra was talking with Jilly Rizzo, not an attractive fellow but loyal to Sinatra, a watchdog.

As I reached the top of the stairs, Jilly gestured toward the crowd with his head. Sinatra walked straight to me, extending his hand. "Hello, John," he said. "Joe said you'd be coming."

I turned to Raposo, the beaming *paisan.* I said, "Really, now."

Joe gave me a drink, and I joined a semicircle around Sinatra in the foyer. He was telling Hollywood stories to the group, an appreciative gathering of accomplished people, now an audience, reacting in unison, oohs of incredulity, happy anticipation, and then full laughter, as if in a theater. I don't remember what Sinatra was telling them. I only remember working rapidly with my whiskey. Eventually I suggested to Alan Lerner that he show Sinatra the Parliament cigarette trick. He went first, and I followed as the educated student. I came close to asking Sinatra to try it but did not.

"Let's talk," Sinatra suddenly said a bit later, and led me to a sitting room overlooking Sixty-second Street. "Shoot," he said, taking a seat.

I understood that he wished me to ask him anything at all.

Sinatra was dressed in a dark suit and wore an orange tie and white shirt. He had taken a chair only a foot or so from mine and had put down a crystal glass by his feet, on the lush green carpet in the room.

"What are you drinking?" I asked.

"Vodka," he said.

"Are you retired for the rest of time, or what?"

Sinatra, in the midst of a sabbatical, had not sung publicly for months.

"There are no more good songs, you know what I mean?"

"Will you give me thirty seconds?" I asked, leaning forward so that our faces drew closer.

"Shoot," he said, more softly than before.

"Listen. Okay? 'Spring Will Be a Little Late This Year,' 'By Myself,' 'Alone Together,' 'With a Song in My Heart,' 'A Ship Without a Sail,' 'Better Luck Next Time,' 'All Through the Night,' 'After You, Who?,' 'Love Is Sweeping the Country,' 'I Got Rhythm,' 'Fascinatin' Rhythm,' 'Shining Hour,' 'It Was Written in the Stars,' 'Out of This World,' 'Darn That Dream'—by Van Heusen, 'As Long as I Live,' 'Solitude,' 'Prelude to a Kiss,' 'They All Laughed,' 'But Not for Me,' 'Lady Be Good,' 'Sophisticated Lady,' 'All in Fun,' 'Right as the Rain,' 'Tenderly.' You sang 'Tenderly' on the radio once in 1955. Frank, there are many more."

Not the *exact* list, but very close.

"So?" he asked, a bit coldly.

"Those are songs you've never recorded. No Sinatra record of 'Long Ago and Far Away'?"

"Didn't I do that onc?"

"Only on the radio and at the Hollywood Bowl."

"I'll get to them."

"Not retired, you won't."

Silence.

Then I asked, "Why did you rerecord 'The Last Dance'?"

"I didn't," he said with certainty.

I leaned forward again. Our knees were inches apart.

"I'll bet you fifty thousand dollars," I said. I tapped his right knee with my index finger. "Fifty thousand dollars."

Sinatra looked down at the carpet. Then he raised his eyes. "Maybe I did," he said with a hint of a smile. "How do you know all this crap?"

"I only know the music. I think I've only seen two or three of the movies."

Silence.

"Send me that list, will you?"

"It'll be at least the tenth list I've sent."

"Give it to Joe."

"Tomorrow morning," I said.

We talked about arrangers. I plugged my father's songs. We talked about Raposo; Sinatra called him "a genius." I told him that I'd gotten Joe to come to New York and that he'd stayed with me at first. I made the snap decision to tell Sinatra the joke that Raposo had told me in the car on Storrow Drive the day we'd met, the joke about the guy getting on a plane, the joke that ended with "Pardon me, do you mind if I smoke?" In midjoke, I realized that I would have to use the word "masturbate" in front of Frank Sinatra and thought to change it to "jerk off" or "made himself come." I stuck with "masturbate."

Sinatra loved the joke.

"That's how we met, Joe and I," I said.

We'd been in there close to forty-five minutes.

Jilly Rizzo came into the room; again, not a good-looking guy, especially.

Apparently the party had lulled.

Think of it: a happy gathering, festive, showbizzy, Sinatra at the center, and then he disappears.

Lull.

"We'll talk again," I said.

"Give that list to Joe," Sinatra said, leaving the room, as I followed.

In Lord Fletcher's, yet another "Hello, John" from Frank Sinatra. He put his left hand on my right shoulder.

"Leo," he said, calling over another man at the far end of the bar, whom I hadn't noticed but recognized at once.

Sinatra introduced me to "Durocher the manager," as he put it, reminding me of "Raposo at the piano."

What *didn't* I know about him? Very little. Even as an American League kind of guy, I was up on the Lip, as Leo was known. Perhaps I wasn't aware of the vast reach of his shady affairs or entirely familiar with his rage—I'd never encountered it—but the icy-eyed fellow I was introduced to by Sinatra that night stood before me as an intimate stranger, to the extent that I even knew of a recent falling-out with Sinatra, of long letters of apology from the Lip to Sinatra (apparently Durocher had been given a job by Sinatra in a Vegas casino that had allowed him access to loose change, which he had shifted and filtered and caressed into Lip pockets—petty embezzlement, which was, after all, what Durocher was all about). Upon discovery, the Lip had been ostracized from Sinatra's desert crowd, which meant, in effect, that Durocher had had nowhere to go in the small stretch of the Coachella Valley from Palm Springs to Palm Desert. He lived in a three-room condominium on Highway 111 in an apartment I eventually visited, which was furnished, at best, as a motel suite, and offered little trace of its tenant's distinct history. After the freeze-out, which I believe lasted a year, Sinatra had allowed Durocher's return to the social ramble of the desert towns, and now here he was, scowling and aged but back in the good graces of the man who governed his life.

Sinatra left Durocher and me together to join Barbara Marx and a cluster of women near the restaurant's entrance. I told the Lip a little about Jackie Robinson in Stamford, Connecticut, but his eyes flickered nervously around, passing me by.

In a short while we were all seated at an L-shaped table. I was placed directly across from Sinatra and next to Van Heusen. At the end of the long wing of the L, a stubby hulk of a guy drank a full glass of beer straight down.

"Who's that?" I whispered to Van Heusen.

"The crusher," Van Heusen said.

"Why is he called the crusher?"

"Because he crushes people."

We all received roast beef. We were all poured Mouton Cadet red wine.

Sinatra was cordial to everyone. He said to me, out of the blue, "If you ever write about me, you'd have to follow me all over the world."

Surprised, I said, "I could do that."

Write about him. But of course!

"When you hear a record of yours on the radio, do you listen to the end of the song?" I asked.

"Yeah. The other night I heard something, I forget what, but the vocal went off line near the end, and I remembered that I'd been tired."

"What album?"

"I think it was something with Costa."

" 'Misty'?"

"Yeah," Sinatra said, not surprised by my magic.

"What are you recording this summer?"

"We're doing a tune called 'Dry Your Eyes.' "

"What's it about?" I asked.

"It's about Jesus. At least I think it's about Jesus. Neil Diamond sent it to us."

When someone else caught Sinatra's attention, I asked the waiter for a beer, "just like the crusher's."

Beneath the table, Van Heusen's knee banged mine disapprovingly. His wife, Bobbe, threw a grim glance my way from Sinatra's side of the table.

But I didn't care, not one whit. I was having far too fine a time.

We were, as it turned out, a group of nine who dispersed, at meal's end, into separate vehicles. Sinatra's, a Rolls with an "FAS" plate, led the motorcade down Frank Sinatra Drive to the compound, as his estate was known. The motorcade seemed to me as long as the short distance between restaurant and compound. I imagined not having to do any driving at all. Just being in the motorcade would eventually transport me into the compound. I even considered telling Sinatra this when we got there. I thought that he might find in me the very humorist he'd been seeking all his life. I would become a close adviser. I would advise him not to record a song about Jesus. Or anything written by Neil Diamond. I would advise him never to take calls from Neil Diamond. I would advise him to have Neil Diamond whacked.

We were shown to a large recreation room. On a pool table, a number of piles of record albums were sloppily stacked. Peggy Lee, Stravinsky, Basie, the Four Freshmen, in no particular arrangement.

A number of comfortable black leather chairs were informally settled in what proved to be the back of the room. Nearby, standing in a sunken bar, Sinatra was making drinks to specification. Behind him, highball glasses were engraved with his familiar slang. "It's a gasser," "Ring a ding ding," "Chairman of the Board," "Ol' Blue Eyes."

One by one, his guests were served. Finally Sinatra looked up at me.

"A double Johnnie Walker Black, with soda. And I'll have mine in an Ol' Blue Eyes glass," I told him with a dreadful wink, sending him up right there in his own recreation room. Oh, what a merry prankster!

Sinatra made my drink, his eyes cast down.

Had he taken my warm-spirited, kindhearted mirth the wrong way? How *could* he have? He knew I loved him.

"Thank you, Frank," I said, when he held my drink up.

No more tricks, that's for sure.

A movie screen was lowered in the front of the room, beyond the Four Freshmen albums.

I took the black leather chair next to Barbara. Sinatra sat on her other side.

We were going to see a full-length film, *The Missouri Breaks*, with Marlon Brando and Jack Nicholson.

"Directed by Arthur Penn," Sinatra said when Penn's name came by.

About a half hour into the movie, Sinatra began to tell us, all of us, what was happening, though he'd never seen the film.

"You see, Nicholson is getting off the horse and he's going into the bar. Brando doesn't like what he sees, but he's not going to say anything."

Sinatra was right on top of it. Arthur Penn's dreadful movie seemed to go on forever. I remembered that I'd read that Harry Cohn, the legendary chief of Columbia Pictures, had done, in his own screening room, exactly what Sinatra was doing now. They assumed, it seemed to me, a kind of possession, but, more than likely, something grander. I remembered the Password League of my childhood; my broadcasts of the games, the whole thing in my control. Harry Cohn and Sinatra were broadcasting their own games, in their own leagues, on their own networks, to their own audiences. They towered above the movies. The stories were *theirs* to tell.

When, finally, *The Missouri Breaks* ended, Sinatra disappeared with Barbara.

"Let's go," Van Heusen said.

"But I want to talk with him," I said.

"He gave the signal."

"What signal?"

"For us to get out."

"How do you know?" I asked, getting out.

"Trust me. He gave the fuckin' signal."

We all drove away, Sinatra gone.

I waited several weeks for my writing assignment. I was ready to put off my novel and follow Sinatra "all over the world."

Van Heusen told me that Sinatra would call me when he needed me.

"What signal?" I asked him again.

"It's invisible," Van Heusen said.

No call.

Not for years.

18

CARLY SIMON ONCE TOLD ME THAT, FOR HER, SINATRA WAS A FATHER figure. I realized that I'd hidden that truth about myself out of embarrassment. This unusual, prickly guy, whose music I so admired, turned out to be a father figure as well. God help me! When he was singing Arthur's songs, what was he? A kind of LSD carbon, communicating paternally from the middle of all the junk in my head. Carly had been brave enough to say it on the phone, which released me into its reality. I had hidden away from the glare for years.

In the desert, over the Fourth of July Bicentennial celebration in 1976, I had decided to call my novel-in-progress *Hiding*. Look at all the hiding I've done, I thought: Beverly Hills, Robert Delvecchio, the dorm staircase, the hotel ballrooms. And alcohol, which was, I imagined, like a large cave way up in the mountains that no one knew about but me, but I had it all set up with Scotch and beer and radios and books and avocados and fresh trout from a brook just outside the cave and tomatoes from the garden on top of the cave.

At a party at Candice Bergen's house in Hollywood, to which I had somehow been invited a month or so earlier, I had asked about her ventriloquist father, Edgar Bergen, who had been quite a figure in my young radio life. She told me that she'd felt in competition with Charlie McCarthy, the dummy, and that she had imagined him to be a brother of sorts. Then she said, "Sometimes at night I got up because I heard my father yelling. There was a light on under his study door, and I realized that he was fighting with Charlie McCarthy."

Wasn't that hiding? Expressing yourself through an inanimate object? It was clear to me that in my book, the character of Emily Keller would be the daughter of a ventriloquist, and I would give her her father's peculiar talent.

Part one of *Hiding* had been sold as a self-contained story and eventually published in the November 1975 issue of *The Atlantic Monthly.* I finished the novel on a May morning in 1978 in a house on Pasa Tiempo in Palm Springs that I'd rented with Merry Rogin. I had asked this marvelous, sexually exaggerated girl to marry me, but she'd declined in a husky whisper. I don't remember what she said, but I remember accusing her of being "illogical." She said, "You can't even pronounce my name." Which was true. The Merry came out Mary. Then for a little while Miriam, her real name, and finally Myrtie, something from her childhood. But still there lay that tricky "y" in Myrtie. I'm not clear about anything anymore.

As it happened, the morning I finished *Hiding,* May 8, was Merry's twenty-fifth birthday, and I took the call from Jimmy Van Heusen that invited us to dinner at the Copa d'Oro, "with Spiro Agnew and his old lady." Jimmy had developed a fondness for Merry (and the ability to pronounce her name), based in part on her grand bosom and terrific, throaty laugh, on her dark and darting eyes, on her childlike vitality, an energy that her constant marijuana use had been designed but had failed to subdue. Jimmy's very special interest in Merry was increased, I have no doubt, by the joints that I, as messenger, surreptitiously slipped into his hand whenever we were together, all from the great Roginian factory on Pasa Tiempo. More than once, Jimmy said, when Bobbe was out of earshot, "that kid Merry has the best fuckin' shit in California." After all, Merry and I reasoned, Van Heusen was deprived of anything that could reasonably be described as a good time. "We're his entertainment," she pointed out.

Oh, the intensity of that girl! The husky whisper, dramatizing noodles and sandals and sunlight and chewing gum, engaged me conspiratorially, it seemed, in the conveyance of sweet secrets. I accused her of having been born in italics. "What's the big deal?" I occasionally asked. "If you don't know now, you'll never know," she replied with no venom. No venom practically ever. I think it's possible that Merry Rogin was one frightened twenty-five-year-old, just beginning to negotiate on her own terms. I held a good part of the map she wished to examine but kept it from her in fear she'd find a way to pass me by.

"We're having dinner with the Agnews," I told her.

"You're always doing stuff like this. The Agnews? Get out of here."

"You'll see," I said to the naked girl in the swimming pool with a joint in her hand.

At the Copa d'Oro at 8 P.M., Merry Rogin and I were introduced to the former Vice President of the United States and his wife, Judy. Homely and forlorn, they sat across the table from us, Merry's red marijuana eyes taking in the special guests, Van Heusen seeing it all, not saying a word, Bobbe, her gold-plated Derringer stashed, I knew, in the handbag at her elbow.

Agnew loved old songs. When the subject turned to music, he sang "When the Red, Red Robin Comes Bob Bob Bobbin' Along" in its entirety, as if it were a brand-new tune he wished us to know. He didn't smile at all, during his song or after it. He was a pragmatist in the dullest sense, an uninteresting man in exile, a neighbor of the Van Heusens, beholden to Sinatra, who'd befriended him before his boat had capsized in the Chesapeake Bay. A man in a gray suit, mirthless and obsolete, "Ted" Agnew viewed Merry Rogin with an obvious delight as she sat there smiling across from him. Yes, she's a Jewish girl, bozo, I felt like saying, and what a beauty, right? Instead, I gave Merry a lengthy birthday kiss, quite a sexy kiss for the Agnews to consider.

And oh boy, when the surprise birthday cake arrived, did Agnew jump into "Happy Birthday"! Even his wife managed a sound. I would be forty on June 28, and Merry was fifteen years younger. We were, at the very least, pretty, in the way that most of us forget we ever were. I can tell you that so-and-so was attractive at a certain time or that I looked okay on a specific evening. What I cannot tell you is why I've forgotten most of it. I am left with lovely shadows, which I can arrange to my liking. I can glamorize the women without being able to convey how they really appeared. I think this is true of a great many people, who, coming upon themselves in old photos, are stunned by their ancient allure and stung by the wounds incurred that have turned the snapshots into haunting dreams.

"When I finish my book, I'll do it," I had told the owner of Michael's Pub in New York, who, having heard an album of my singing, was calling to invite me to appear in his cabaret.

"The wooden horses will go up," I told Lester on the phone from the desert, and we both laughed. I'd been warning him for years that if I ever took to the stage, the crowds would need to be restrained. Lester had taken an opposing view.

I had rented an upright piano for the house on Pasa Tiempo,

and often I'd sat on the bench, rehearsing what I might perform at Michael's Pub. Certainly I'd have a better pianist and a small group, maybe a guitar, bass, clarinet, and drums. I'd have a chance to sing some of my father's songs that weren't well known, and one or two unpublished things that I knew to be first-rate. I worked up a group of titles and ran them by Van Heusen in his untidy little study. He suggested "If There Is Someone Lovelier than You," which I'd forgotten about, and his own "Suddenly It's Spring," which I found difficult to sing because of its tricky intervals. If I were to appear in New York, I'd better be comfortable from top to bottom, I told him. "It's easy," he said and sat down to play and sing "Suddenly It's Spring." Van Heusen's playing was unpretentious. His singing voice was lilting and lovely, defying his gruff profanity, his mischief.

Michael's Pub was operated by a trim, good-looking fellow named Gil Weist, whose reputation as a monstrous, tyrannical imbecile had not eluded me. I found him, in late June 1978, approachable, cordial, and delighted that I'd be playing his club for two weeks, beginning Tuesday, July 4. I looked upon the engagement as a quiet little secret that no one would know about. Friends would come, I'd sing my songs, and Lester would have the last laugh: no horses.

A small ad in the *Times* caught my eye.

"No, no," I said to Lester. "I'm just going to embarrass myself. Why take an ad?"

"It's a business," he said.

"But who's going to come, aside from you and Merry Rogin?"

"I guess he's counting on your radio audience."

I hadn't thought of that. Was anyone ever so, well, young?

"Disaster," I said.

"If that be the case, you won't have to worry about the horses,"

Lester said, having by then achieved a noticeable presence as a radio jazz personality. "I found my sound," he had told me along the way, meaning Sonny Rollins, Miles Davis, John Coltrane, Lester Young, Zoot Sims. In fact, Lester had become the radio voice of jazz on several New York stations.

I thought of him a few moments before my first performance. He wasn't in the audience, though he'd promised to show up "during the en*gage*ment." His jazz was raw and pure, while my songs were so sentimental. It occurred to me, as I was announced by the hidden Gil Weist, to go out there and actually speak about the matter to the fifty or so people who had gathered on a July Fourth evening. "Ladies and gentlemen," I'd say, "what I'm going to do for you tonight is a bit on the sentimental side, compared to my friend Les Davis's jazz." I would trade off Lester's success. I would win the sympathy of the audience.

Instead, I sang the show at top speed and did second and third shows that grew progressively relaxed. I dropped in a few stories about Arthur Schwartz and the other songwriters and sang the Brant Lake Camp lyric by Larry Hart to "I Guess I'll Have to Change My Plan."

I had no idea that *The New York Times* would send a critic. The respected John Wilson had been there for the first two shows. His favorable review appeared in the Thursday paper, and that night the horses, quite literally, were up. I used the word "throngs" when reporting back to Lester, and not inaccurately. The lines stretched from the inside entrance hallway out to Fifty-fifth Street.

"Throngs?" Lester asked incredulously.

"Come and see, my dear man," I said. "It seems I've found *my* sound."

The two-week engagement sold out quickly, and subsequent stays of up to three or four weeks were nicely populated. A live album was made that I'm still not embarrassed by, and an intimate friendship leapt out of the music to help me through a public existence both facile and rigorous in which I have seldom felt lonelier, even as a child. The pianist on whom I'd settled, cynical, passionate, round-faced, occasionally bearded, frequently overweight, often hilarious, gentle, laughing, professorial, indignant, wild-eyed, and now and then raucously inebriated, was a New York musician named Tony Monte. He grasped the diction of my singing and respectfully joined in. An economic Basie child, he was exciting to hear, night after night, year after year, for more than five hundred performances at Michael's Pub and perhaps a hundred more at the Ballroom, Rainbow and Stars, and Fat Tuesday's, all in Manhattan. I depended on him, this spewing little man, during hundreds of hours of rehearsal, much of the time wasted in convulsions of laughter. I depended on him on the stand to guide the band, often as many as eight other musicians, including, during one engagement, an all-woman string quartet. I depended on him most of all to steer me through the haze of flattery, the eager faces with long stories to tell as others waited in happy agitation. Here now, an old friend, with a new wife named Stephanie, a shy, light-skinned woman in a dark green dress, waiting to shake my hand, to utter her few stumbling words, and then to back away after they'd been spoken in a surprising French accent. Here now, an old girlfriend with a new girlfriend. One of the last things she'd said to me a few years earlier was "You don't resonate to the larger picture." Now she stood before me between tables at Michael's Pub, wishing to say "We enjoyed the show." She put her arm around her friend's waist. "This is Charlotte," she said, proudly, possessively. "Susan and Charlotte?" I asked generously, receiving a reply in the silence of their pleasure.

And here now, my father.

"Jonno boy!"

What a hug he got from me.

I had called him up onstage to play "Dancing in the Dark," for which he'd received a standing ovation. Now he held me close, his forehead glistening with perspiration, his blue eyes excited as people gathered around to shake his hand, to seek an autograph. He was seventy-nine during my third engagement at Michael's Pub, his hair dyed boot black on behalf of youth, his frailty apparent in his cautious navigation of departure, crossing the back of the restaurant, mistakenly passing through the front bar, called the Bird Cage, before maneuvering himself onto Fifty-fifth Street and into the difficult task of hailing a taxi. I watched him go. He was delayed once by a couple his age, Arthur's music in their bones, which is, I guess, what they wanted to tell him.

Tony Monte steered me into the kitchen, through the piles of plates, around the discarded fat of roast beef that had fallen to the floor, below the clatter of cleanup, the Greek and Spanish roaring above the rattle, the wet floor a minefield of puddles that menaced the sleek black shoes of entertainment.

Monte and I, in the cubbyhole of a dressing room meant for the kitchen help, talked of lowering the key on "Somebody Loves Me" or cutting a trumpet solo out of "I'm like a New Broom." I implored him to reassure me: Had I sung well? What about the lyric mistake I'd made in "I Wish I Were in Love Again"? Did I *look* okay?

"Yes, yes," Monte assured me. "What the fuck."

Later, alone, I stood outside the swinging kitchen doors, waiting for the second show. Monte and the band were out there playing an opening number. I realize now how quickly I had come to love him.

. . .

"The dago's on the warpath," Jimmy Van Heusen told me on the phone.

"Why?" (I knew).

"He's pissed off about something you said about the *Trilogy* album on the air."

"What's he going to do?"

"He's talking to the guy who owns your station."

"John Kluge?"

"That's the guy."

We were both in the desert on a rainy Monday night. I had flown out after my Sunday show for a week's vacation before a Michael's Pub three-week run. That night I was planning a marathon read of Richard Yates, the books I'd never picked up, including *A Special Providence* and *Disturbing the Peace*.

On my program the day before, I'd praised Sinatra's ambitious new three-record set, *Trilogy,* except for record three, a musical essay called "The Future," which I'd found to be a shambles of self-regard and said so on the air. Now the dago was on the warpath.

Minutes after Van Heusen's call, the phone rang again, my own secret little number.

"I don't care *how* much you respect me, you fuckin' *schmuck*! I don't care *what* you know about my music, you fuckin' *ass*hole!"

And a good two or three minutes more. I held the receiver away from my ear and said nothing. I was trembling. I was terrified.

Sinatra finished and slammed the receiver down.

I sat on the side of the bed among the works of Richard Yates.

Then a third call, almost by design: the general manager of WNEW, Jack Thayer.

"We have a problem," he told me, probably from his home, at around 10:15 New York time, which meant he'd been on the phone a lot during the evening.

"What's the problem?" I asked.

"Sinatra," he said.

"Sinatra?" I said, believing my bewilderment.

"You've got to take a sabbatical," he said, in a grave tone.

Thayer was a giddy EST guy, moderately obese and leaking fraudulent goodwill. All of his memos and letters and his personal letters and his postcards, even his termination notes (two of which I saw), were signed Jack ON YOUR SIDE Thayer. The grave tone, so out of place from this, let's face it, silly guy, was sobering, convincing, ominous.

"What is this about?" I asked.

"It's about what you said about the *Trilogy* album yesterday."

"Have you listened to a tape?"

"Many times."

"I spoke the truth."

"That's not the issue."

"What *is* the issue?"

"John Kluge is the issue."

"In what sense?"

"He wants you off the air."

"Am I fired?"

"You're on sabbatical."

"What does that mean?"

"You'll be working on your book."

"But I'm not working on a book."

"That's not the issue."

"Should I come back and fight this?"

"Do you think it would do any good?"

I had no reply.

I went back the next day, on sabbatical.

The columnist Liz Smith got ahold of the issue. I spoke to no one, but Sinatra did, wiring Liz that he had "the know-how" and I was just a "would-be singer."

What an uproar!

People magazine juxtaposed photos of Sinatra and me. *The Wall Street Journal* ran an op-ed piece that pointed the finger at Kluge.

My opening night at Michael's Pub was packed with press, to whom I'd been legally advised not to speak. On that day, April 1, 1980, the city was hit by a bus and subway strike that was universally inflaming. The mood in the club reflected the chaos, as flashbulbs and TV reporters disturbed the music and especially the singer. Gil Weist, standing by the phones, all of which were unstoppably lit, wore a satisfaction that bespoke a man whose finest hour had arrived.

In the days that followed, I developed headaches that nothing would relieve, due, I think, to my confusion. My father figure had risen up against me because of something I'd done. He was in the Waldorf-Astoria "in a rage," I was told by a Sinatra confidant with whom I was friendly.

Kluge and WNEW received thousands of letters and calls, all of which excoriated the iconic singer and supported the meager disc jockey.

I remained on sabbatical until June, when I was suddenly, mysteriously, welcomed back by the station and given a raise and an ON YOUR SIDE hug from Jack Thayer.

At a concert in Carnegie Hall on June 25, Sinatra introduced William B. Williams in the audience. "He's no Aaron Burr," he said as an afterthought (I have the video). He meant, of course, Benedict Arnold, but I perversely felt a delight that he had mentioned me in Carnegie Hall, however indirectly.

On September 16, 1987, again in Carnegie Hall, Sinatra, having been told I was present, introduced me during his informal chat in the middle of the show. He said, "There's a man here tonight who knows more about me than I do myself. Jonno, where are you?" The spotlight picked me up quickly in an aisle seat in the fifth row. "Stand up," he said. "Turn around so they can see you."

Because the hall was filled with my constituency, I was warmly received.

After I sat down, Sinatra had something more to say: "Don't mess with Jonno, I'm tellin' ya."

He had picked up the "Jonno" from his confidant who was my friend.

He then introduced Betty Comden in the audience, the woman in whose home, thirty-eight years earlier, my father had come upon Mary Grey.

Late that night I told Lester on the phone that Sinatra had said "Jonno boy," and Lester believed me.

Much of my singing was defensive singing; that is, working around the villainous nose and throat cabal that, to greater or lesser degrees, challenged my intentions. Somewhere in the middle of the second song (the opener was generally a relaxed little swinger, such as "This Can't Be Love," "I May Be Wrong," or "I'm Old-Fashioned") I was able to fathom the strength of the opposition on any evening. There were maybe fifteen shows during which I felt entirely confident. Those shows were created by prednisone, which wiped away the mucus on my vocal cords. I was able to find any note, sustain any line, and depend on a full vibrato. Defensive singing was all about limiting my range, going more staccato throughout, lowering a high last note a full octave and disguising the retreat from the high note by a visual melancholy or contemplation that would validate the choice. It forced me to move quickly through vowels (let's say the "o" in "love") and fasten securely onto the closed "v" particularly on a high D, E, or even F. In the word "night," the vowel "i" would change quickly into a "y" which would sound like an "e" that would provide a safe landing on the "t."

In the small space of a cabaret stage, I tended to wander as much as possible, to distract the listeners' attention from the defensive singing by providing them with an unexpected physical restlessness. I would turn to face Tony at the piano during his solo, under the guise of admiring his playing. In fact, with my back to the audience, I was able to clear my throat a little, the microphone down at my side while Tony played. I'd smile at him appreciatively, and he'd smile back with a "what the fuck" written on his retinas, which made me laugh, a laugh that I was able to use as a cough, before turning back to the audience for my second chorus.

That Gil Weist, through the eight years I was at Michael's Pub, treated maître d's, waiters, musicians, and often customers with arrogance, and a contempt that bubbled with rage, is not a matter in dispute. Although he was civil to me, I was ordered, on one occasion, to give an entire evening of three performances without the sound system working, and I appeared each time very much like a fellow at the far end of a long living room making some kind of obscure musical presentation. What started as full houses, to which I explained the problem, became merely a handful of front-rowers who hung in with an obvious lack of interest. Groups of people left in the middle of ballads, noisily disengaging themselves from their places in the room, stumbling out through the lake of tiny tables.

On another occasion, a snowy Tuesday night, there was no one at all in attendance and only a single waiter in the house, and Val, the boorish maître d', who cowered under Weist's sadistic rule and then, in the owner's absence, used it himself. I was ordered by Val to perform a show for no one and did so, treating the event as a rehearsal for new material, some of which we later used, as a result of our empty house.

Imagine all of this, year after year, around the world, if I had taken on a career outside New York. The Ramada Inns, the airports at five in the morning, the phone calls to answering machines, women not picking up, listening, determined not to speak. *You have no right calling me, buster.*

Yes, I know.

My life as a singer. Panic, aloneness, whiskey, fleeing in the dead of night, the songs again and again, floating high like smoke rings in the cabaret, over and over and over.

Japanese men came to Michael's Pub in groups of ten or more. Throughout the music they spoke enthusiastically in Japanese, as if nothing were going on. They showed up on weeknights, joining silent, elderly men and women scattered about. The Friday- and Saturday-night crowds, known as the "OBs," for "Other Boroughs," came to town to hear my show. They were a joyful presence, the largest in number, and the most detested by Gil Weist. Being from the Other Boroughs, they weren't, he thought, of his kind, yet they entered his store with money to spend. The irony nearly destroyed him. His oily graciousness for anyone even slightly well known would turn into ferocity for any OB with even the lightest problem, such as a need for a second glass of water. On one occasion he was knocked to the floor by a towering guy who'd endured him all evening. Weist scurried away, his right eye bleeding, just as I was about to begin the second show. Introduced by Monte as I hit the stage on the run, Tony said to me, with a wave of his right hand, "A mere disagreement." Weist was there the next night, a bit banged up and without comment. My "Hi, Gil" went unanswered, though our eyes met. It was clear that I was being held responsible for the events of the night before, and a reciprocity was inevitable. Indeed: no Scotch and soda on the stool by the piano and a suddenly faulty sound system that muddied my singing.

What I did was just continue. I worked in his place, I did what he said, no matter his indelicacies. If I wanted to sing songs in front of other people, I had to be prepared for schizophrenic management, firings on the spot, noisy disputes, and perhaps confrontation.

My spectacular moment built over the last week of a twelve-week engagement during which other singers had joined me for a Rodgers and Hart extravaganza.

"Weist has a war going with the musicians' union," Tony Monte told me on the phone. It was the word "welfare" in the phrase "pension and welfare" that infuriated him. He refused to make any payments at all. In a special contract designed to keep him signed up, the union had agreed to wave the welfare payments but not the pension. Weist had signed because he had mistakenly thought that he had found a loophole by making all the musicians independent contractors. In other words, he wasn't the employer, we were all self-employed. As it turned out, the courts had ruled a long time earlier that what Weist believed was true with regard to the *withholding taxes,* but the agreement with the union was separate and the P-and-W issue was yet to be decided. Weist had chosen to challenge that concept during my long run by claiming to have hired a self-contained show, with him only distributing money. He'd insisted that he wasn't the employer. Looking at the musicians and the lineup of talent, the union didn't believe a word of it.

On Friday, January 3, 1987, one day before closing night, Weist received an invoice from someone at the union who charged him pension and welfare and calculated it on an increase in the wage scale (unbeknown to us) that had taken place while we were there. When Tony Monte walked in Friday night, it became his fault. Weist wasn't going to pay. He wasn't paying any welfare. There would be no withholding, which sounded as if he wasn't going to pay any of us at all.

"The union offices were closed," Monte told me later. "At that time I had a corporation. To protect the musicians' payroll, I decided to issue a corporate check for the P-and-W, payable to the union, that in effect made me the employer. I intended to slip out of the scheme on Monday by stopping payment on the check. When I came in on Saturday, I gave Weist the check and announced that he was off the hook. Weist immediately saw through the thing and wouldn't accept the check unless I signed a letter from him stating that I was indeed the employer. I agreed, intending to tell the union on Monday that all of this had been done under duress and the whole thing was null and void. While waiting for him to come back with the letter, I told you what was going on. You saw Weist as the bully that he was. You said, 'All cowards are bullies.' You ignored my pleas to let it lie. You told me that I wasn't going to sign anything and that there'd be no music unless everyone was first paid in cash. All of this took place in very hushed tones, as you know." Monte, impassioned and gesticulative as he told me all this, finished quietly, almost solemnly.

It was about 8:50, and the show was scheduled to start at 9:00. I said that we had to tell the other musicians and singers at once. They were Tony Tedesco, Jimmy Mitchell, Jerry Bruno, Margaret Whiting, and Mark Murphy. I implored them to join us. I said it was possible that Weist might not pay us and that we needed to get the money first. Margaret, now a woman of a certain age, was puzzled, but she agreed. Mark agreed, but he didn't seem sure of anything. The other musicians leapt at the chance (the union would take Weist to court).

Michael's Pub was packed, and the second show was oversold. Celebrities were everywhere (we had recruited a few): Tony Bennett, Mel Torme, Linda Ellerbee, David Susskind, Joe Williams, Charles Kuralt, Lionel Hampton. Now it was 9:05. Val came into the Bird Cage, where we all were. "Okay, Monte, get the musicians—let's go!" "No," Tony said. Val tried to be nice: "Come on, play the music, everything will be okay."

Then Val left. After another endless ten minutes he returned, with the same result. Weist came in about ten minutes later and asked Margaret to go on with her pianist. She said that she couldn't because she needed all the instruments. Weist asked Mark to go on as a singing pianist. Mark said he wasn't really a pianist. Then I asked Mark what he was being paid. "Three thousand dollars," he said softly. "I'll pay that amount in cash if Weist defaults for no play." He agreed. He still wasn't sure of anything.

Now it was 9:45, and Weist was by the phones watching the full house, and I guessed that he was adding up the covers to see what the room was worth in the event of a cancellation. Then he came into the Bird Cage and threatened to cancel the show, implying grave consequences for all of us if we didn't start immediately. I told him that if he paid us, we'd start. He left the Bird Cage, and this time he went upstairs to his office. He returned to the phones at the front desk in about five minutes. He had seven envelopes stuffed with cash. He sent Val in to fetch us to be paid, one at a time. Everyone but me. Val called for places, but no one responded. After another five minutes, Weist sent Val in with my envelope. I counted the money. Then we took the stage. There was really serious applause as we entered. It was 10:10.

After the first show, which I ran much longer than usual, thus screwing up the lines for the next show, nobody wanted to hang out in the Bird Cage, and Michael's Pub was in complete disorder, with the second-show people trying to get in while the first show was letting out. There were some people trying to skip out on their checks, and Weist was yelling at Val, so I suggested that we all go to Clancy's on Third Avenue. Everybody came. And we did a wonderful closing show that ended at 1:00 A.M.

The union eventually took Weist to court. Weist lost the case. I've never seen him again. Monte hasn't either.

19

IN THE FALL OF 1979, I MARRIED MARIE BRENNER. OUR DAUGHTER, Casey, was born in September 1982.

Marie and I separated in 1983 and divorced a year later. In December 1984, I married Ellie Renfield, who gave birth to our son, Adam, in January 1987. Marie remarried in 1985. Her husband remains Ernie Pomerantz, who for years was a terrific stepfather for Casey, whose full name is Katherine Ann Schwartz. The Ann is for Marie's close friend Annie Arensberg. Adam is Adam Arthur Schwartz.

Marie is a journalist, principally for *Vanity Fair.* Ellie is a theater director whose résumé runs the length of the pages of an O'Neill play.

That marriage is both beautiful and desperate is well known. You can be assured that in my years with these two women, the complexities of intimacy were often challenged, mostly by grace and truth. Ellie and Marie are friends but not confidantes. Casey and Adam are loving siblings who have conspired, laughed, and taught each other a thing or two. Both Ellie and Marie knew my father, who was crazy about them. There are three or four photographs of Casey, as an infant, being awkwardly held by her grandfather. Adam was born three years after Arthur's death.

There they are, my family, quite above the fray of these pages, their privacies forever their own, and mine.

A Sunday morning in February 1984, bitter cold. Snow had fallen since sunrise. My program was in midstream, 11:15, and I hadn't heard from my father, who, now that he was living in New York permanently after several years in London, had become a member of my audience, one of only a few with access to the private telephone line. "Jonno boy," he'd always say, "are you all right?" Which irritated me. "Why do you keep asking? I'm fine, I'm fine. How are *you*?" Which was the point. "Not so good, Jonno boy. My legs ache. The man with the pitchfork is here. I'm thinking of leaving Mary and moving into the Carlyle. Oh Jonno boy, I can't get a show on."

Arthur's themes.

"Hold it a sec," I'd say as a record ended. "Billie Holiday's only recording made in a studio with just a piano. 'I Thought About You.' You know, if you listen to the recording back to back with Sinatra's 'Empty Tables,' which is one of only two *he* ever made in a studio with just a piano, you'll find them almost talking together. The songs have the same blue midnight about them, they're both in B flat, and they're both written by Johnny Mercer and Jimmy Van Heusen. Listen to this, Sinatra's 'Empty Tables.'"

"I've never heard this," Arthur would say when I got back to him.

"It's Mercer's last lyric," I'd tell him.

There were always two calls, the first at 9:30, the second a little after 11:00. On that winter morning, there'd been nothing at all.

I phoned the Lotus Club, where Arthur stayed, risking the voice of Mary Grey. No one picked up in their suite.

I was pretty sure that my father had died or was dying. An instinct.

I called New York Hospital and discovered that he'd been admitted early in the morning to Sixth Floor Neurology. He'd had a cerebral hemorrhage.

I arranged for an on-air replacement, who arrived quickly.

I walked from Forty-second and Third to Sixty-eighth and York in an increasingly heavy snow. "Mommy, I'm now walking over to New York Hospital from the radio station where I work. You'll never guess what happened," I said out loud to my mother, Katherine Carrington, about whom I hadn't given a great deal of thought for a number of years. I spoke conversationally, as if we were dining together. "Arthur's had some sort of stroke. I want you to know that Arthur had great success throughout his life, and he told me that all of his music was written for you. Isn't that something?" Then I told her it was snowing.

Mary Grey was in the waiting room. She said that Arthur had experienced "a seizure" but that "he'd be fine."

Dr. Frank Petito (who is currently my own neurologist) pulled me aside about an hour later, wanting me to know that my father's wife had been behaving erratically.

"Has she called you a cocksucker yet?" I asked.

"Yes indeed," he replied drolly (I've come to know his droll).

He went on to report that my father's stroke had left him paralyzed on his right side and unable to speak, and that he was undergoing a CAT scan.

A ruckus at the far end of the hall. An odd holler, the words indistinguishable. Arthur Schwartz was being rolled to his room by two nurses and a male attendant. His eyes were wild with panic.

"Get the fuck out of here," Mary Grey said to everyone after Arthur had been transferred into bed and made as comfortable as possible. I remained in the room, as close to murder as I'd ever come.

"I said out," Mary Grey told me.

"One more word, and you're a dead woman," I said, standing.

I bent over Arthur, whose eyes were filled with tears.

"There's nothing we can do about her now," I said to him with a smile. "The idea is for you to get better."

Arthur said something in a garble.

"Say it again," I told him.

Again a garble, but within the garble I sensed a question.

A question he eventually asked by wiggling the fingers of his left hand, his eyes wide open, waiting for a response. He was asking about playing the piano. Would it ever be possible again?

"Of course," I told him. "More like Irving Berlin than Gershwin, but you'll do okay."

I expected Mary Grey to have something to say and turned to discover that she had left the room, perhaps, I thought, to get the police to have me locked up for threatening her life. Who would testify on my behalf? Not this old bewildered man, who lay there knowing the truth, wiggling his fingers, making silent music.

Arthur's hospital wrist tag looked cheaply ornamental. His bare feet revealed uncut toenails that reminded me of Joe Raposo's. His hair, unkempt, showed its white roots under Mary Grey's black dye.

"It's snowing," I told him.

"It is?" he answered, clearly.

"What?" I said.

But his reply was garbled. He tried again, with even less success. The tears he had shed remained on his face below his eyes. With a towel from the bathroom, I brushed them away.

The usual hospital parade began: Petito, nurses, medical observers with notepads, my brother, Paul, and of course Mary Grey.

Arthur was eventually sent to the Burke Rehabilitation Center in White Plains, where he refused to participate. My visits with him were brief and cheerless, the sorrow hanging oppressively in the air. Only his eyes remained alert and oddly youthful, a phenomenon I've noticed during subsequent visits to others similarly afflicted.

His illness kept me talking to my mother, after thirty-one years of silence. I told her all sorts of things, mostly at night. I loved talking to Katherine, and not only about Arthur. I edited out Paine Whitney from my own history, and of course the first woman I'd married.

When Arthur died, on September 4, 1984, Mary Grey and Paul were there. Paul's call to me came through at about nine in the morning.

"He didn't make it," he said, which I told my mother later in the day.

20

MY DOUBLEDAY PUBLISHER, SAM VAUGHAN, CALLED ME UP A FEW months after Arthur's death. He told me that he was moving over to Random House as a senior editor and vice president and was wondering if I'd like to come with him. He said that he was taking two authors, William Buckley, Jr., and, he hoped, me. Sam had published my novel *Hiding* under a far better title, *Distant Stations,* and though the reviews had been good to very good, the book hadn't had a commercial success.

Still, here was Sam on the phone, knowing of some new stories I'd written, aware that I was keeping at it. A novel I'd wobbly begun became, at Ellie's suggestion, a collection of short stories that Random House published in the fall of 1988 as *The Man Who Knew Cary Grant.* Again, good reviews, this time all of them, but no buying fever whatsoever in the marketplace.

I went out to the desert in late September to start something new and wrote about forty pages in two weeks, quite a lot for me.

Everything that happens around a typewriter (I still use a typewriter, a Hermes 3000, the best) is in slow motion except my departures from the chair, occasioned by the slightest fatigue, a knock on the door, a ringing phone, a hunger for sushi, a box score to be examined, a gift to be bought, a car to be fueled, a song to be learned, batteries to be bought and installed in three radios, calls to be made, beer to be chilled, the refrigerator to be organized with the beer on top and Diet Cokes on the second shelf and fresh tuna at the coldest spot in the back and ice trays filled with water, and a ringing phone, and calls to be made, and five newspapers to be read, and a film to rent, and a film to view, and a nap to take, and Chinese food to order, and letters and eventually e-mails to write, and stamps to buy.

Forty pages in two weeks. I found it heroic (I thought of Thomas Wolfe, so many years ago, lunging through the midnight streets of Manhattan shouting "I wrote ten thousand words today").

In this heroic spirit, with a handful of cassettes, a bottle of Scotch, a bucket of ice, two quarts of club soda, and six Corona beers chilling in the bucket of ice, I drove out into the desert on a hot, dry evening and over the mountains, heading toward Vegas. What a hoot! I blew my horn on the empty road.

My glass of whiskey sat on the passenger seat, wrapped in a towel. I had snuggled a large bag of Fritos between the passenger door and seat, so that, from my point of view, everything was perfect.

Let the music play on! Elgar, Samuel Barber, the last three Shostakovich string quartets, Sinatra's last great album, *She Shot Me Down,* Miles Davis's *Sketches of Spain.* Not light stuff, that little group of cassettes. What in the world must I have had in mind?

A whiskey and a beer during a rapid sunset. I drank and drove for a long time, pulling over now and then to use the rest room in a gas station. I believe I bought a sandwich, but I don't recall its taste. Did I eat it? Did I really buy a sandwich?

Some time later, I pulled off the road for gas and noticed that I'd almost finished the bottle of Scotch. But it was only a fifth, not a quart, I reasoned, so it didn't count, not even taking into consideration the beers, all of them gone.

I drove in the desert dark, away from the main road, on some sort of dirt pathway behind the gas station. About a half hour into it, I pulled off into a sandbank to rest and found that I was stuck, digging a deeper and deeper hole by accelerating frantically.

I got out of the car and wandered around. Eventually I threw up and lay down a few yards away, but I was so dizzy I couldn't fall asleep. "I've got an island in the Pacific / And everything about it is terrific," I remember singing.

I woke up in strong desert heat, covered in sweat, vomit, and excrement. And then tears. The pity of self-pity.

If you call a rehab center, such as the Betty Ford Center, your evaluation begins the moment you open your mouth on the phone. I spoke with a man named Malcum in a quiet, reasonable radio voice. I told him that I felt I was drinking "a bit too much" and that "it behooved me to entertain the idea of assistance" but that I was in "no crisis," that I was in the California desert, and that I could "come right over" at their convenience. Malcum spoke with the gray neutrality of all who work in such installations, neither happy to hear from me nor irritated that I'd called. He asked about my medical and psychological histories, the length and severity of my relationship with alcohol, and whether there'd been "a defining incident" that had led to my call. I told him that there'd been no defining incident and that since I was thirty years old I'd occasionally "overstepped the boundaries of consumption, if you know what I mean." He told me that the cost of a twenty-eight-day stay at the Betty Ford Center was $6,500, and I said that that was no problem. Malcum told me that when there was "a bed," he'd get in touch with me. He took all my phone numbers and addresses, my Social Security number, and the name of my wife, Ellie, and my former wife, Marie. I had no other living relatives except my children.

How great! Time in the desert to write and drink, help on the way, who could ask for anything more?

A few days later, during a National League play-off game on television being played in the rain and mud of Shea Stadium between the Mets and Dodgers, there occurred, for me, a defining incident.

Keith Hernandez of the Mets, during the sixth inning of the third game of the series, slipped on his way to third and then, in painful slow motion, tried to crawl to the bag, slushing through the wet infield earth, lunging, sliding, plodding, groping, and arriving, finally, at the waiting glove of the Dodger third baseman, Jeff Hamilton, who tagged him out.

Clearly I had fallen into the sandbank of alcohol on the scorched desert earth somewhere between Palm Springs and Vegas, somewhere near Harvard Square in Joe Raposo's apartment, somewhere near somewhere near somewhere.

Late that night, after a lot to drink (remember, help was on the way), I imagined Jeff Hamilton as the mysterious black hole that sucked up the stars, that suffocated the stars. There was no oxygen in the black hole, just the crushing of the skulls of planets in the silence of death. But no matter. I'd be okay. A steak was on the barbecue, the Basie band was playing, I had at least a week before the Betty Ford Center, and I could really do some good writing while I was actually in the place. I'd set up a table in my room for my typewriter, no whiskey, of course, and I'd just turn out the pages like I'd been doing. *And* I'd found that my union, AFTRA, had me covered for every cent of the $6,500. So who was kidding whom? This was a great deal, any way you looked at it. Marie and Ellie were all jived up in New York. One of them (I don't remember which one) said that I wasn't the coward she'd thought I was.

Jonno boy *kicks* the ball out of Hamilton's glove and is *safe* at third! That's what I said out loud on my patio, under a full moon, under a sky filled with stars.

The Betty Ford Center turned seven years old in 1988. It was a construct of four dormitories, McAllum, Pocklington, North, and Fisher, two of which, Pocklington and North, were coed, one of which, Fisher, housed women only, and one of which, McAllum, was all male, which is where I was sent. The admissions building was called Firestone, and the Cork building, right next to the Barbara Sinatra Center for Abused Children outside the Betty Ford Center, was used for family programs during the third week of a patient's stay.

The grounds were beautifully groomed. Sweeping green lawns near McAllum rolled down to a duck-filled pond around which were three or four benches. High hedges surrounded the property and created a sense of enclosure, though in fact it wasn't hard to escape or return, or to peer in and out.

My one roommate was a black kid, about twenty-two, from Los Angeles. The other eighteen men at McAllum were Americans ranging from twenty-five to fifty years old and an older Japanese fellow who spoke in clear soft English. Twenty of us in all at McAllum and twenty in each of the other dorms, forty men and forty women at the center at all times. The place, as I described it to Marie on the phone, was a long tube; into one end were squeezed incoming patients, while out the other end tumbled the solid new citizens of sobriety.

Can you imagine this? I was denied my typewriter. It was stored away "for safekeeping." I put up a fuss.

There were housekeeping chores for me to do: mopping and

sweeping, cleaning the coffee kitchen, making an immaculate bed for Brant Lake Camp–like assessment.

Except on weekends, no phone calls were allowed, in or out. On Saturdays and Sundays you stood in a public area by a wall pay phone.

Meals were foul, particularly lunch and dinner, with flavor removed, I'm convinced, by an expert in the field: lettuce, tomatoes, meat loaf, rice, for God's sake! Baked potatoes, for God's sake! Carrots, string beans, chocolate pudding, apple pie. I'm *serious* here.

The Betty Ford Center was an endless AA gathering, with little meetings, lectures, open-to-the-public AA meetings on Friday nights, meditation walks around the meditation path that circled the installation. Casual AA talk took place in small casual groups and the tough stuff in the twice-a-day group meetings that divided McAllum into two sections of ten, with a counselor for each. Those menacing hours were designed to strip away pretense, facade, credential. They were mortifying, harrowing, vicious. During my second week, a favorable review of *The Man Who Knew Cary Grant* appeared in *Newsweek.* I discovered it on a table in Firestone, near Admissions, and took it for my own to wave grandly in group, only to have it savaged by a swollen, mousy guy who only the day before had waved his own grand document in the air as one of Hollywood's "elite" gynecologists; he was, indeed, Sissy Spacek's.

In group I was a fancy talker. "I'm ambivalent about this potentially destructive process," I believe I said on one occasion. I know I said, at another time, "I don't think I can introduce any elaborate epiphanies under these accusatory conditions."

Everyone tore into me, Sissy's gynecologist with special glee. I was called a pompous asshole, a condescending schmuck, and furthermore, the review in *Newsweek* didn't mean shit because nobody read *Newsweek,* and what did it matter what the fuck I'd written when what we were all there for was to get sober? I said quakingly that I hadn't had a drink in five weeks and in fact I had come to the Betty Ford Center to do research for a possible novel. Then get the fuck out of the group! I was told by one and all, except for the counselor, a controlled crew-cut sergeant named George Vandel, who had, only forty-five minutes earlier, on behalf of truth, felt it necessary to tell us, out of the blue, that his wife was "extremely obese."

The clamor subsided, though a distrust, and probably a dislike, of me began to spread through all of McAllum. I was never invited into casual twos and threes (though I could have plunged in).

A widespread antipathy might have been muted by the attention given to the arrival of Elizabeth Taylor, a new patient at Pocklington. She came to meals in a wheelchair, navigated by a male patient she would eventually marry. She was puffy and tired, having apparently fallen down in her home. Her eyes were youthful, like my father's in the hospital. She appeared to be unembarrassed by her circumstances. We were all told that she was making her second visit to the Betty Ford Center. I spoke with her once, noticing *Newsweek* in her large open pocketbook. I told her of my review. She smiled as if I hadn't spoken. "I'm glad to have met you," she said, and signaled her navigator to roll her along.

Twenty-eight days. Not possible, it seemed to me. The horrifying stories in group: the terrible admissions, through tears, of family destruction; of vehicular catastrophe, leaving children dead, lying in the street, crushed and bloodied beyond imagination; of unspeakable loss, wives and fathers, lovers and infants blown to pieces, their carcasses carried by the wind to junkyards; holy marriages desecrated by liquor, cocaine, heroin; glass, oh God, glass, decapitating a falling six-year-old girl who'd been hurled through a plate-glass window, while, only seconds earlier, the child, Abby, had been sitting on the side of a bed watching *Sesame Street.* A Texan, a burly father of six, had prowled the night streets of Houston for three years in search of lithe, inviting boys, the midnight crawl a profound humiliation. So many lithe, inviting boys in Houston's darkest corners received money, all the money the father had put away, his oldest son ready for Texas A & M, the tuition so terribly misplaced. He wept in group until it was time for lunch.

I had to leave the place. "I'm leaving," I told George Vandel. "Why don't you call your wife and tell her?" he asked. Which I did. "Ellie, I'm leaving," I said. "But you're only half through," she said. "Ellie, this place is a city of tears." "I want you to stick it out. Call Marie." I called Marie. "I'm leaving," I said. "Stay the course," she said. "Marie, this place is a city of tears." "Stay the course," she said.

I packed up in my room.

"What are you doin'?" my roommate asked.

"I'm leaving," I said.

"I don't know," he said.

I stayed through the night. In the morning I told George Vandel that I wasn't going.

"Good," he said, but not matter-of-factly. I felt that he was invested in this decision, that I was not dehumanized.

Later on in the morning, I talked in group about hiding, and no one came down on me except Sissy's gynecologist, who said that I was "bullshitting."

"No, he's not," someone else said.

One morning on the meditation path, after breakfast and before group, I walked behind the others under a hot desert sun. A recreational hot-air balloon floated above, bearing happy people. I had rented one years earlier for friends and me. When the balloon landed, we'd had champagne in the station wagon that had followed us south. The happy people, perhaps two hundred feet above, waved. I waved back. As I waved, I saw in the sky my father's green liquor cabinet from the penthouse on Ninety-fourth Street, filled with bottles of VAT 69 Scotch. The cabinet floated behind the brightly colored balloon that was striped yellow, blue, red, white. The green cabinet wasn't a vision. It had risen from the desert, my own dear desert, in pursuit of the happy people, who waved until they were out of sight. Had they known we were incarcerated down below? Could they see the green cabinet?

The green cabinet of 1948. I'd been ten years old, wearing pajamas and pouring Scotch.

I brought it to the group without fuss or fanfare. But consider this: there was no blood on my hands, no Houston midnights, no plate-glass windows. What was my little thought worth, after all? Hardly anything, except to George Vandel, who lingered over it.

"That's what the meditation path is for," he said.

"I wish I'd been in the balloon," I said.

"Not the green cabinet?" he asked.

"No," I said truthfully, "the balloon."

Years earlier, I'd been taken by Charlie Jackson to a closed AA meeting. Closed meant no one but alcoholics, but Charlie, the author of *The Lost Weekend,* had clout, and I went along just to see what this crazy AA stuff was about. It was about truth, I figured later on. Charlie, a small, balding man in his fifties, replied, "It's about hanging on to life."

Hanging on to life.

Had I had a defining incident? Obviously, out there in the desert somewhere near Vegas. Was I really an alcoholic? Really and truly? No question. Would I stop drinking, "one day at a time," after the Betty Ford Center? No.

Ellie showed up for family week. I posed as reformed. We ate tasteless lettuce together, and in the Cork Building, Ellie got a whiff of the program.

At the end of my stay, I left with my Betty Ford coffee cup, my medallion, and twenty-eight days of sobriety.

We reached our lodge at 7:30 in the evening. I told Ellie I wanted to go shopping. She lay down on the bed and fell asleep. Ever so quietly, I took a handful of ice cubes from the freezer and dropped them gingerly, noiselessly, into a glass. I drove to the Locomotive Liquor Shop, about a half a mile away, and bought a pint of Johnnie Walker Red Scotch and a bottle of Canada Dry club soda. Sitting in the car, I rested the glass on the passenger seat and opened the pint of Scotch. As I moved my hand to the glass, the pint slipped away from me and, headfirst, slid into the stick gear between the seats. Glub, glub, glub. I was frozen, watching, as the pint emptied into the bowels of the car. I watched all of it disappear. Then I got out of the car, went back into the store, and bought an identical pint of Scotch. This time, in the car, I held the bottle with two hands, poured a drink, two ounces or so, onto the ice in the glass, and filled the glass to the top with soda. Then I took the pint and the bottle of club soda through a dark alley near the store, put them down on the cement, and returned to the car. I sat in the car in silence, having my drink. It took about a half hour. When I finished, I took the glass through the alley and put it down next to the still pretty full pint of whiskey and the three-quarters-full bottle of club soda.

Before I turned the key, I wondered if the car would explode—alcohol and gasoline.

It did not explode.

I drove to Von's Supermarket and bought all kinds of things, and after a lengthy mouthwash with Listerine, I drove back to the lodge. I made dinner. And woke Ellie. We ate together, and then we went to bed. In the middle of the night I awoke with the fear that the smell of whiskey in the car in the morning would give me away. I got up and went out to the car. I opened the windows and moved the car from its usual location to the far end of the empty parking area. Then I went back to sleep. In the morning, on the way to breakfast, we walked to the car. "Someone's used the car," I said. "I parked it over here, not down there." "How would someone have the keys?" Ellie asked. "People at the lodge know I leave the keys on the floor of the car, tucked in. The keys are here. And look at this, the odometer. I checked it last night. Someone put thirteen miles on this car overnight. It was obviously a drug pickup in Cathedral City, six and a half miles there, six and a half miles back. Look at the odometer." Ellie looked. Ellie, who knows nothing about odometers and doesn't drive, never has, said, "I see." "No damage done," I said. "Do you think you ought to report it?" she asked. "Nah, it's okay," I said. "I think I know who did it. Roberto in housecleaning. It's no big deal."

There was no whiskey smell.

We had a nice breakfast at Louise's Pantry.

I think that the twelve-step program at the center of AA is one of the most remarkable ideas of the twentieth century. It occurred to a man named Bill Wilson in 1935, and it crept along quietly for a number of years until national publicity, in the form of a 1941 piece in *The Saturday Evening Post*, gave it recognition. Alcohol was its first target, but cocaine and other drugs are now as well represented in rehab centers as the original bottle of booze. The success of these centers is well below 50 percent, and I am one of the failures. I am not happy in groups; AA is nothing but groups. I am an enemy of most systems; AA is nothing but a system. I don't believe for a minute that alcohol is a disease; AA believes nothing but. I feel that AA wants to help themselves *to* you; AA believes it wants to help. I believe that drinking can be cut back and not out; AA believes no such thing. I believe that AA has saved thousands of lives; AA knows it to be so. I believe that lonely zealots populate the postrehab world of recovery; AA believes they are only "tough lovers."

I know that I still dream of November 1988: the early shadows of the night outside the dining room, a plate-glass window mutilating a ventriloquist, Sissy's gynecologist turned into a six-legged squirrel, a hot-air balloon dipping low to rescue me.

AA knows it, too.

21

"WHEN OTIS REDDING DIED, I THOUGHT I COULDN'T GO ON," BILL Clinton said to Carly Simon in August 1998.

News of Sinatra's death, on May 14 of that year, arrived by phone in the middle of the night. I went down to *The New York Times*'s WQEW, where I'd worked since the station's inception in 1992, and went on the air about 4:30 in the morning. His passing, not unexpected, aroused my deep affection. What marvelous recordings he'd made! How remarkably he'd changed the sound of popular music all over the world for half a century! In various spurts of appreciation, I said all of this on the air, alone in the studio with every record, released and unreleased. I was soon joined by a string of television crews representing all the networks, local stations, and many cable companies. I remember, despite the pressure of conducting a radio program without an end while addressing camera after camera, the heavy hearts in the eyes of all who came to ask questions. This was a personal loss, and even the youngest interviewer, a man about twenty-five, exhibited a sorrow in the funereal rhythm of his words. Dan Rather's man, the gentlest and most specific of them all, was endearing in the depth of what he asked.

Sinatra had spent his last days alone in a room with a guy named Tony Oppedisano, eating ice cream and watching television. His short-term memory was shot, and his health was fading. He stayed in his pajamas a lot of the time, though he pulled himself together for a striking photo, shot for *The New Yorker* by Richard Avedon. That his last words, reported by his daughter Nancy, were "I'm losing" did not surprise me. They acknowledged his lifelong battles—often he'd had a dozen going at the same time. Throughout his life, Sinatra had conducted a relentless prizefight, legitimized by his iconic stature. He had fought tough, he had fought dirty, sensing another's weakness, sometimes lashing out below the belt. He had fought truthfully and bravely for what he saw as justice, and generously he had fought financially against the tragedies not only of his friends but of absolute strangers.

On the night of May 15, when, finally, I left the radio station, I saw at once that the Empire State Building was bathed in blue light.

In November 1996, the president of Lincoln Center called to make a date for lunch. Nat Leventhal, a slender, shy man leading a public life, came to the restaurant with an unprepossessing associate, a woman named Jane Moss, who smiled her way through a playful meal, hardly saying a thing. I knew of her, in fact had even met her along the way, as a behind-closed-doors operator and a classicist through and through. The boys at the table, throwing Van Heusen, Harold Arlen, and Arthur Schwartz around, were speaking, I saw clearly, a language unimportant to the smiling politician, who was there to comply with the president's whim.

Nat had sought me out to act as artistic director of a new "American Songbook" series at Lincoln Center that would honor famous composers by gathering performers from all kinds of music to sing their songs in front of large orchestras and audiences. I would weave stories and biographical information through each show that would illuminate, to some degree, the lives of Richard Rodgers, Harold Arlen, Frank Loesser, and eventually my father.

That the shows got on at all still amazes me, in view of the brief rehearsal time and the diversity of singers, from hard-core jazz to cabaret to opera and theater.

We started with Harold Arlen and went on from there. *The New York Times* was cool, then less so, but never, until the end, enthusiastic. The critic, Stephen Holden, objected to the heaviness of it all, the excessive formality in the casual world of popular music, which was, in fact, the case.

But along we went, to inevitable standing ovations and warm letters of appreciation, sent both to Lincoln Center and to me at the radio station.

WQEW had struggled through six years of adequate ratings and revenue, playing Peggy Lee recordings in a Celine Dion world after WNEW, enfeebled and failing, had left the air in 1992.

In the late summer of 1998, the ground began to shift, unnoticed in the office. I picked up a rumor through two friends at *The New York Times:* the company was going to sell WQEW to Disney, which wanted it for its children's radio network. Nothing was certain, and I kept silent, hoping for the best. The fact was that if the format changed, if the sale went through, the standard songs in which I'd trafficked all my life would be dealt quite a setback. No other New York radio station had taken the risky choice of appealing to the older demographic rather than the coveted twenty-five-to-thirty-four-year-olds. I have always felt that older listeners, their younger years caressed by Gershwin, Rodgers, Sinatra, and Ella Fitzgerald, had money to spend; that they should be targeted, sold to, even curtsied to by Madison Avenue. If programmed without the trashy hit records that enervated WQEW, if only the good stuff—the infrastructure of albums by the finest popular singers of the era—got on the air, any radio station's sound would become eloquent, and newer, younger listeners would wander in and begin to understand.

It turned out that *The New York Times* leased WQEW to Disney for about $48 million over a six-year period, and we were out of business at the end of 1998. There wasn't much ceremony to our closing down; the place was demoralized and beyond final tribute.

I had about 3,500 albums on the premises, all of which were moved into storage in Queens. I had slowly been replacing them all with CDs, which came uptown to my office in the West Fifties.

To me, the station, a mediocrity focusing on crummy hit records in order to preserve the last possible octogenarian in New Jersey as listener, deserved to fall silent. My contract had eased me around the worst of it, allowing me to program my own show, but the other "music presenters" had been told to play the same Patti Page and Frankie Laine records over and over again. The process had drained the station of imagination, spirit, warmth. Lobotomized from the start by its program director, WQEW emitted no energy. It sounded dull almost all of the time, despite Sinatra, Basie, Armstrong, and Fitzgerald. When I argued with the program director and implored him "to take some chances and play new versions of standard songs and go deeper into the albums and cut down on hits," I was told that "conventional wisdom has it that hits make you a success." "That's why it's called conventional," I said urgently, during a conversation that took place during the brief time when I knew we were going off and the program director did not.

Lester, who had moved to San Diego "in semiliterate retirement" and who had appeared as my vacation replacement on WQEW between 1992 and 1998, was in town at the end. We had drinks together in my office one afternoon in January 1999.

My dearest friend sat on the couch with a vodka and tonic.

He asked, "Do you think Sinatra's death had anything to do with this?"

"Sinatra as metaphor," I said. "But no. It could very well be that the *Times* had this in mind from the beginning. Grease the pig and sell."

"Do you mean to tell me that they concocted the whole thing in 1992?"

"No, not really," I said. "We simply didn't turn the proper buck."

"And what was the proper buck?"

"I guess you could say forty-eight million dollars," I told him.

"I guess you could say we fell short," Lester said.

Which put an end to our brief evaluation of what conceivably might have gone wrong.

"I want you to hear something," I said as I got up to put on a CD.

"Do you realize how many times you've hosted a private radio show for me?" Lester asked with benign detachment.

"I am a disc jockey, Lester," I said. "I wish you to *feel* music the way *I* do."

"But Jonno, that's impossible. Your level of excitement is way out of my casual league."

"That may very well be," I said, "but at least you could have the common decency to listen."

"Oh, but I do," Lester assured me.

"I stand before you now at my music system," I said. "I have stood before you in front of my Victrola, my record player, my hi-fi, my stereo, my components, my unit, and now my system. You have always been gracious."

"Well, I . . ."

He trailed off, sipping his drink, my sixty-eight-year-old bosom buddy.

I played him "Out of This World" and "So in Love," sung by Nancy LaMott.

"Jonno," Lester said, after a moment, so softly.

"Well, yes," I said. "Adult, no?"

Lester didn't respond.

"My father would have loved her. She does what the composer felt in his heart of hearts: a love for someone, trepidation, desire, nobility, longing. All of it, as you heard, in two songs that are thematically immense. Now and then my dad touched upon the immense."

"He did," Lester said.

I hired my brother, Paul, to conduct the thirty-five-piece orchestra for the Arthur Schwartz celebration at Lincoln Center on two nights, Friday and Saturday, January 12 and 13, 2001. His mother, Mary Grey, had died in November 1994 after losing control of her car on a rain-slicked New Jersey road.

"I'm *free*!" Paul had shouted to me on the phone, announcing his mother's death.

We hadn't known each other very well until that time, though we had both been wounded by Mary Grey. Still, Paul was her son and I was the outsider. Keep in mind the eighteen years between us—1938 and 1956. We'd been cautious half brothers until Mary Grey's car crash. We were then able to begin to talk.

Paul had received a sophisticated education, mostly in Europe, after Arthur and Mary Grey had moved to London in 1968. The Westminster School, the Royal College of Music, the Accademia Musicale Chigiana in Siena had all welcomed Paul's attention. In 1981, he'd become the assistant conductor of the Washington Opera, and, a year later, the William Steinberg Fellow of the Pittsburgh Symphony Orchestra under André Previn. He had aspired all the while to be a composer of "Stockhausen-like impenetrability" and, as I recall, succeeded.

It must be said, and incredulously accepted, that my brother conducted 1,573 performances of *The Phantom of the Opera* at the Majestic Theatre in New York. I saw only half of one performance, finding the show bogus and musically vulgar.

I include Paul's credentials to show how richly qualified he was to conduct at his father's centennial celebration in Alice Tully Hall at Lincoln Center. We became collaborators on Arthur's behalf and spoke of what would have been his enormous pleasure at the event.

By then we were solid friends, having combed through the disgraces of Paul's mother. I discovered that I hadn't been her only target, and with that knowledge I embraced Paul as an intimate. We caught up with each other, until, finally, we inhabited the present tense as companions and advisers. To see him in a tuxedo standing before the orchestra on opening night, the curtain seconds from rising, filled me with the first recognizable joy of early family that I had ever experienced. Here was Arthur's other son, baton at the ready, tall (taller than I), motionless, expectant, prepared.

For two hours on both of the evenings, the music of Arthur Schwartz filled, it seemed to me, *all* of Lincoln Center, swooping through Juilliard, encircling the fountain in the plaza that was stilled for the winter, ascending the halls and staircases within the Metropolitan Opera, and drifting up through the heating vents into the office of the chairperson and Nat Leventhal's empty quarters, laid bare by his retirement only a month before. My father's music rose up into the winter night, rising ever higher into the sky.

I will not deny the standing ovations or my kiss to Paul's cheek during the extended bows.

The houselights were on, revealing my children in the fifth row, my daughter clapping her hands above her head. We were going to meet in my office in a half hour, just the two of us, to dissect everything. Her arm was around her younger brother's shoulder. Casey was nineteen, Adam fourteen. They had, from different homes, come to love each other.

Visitors swarmed into dressing rooms. Paul's two very young sons ran across the stage, shielded from sight by the final curtain.

I caught a lucky break with a taxi and beat Casey to my office by about twenty minutes.

I changed from my tuxedo into jeans and a summer sport shirt from the Gap. I combed my hair and brushed my teeth.

Like Marie, her mother, Casey begins many of her arrivals well before she comes into sight. On the night of January 13, 2001, she stepped off the elevator way down the hall, singing "A Shine on Your Shoes." By the time she appeared in the frame of my open door, she was well into the song. There she stood, facing her father, who was back in his raggedy attire, right down to sneakers and sweat socks. "Daddy!" she said as she ran into my arms, a freshman at college, her grandfather's music still flowing from her, before it turned to praise and into the articulate perception that for years she had brought to even the most unassuming occasions. She recognized disguise and was unafraid to acknowledge her own, but I had not yet stepped forward without camouflage.

On this night, sitting across from each other for a number of hours, I spoke truthfully and expansively to my daughter. I had stories to tell her and music to play her, of all kinds. Turkey burgers arrived with hills of French fries and many whole pickles wrapped in aluminum foil.

We talked about books and "the tons" (as I said) of the hardest things to do as a writer, which Casey was thinking of becoming. For the first time, we spoke of her parents' divorce, and I of Paine

Whitney and the Betty Ford Center and Robert Delvecchio and Anna Gold and Merry Rogin and Lynn Taylor, and of the man with the pitchfork, and of the night of my mother's death. We listened to Arthur's music, and I brought out the few photos of the two of them together, Casey as an infant, in his arms, both looking bewildered.

It was three in the morning, will you look at that!

I drove Casey home up the quiet avenues.

I bought a hot dog at Eighty-sixth and Third from the Papaya King that was mysteriously open, and ate it in the car, listening to the Allman Brothers on the radio.

My household was asleep.

I called Paul, but his wife picked up the phone sleepily, so I hung up.

I put on Sinatra's "I See Your Face Before Me," sitting alone in the living room. "We're not getting over," my father had said outside the Majestic Theatre on *Jennie*'s opening night. "She was so so so so sick," he had said the night my mother died.

Forty-seven years ago.

I heard my father playing the piano, confident, fearless. The sound of my blood.

Eventually I went to bed.

Acknowledgments

Unbounded gratitude is extended, for diverse and heartfelt reasons, to Dennis Ambrose, Ken Auletta, Marie Brenner, Larry Brooks, Marsha Brooks, Chris Cerf, Michael Feinstein, Sharon Fisher, Nancy Franklin, Ann Godoff, James Isaacs, Jonathan Jao, Jon Karp, Jesse Kornbluth, Owen Laster, Dave Logan, Barbara Lorenzo, Jim Lowe, David McClintick, Daphne Merkin, Tony Monte, Arden Ostrander, Ellie Renfield, Virginia Robertson, Adam Schwartz, Casey Schwartz, Paul Schwartz, Joanna Simon, Sam Vaughan, and Jill Whedon.

ABOUT THE AUTHOR

JONATHAN SCHWARTZ has, over thirty years, gathered a wide and attentive radio audience for his programs devoted to the American Songbook. His novels and short stories are frequently animated by the music he knows so well. His own three CDs, secretly released, pay respect to the highest level of popular song: Jerome Kern, Richard Rodgers, Harold Arlen, and his own father, Arthur Schwartz. He is currently heard on WNYC-FM in New York and on XM Satellite radio nationwide. Jonathan Schwartz is married and lives in Manhattan.

ABOUT THE TYPE

This book was set in Fairfield, the first typeface from the hand of the distinguished American artist and engraver Rudolph Ruzicka (1883–1978). Ruzicka was born in Bohemia and came to America in 1894. He set up his own shop, devoted to wood engraving and printing, in New York in 1913 after a varied career working as a wood engraver, in photoengraving and banknote printing plants, and as an art director and freelance artist. He designed and illustrated many books, and was the creator of a considerable list of individual prints—wood engravings, line engravings on copper, and aquatints.